BRIAN CALFANO AND VALERIE MARTINEZ-EBERS

HUMAN RELATIONS COMMISSIONS

Relieving Racial Tensions

in the American City

COLUMBIA UNIVERSITY PRESS
NEW YORK

Columbia University Press
Publishers Since 1893
New York   Chichester, West Sussex
cup.columbia.edu
Copyright © 2020 Columbia University Press
All rights reserved

Library of Congress Cataloging-in-Publication Data
Names: Calfano, Brian Robert, 1977– author. | Martinez-Ebers, Valerie, author.
Title: Human relations commissions : relieving racial tensions
in the American city / Brian Calfano and Valerie Martinez-Ebers.
Description: New York : Columbia University Press, 2020. |
Includes bibliographical references and index.
Identifiers: LCCN 2020001205 (print) | LCCN 2020001206 (ebook) |
ISBN 9780231191005 (hardback) | ISBN 9780231191012 (trade paperback) |
ISBN 9780231549196 (ebook)
Subjects: LCSH: Social problems—United States. | Civil rights—United States. |
Discrimination—Law and legislation—United States. | Racism—United States.
Classification: LCC HN43 .C35 2020 (print) | LCC HN43 (ebook) |
DDC 306.0973—dc23
LC record available at https://lccn.loc.gov/2020001205
LC ebook record available at https://lccn.loc.gov/2020001206

Columbia University Press books are printed on permanent
and durable acid-free paper.
Printed in the United States of America

Cover design: Julia Kushnirsky
Cover image: Police keep riots under control in the Watts area of Los Angeles,
Calif., Aug. 1965. © AP Photo

CONTENTS

ACKNOWLEDGMENTS

No project of this size comes together without the assistance and guidance of several people and institutions, and this manuscript is no different. We first extend our deepest gratitude to Columbia University Press editor Stephen Wesley for his patience, support, helpful suggestions, and patience (yes, twice). Brian Humes and the National Science Foundation were integral in enabling financial support of the large-scale survey experiment we conducted in Los Angeles. The faculty, students, and staff of the California State University, Dominguez Hills, made particular contributions through their engagement in the research featured in chapter 6. Colleagues, staff, and students at our home institutions—the University of Cincinnati and the University of North Texas—offered helpful opportunities to discuss aspects of the manuscript and provided feedback at various stages in the writing process. And we owe a debt to the thoughtful recommendations from the three anonymous reviewers for Columbia University Press who assessed the manuscript at both its proposal and revision stages.

Iris Roley of the Cincinnati Black United Front deserves special mention for her leadership on the Cincinnati Community Perception Survey, which features in chapter 6. Finally, none of the research would have occurred without the willing collaboration of commissioners, directors and staff with the City of Los Angeles Human Relations Commission, the City of Fort Worth Human Relations Commission, the City of Pittsburgh Commission on Human Relations, and the City of Cincinnati Human Relations Commission. Those who work on these commissions give of their time and energies to improve intergroup relations in the communities they serve. It is to them that we dedicate this book.

HUMAN RELATIONS COMMISSIONS

INTRODUCTION

———

Too Big a Task?

The meeting room was filled to the brim with people of varying body postures. Some seemed eager to get a problem off their chest. Others seemed content to simply watch. All appeared to know that what they were about to take part in was about as familiar as a Sunday church service. This community center room had rows of chairs arranged like pews, and chairs also lined the room's left side. At the front were a couple more rows of chairs facing the audience, but no one was yet in these seats. With the number of people milling about or already seated, several interested parties were left to stand in the hallway to listen for a bit of what this gathering might produce. No one was put off by this. It just seemed to be the normal state of affairs. As the last seat or two filled in, a few attendees huddled closely together whispering intensely about something that seemed like a life or death concern to all of them. Others milled through personal papers or the local newspaper. Several greeted each other with hugs or hearty handshakes. At 10 A.M., as if on cue, a door on the left front side of the room swung open and a line of Los Angeles Police Department (LAPD) personnel, including precinct captains, strode in, filling the seats in the front. They were followed by a man in a three-piece suit and cufflinks. Standing in center front, he welcomed everyone, bowed his head, and asked everyone to join in prayer. After invoking the name of Jesus Christ for wisdom and guidance over their work, the latest meeting of the Watts Gang Task Force convened.

For the next ninety minutes, police, community leaders, academics, and local clergy took part in their weekly give-and-take discussion (sometimes you might call it a passionate exchange of views) about issues ranging from the latest altercation between members of rival gangs in one of the neighborhood's four public housing projects, information from LAPD precinct officers on recent arrests and other interactions the department has had with residents, and general discussion of what community members can do to help stave off disputes before they escalate. On more than a few occasions, the discussion was steered by attendees who seemed to command a great deal of respect from everyone in the room—longtime residents, most of whom had lost children to gang violence in the neighborhood. These people, with lines of experience and pain on their faces and in their eyes, offered a familiar refrain: we have to do something to get Watts out of its rut, especially the violence that robs children of their future.

And, make no mistake, violence continues to plague Watts. The area's median age is just twenty-eight. There are long stretches—months—where the area goes without a homicide, only for innocent residents to be gunned down in sprays of bullets by passing cars. After such tragedies, task force meetings are hotbeds of grief, recrimination, and calls for calm and reconciliation. In many ways, the process is a familiar cycle, with the same participants making the same general statements, and the same police and local officials listening with intent.

But sometimes there is a break in this informal status quo. At one meeting, a Latina and her daughter, neither of whom spoke English, stood at the back of a task force meeting waiting to speak during the open comment period. Both were agitated, tired, and desperate to have those in the room (most of whom did not speak Spanish) understand their plight. An interpreter working for the city walked over to the two and ascertained what was wrong; then the interpreter lifted up a clear plastic bag with some drywall in it. The women had been eating dinner the night before in their Watts apartment when gunfire erupted outside. Bullets entered the apartment and embedded in the walls and ceiling. There was no evidence the women were targets of the shooters, but that did not matter. In a place where they did not speak the dominant language and had few, if any, contacts with community or city services to help guide them through this trying time, the bullets were a reminder of the women's vulnerability.

Equally as shocking as the women's story was the palpable lack of empathy or acknowledgment of the issue by many of the other neighborhood residents in attendance, most of whom were African American. Although Watts' population is roughly three-quarters Latino, it is African Americans, with their relative advantage in leveraging community resources like houses of worship into political representation and influence, who are arguably Watts' most visible representatives. This arrangement can leave Latinos without a sense that city and community institutions are interested in their well-being, which is only reinforced by language and cultural barriers among new Latino immigrants.

But observing this meeting and others like it, there's a sense that some of the concerns expressed are part of a familiar set of complaints, a litany of refrains that almost seem like a ritual for regular attendees. One wonders what, if anything, can be done to truly change the dynamic in Watts—or even among the task force, for that matter. And we are certainly not the first to document the rather circular nature of progress for racial and ethnic minorities in urban America.

Watts and its surrounding neighborhoods, what is now called South Los Angeles (a name change from the former "South Central" to disassociate the area from harsh stereotypes), are key to the lore of America's urban centers as ungovernable cauldrons of crime and decaying infrastructure. The 1965 uprising of mainly African American residents over police abuse helped cement "Watts" as a code word for neighborhoods where blacks and other minorities burn down economic and institutional order. Even after the fires stopped in the 1960s, Watts served as an infamous symbol of gang-related violence brought on, critics assailed, by government attempts at social engineering in the form of public housing projects. The drug-fueled shooting sprees between rival gangs and the paramilitary tactics used by the LAPD under longtime chiefs William Parker and Daryl Gates eventually brought community leaders, residents, and politicians together to attempt to find some understanding of what each group could do, working in tandem with a reformed LAPD, to address community concerns before bloodshed and unrest develops. To be sure, the community, the police, and the city have worked hard over the last thirty years to coproduce a renaissance of sorts in Watts. Like any situation, nothing is as extreme as stereotypes can make it, and this is true of Watts's one square mile.

In fact, driving down Compton Avenue through the neighborhood, you might think that you're in the Holy City. The street is lined with churches and worship centers. In the absence of a robust retail or commercial district, these churches, along with the restaurants and auto repair shops nearby, are the Watts community anchors. It's not Wilshire Boulevard, but neither is it the den of run-down crack houses some might mentally conjure when they hear "Watts." Neither is there the degree of blight and structural abandonment that has historically plagued northern and eastern cities such as Detroit, Baltimore, and Camden, New Jersey. The California sun and conga line of commercial jets on their approach to nearby LAX help too, giving the area a bit of the wonderland feeling the rest of Southern California exudes.

But whatever progress Watts and the surrounding communities have enjoyed, and whatever spiritual and organizational resources they bring to bear, are not enough to guarantee there will never be another civil uprising over systemic issues such as poverty, crime, and distrust of the police. In its way, the Watts Gang Task Force resembles the larger neighborhood as a collective with potential but one that is also weighed down by the realities of trying to bring lasting, positive change to a situation where some people may be beyond the point of living out different circumstances. In some cases, the limitations may be physical, as with addictions of various types. In other instances, the challenge may be emotional and psychological, especially if one's coping mechanisms are ill-equipped to deal with the stresses that come with poverty and concerns for safety. But trust may also be a problem—namely, lack of trust that "the system" can ever be changed to the point of bettering the lives of those who have been dealt a tough hand.

The Watts Gang Task Force exists, in part, to be a bridge between residents, police, and the City of Los Angeles. The task force was started and supported for several years by staffers at the City of Los Angeles Human Relations Commission (LAHRC). Like most of the work the LAHRC does, the task force was designed to provide an outlet for different perspectives to be heard in a respectful environment, and where community members could come to air concerns and provide input into new ways that the city and LAPD would engage residents. In this way LAHRC's groundwork provided much of the rhetorical glue that enabled initial buy-in for the task force's mission. But the commission was not empowered to do more than that. It is, as we demonstrate in later chapters, a commission with a mandate to foster discussion but not to dole out punishment. Ironically, the LAHRC came into existence as a result of recommendations follow-ing the 1965 Watts uprising, so it is perhaps apropos that the commission was a starting influence behind a task force that, while showing great promise, appears to not have the necessary answers or capacity to address the larger, structural inequalities that drive the present conditions in Watts and similar neighborhoods.

In fact, using Watts as the opening vignette in a book about human relations commissions is itself greatly instructive for the juxtaposition it provides in describing aspects of the racial, economic, and political cur-rents that are likely too strong for any one government agency to over-come, let alone one that is limited to facilitating group discussions, as is the LAHRC. As we show throughout this book, the tasks before commis-sions, even where the bodies enjoy federal funding and statutory mandates for code enforcement, are much larger than government organizations can address. And yet much of society tends to assume that figuring out how to improve the lives of residents in places like Watts will be the govern-ment's worry—the public sector's mission is to figure out what to do with those less fortunate.

Of course, the problem with this thinking is that government cannot "do it all," especially when systemic factors have led to present conditions. Like the Watts Gang Task Force, human relations commissions across the country can point to specific examples where their efforts have made a positive difference, but none make a direct claim on solving the larger problems that necessitate these commissions in the first place. What's more, it is not even clear that commissions make discernable progress in dealing with some of the major intergroup challenges their communities face.

So why write a book about these government bodies? Our reason can be summed up like this: Just because progress might be fleeting, commis-sions are no less important for understanding the potentials and limita-tions of government to right societal wrongs, one neighborhood, one issue, and one task force at a time. Like most human endeavors, the work of improving intergroup relations, deterring and punishing acts of racial discrimination, and building trust across groups from disparate back-grounds and perspectives is fluid, nonlinear, exhilarating, and heart-breaking (and perhaps all of these in a short span of time). Even in instances where improvements might be on the horizon, there are always those cases like the Latinas at the task force meeting who received little empathy from other community members to remind those who do this important work that their efforts typify what it means to be human.

It is for these tireless and unsung faces of local government's best intentions that we offer this book.

1

HUMAN RELATIONS COMMISSIONS

Creativity in Constraint

I t is hard to ignore the myriad of media reports about intergroup conflicts in the United States, especially in urban areas. Various groups,
including African Americans, women, immigrants, Muslims, LGBTQ+,
and others, struggle to improve or maintain their status in American
society. Improvement will come, in part, through the betterment of relations with fellow citizens, such as through government-led efforts to
improve intergroup relations through the work of human relations commissions (HRCs), the focus of this book. These commissions may be called
by different names (e.g., human rights, civil rights, community relations),
but HRCs are present at the state level in practically every state and in
hundreds of cities and counties throughout the United States. HRCs were
originally established to mitigate racial discrimination through the development of intergroup cooperation, but today their mission has expanded
to ensure fair treatment for a variety of groups, including on issues related
to fair housing access and community–police relations.

The U.S. Department of Justice (DOJ) defines human relations bodies
as having a mission to "promote ways in which people in communities
learn to get along and to safeguard equal opportunity for all." As we see
throughout this book, HRCs are staffed and led by people who earnestly
endorse this mission, but they are not necessarily able to deliver both the
"getting along" and "equal opportunity" parts of the mission easily or consistently. Yet the promise of HRCs endures, despite their limitations,
because the seemingly intractable problem of getting people from different backgrounds or views to find a way to work through their differences
and treat each other equally will certainly remain intractable without
some government effort to address areas of tension and violation.

The DOJ summarizes the three basic functions of HRCs as "resolving conflict, settling complaints of discrimination, and promoting cooperation within the community." Not coincidentally, these three purposes feature prominently in the following chapters to provide a perspective on how successfully HRCs discharge their duties and how commissioners and HRC staff perceive their progress.

Besides race, HRC assistance may now be provided on the basis of gender, age, sexual orientation, religion, national origin, citizenship, and disabilities.[1] Refugees, gang members, and victims of sexual assault are a few more examples of the groups that HRCs may aid. Many—though certainly not all—HRCs receive Department of Housing and Urban Development (HUD) block grants to enforce aspects of the 1968 Fair Housing Act and support the work of the Equal Employment Opportunity Commission as Fair Employment Practice Agencies (FEPA), established in 1965. However, money is tight across HRCs, at least for initiatives that do not directly apply to HUD-related activities. At the same time, metrics of success are a challenge, in part because it is not exactly clear what success looks like. Commissions can more easily document such services as providing someone access to housing options free from discriminatory practice by landlords or holding hearings into allegations of unfair treatment in service and employment by businesses. Much more challenging to quantify and document is the broader charge of improving intergroup relations, for this is the type of policy goal that is just ambiguous enough to allow HRC critics to level charges of ineffectiveness.

For anyone who is either part of an HRC or looking to a commission to improve local conditions, a review of DOJ's stated objectives for HRCs should reinforce the difficult institutional charge from the start.

The objectives of a commission should be:
- To promote and assist in developing an environment of fairness and respect among citizens by ensuring that responses to acts of exclusion, bias, and discrimination are meaningful and consistent.
- To develop ways to measure and monitor community relations, race relations, and civil rights issues, particularly those that are sources of intergroup conflict.
- To involve all segments of the community in understanding and appreciating the benefits of positive intergroup relations.

- To offer a range of programs and services that help communities prevent and resolve issues of human relations, race relations, and civil rights.
- To develop ways of anticipating, preparing for, and relieving community tensions arising from intergroup conflict.[2]

Laudable as these objectives are, they are not the type of outcomes that are easily measured nor are they linear in progression (even when such measurement is possible).

Given the broad scope of mission, it is both curious and understandable that scholars have been slow to assess HRCs. On the one hand, the continuing challenges and effects of racism and discrimination, particularly in American cities, make the lack of scholarly attention to HRCs an oversight of substantial proportions. On the other hand, the fact that commissions are so diverse in stature and scope, combined with the challenges in identifying and measuring their effectiveness, perhaps explains why the literature on HRCs is as thin as it is. To our knowledge, we are the first to focus attention on HRCs from a social science perspective, at least in terms of systematically comparing the work of multiple HRCs in urban settings around the United States. Three guiding questions structure our investigation in the following chapters. First, how do HRCs react to and manage their ever-expanding mission? Second, what are the most promising evidence-based strategies for assisting HRCs and other like-minded organizations to improve the (e)quality of intergroup relationships and build on their existing mandates? Third, what structural opportunities and challenges do HRCs face?

With these questions in mind, we examine the work of human relations policy makers and advocates in promoting positive intergroup outcomes in four major metropolitan cities. Using a cross-section of empirical methods and theories from political science, social psychology, and public administration, we assess intergroup relations and human relations policy approaches, successes, and failures at the local government level. Our findings suggest that the path to improved intergroup relations in urban areas is fraught with complications but that the experiences of HRCs inform how disparate groups may be brought together to forge a common identity and productive purpose through an emphasis on the facilitation of community capacity and political efficacy. But it is also clear that HRCs are generally underfunded, understaffed, underused, and underpowered in terms of statutory authority to advance their policy preferences and agendas. In other words, structural limitations impede HRC work. But this is just part of the story.

BUILDING ON EARLIER RESEARCH

Although the nation's earliest HRCs were established during and just after World War II, there was renewed interest in an urban-centered focus on human relations in response to the tumult of the 1960s, which became apparent following the Watts uprising in August 1965. As part of a broader UCLA-commissioned report on Los Angeles since Watts, for blacks and Latinos, the 1960s

> was a period of growing disenchantment with justice delayed. Material and economic improvements failed to match legislative gains, falling far short of rising expectations. This disjuncture and the resulting frustration boiled over in the form of massive urban unrest. The first major riot took place where few expected, in Watts. . . . Physically, Watts, with its low housing density and open spaces, did not share many of the stereotypical images of an inner-city ghetto. It was relatively free from oppressive Jim Crow-style laws.[3]

Watts was so unexpected, and its economic and human toll so dramatic, that California governor Edmund "Pat" Brown tasked former CIA director and head of the California Republican Party John McCone to lead a commission to determine the uprising's causes and make recommendations for prevention of similar events. Only a few months after the McCone Commission recommendations were released in its 1966 *Violence in the City* report, numerous U.S. cities burned during episodes of protest and uprising during the "long hot summer" of 1967. President Lyndon Johnson empaneled the Kerner Commission to understand why, at the height of government spending on the administration's Great Society programs, major American cities would burn in protest, with thousands of residents killed or injured in conflict with local authorities.

Although established by different government entities in response to distinct episodes of civil unrest by minorities in the nation's urban centers, both commissions offered essentially the same explanation: America's minority groups live in an increasing state of economic dissimilarity, the effect of which is to downgrade a person's opportunities for employment, and, the McCone Commission noted, "a chance to earn the means to support himself and his family, a dignity, and a reason to feel that he is a member of our community in a true and very real sense."[4] But the basic act of holding a job is not enough to counter the antecedents of individual despair and community unrest. The Kerner Commission took aim at underemployment, as distinct from unemployment, as a structural issue that must be addressed before realistic chances for prevention of unrest would be realized.[5] Tackling employment disparities required not only investment in job training and education but government action against hiring practices and union membership.

Not far behind employment as a structural cause of urban unrest is lack of quality housing. Both McCone and Kerner recommended investment in improved housing stock, either rental or owned, and both encouraged developers to create new housing opportunities in the urban core. Of course, the challenges of recouping developer investment and the broader, unintended consequences of gentrification remain a Gordian knot for urban planners, politicians, residents, and HRCs. Access to quality, reliable, and affordable transportation and education were also prominent in both commission's list of recommendations. Although compulsory school segregation based on race is no longer a policy, de facto segregation as correlated with larger socioeconomic factors remains very much a reality in many urban areas. The same goes for transportation, where spotty progress—especially in cities like Los Angeles, where political decisions made decades ago limit public transportation options in favor of a dense highway network—means access to automobiles provides a mobility advantage that minorities must have to compete in the labor market.

In their assessment of Los Angeles, Paul Ong and colleagues find what one might expect: progress on employment, education, housing, and transportation has been made, but conditions are far from ideal.[6] Structurally, change is slow, and direct cause and effect measurement lines between policy adoption and an intended outcome are often hazy, at best.

Indeed, so much is out of the policy makers' control. Much like the broad HRC mandate to improve intergroup relations, the challenge of realizing the broad policy recommendations of blue-ribbon panels is that those who have do the work of making conditions better have a much tougher job than those who set up the broad outline of what "better" should look like.

MULTIPLE WAYS TO ASSESS IMPACT

At this juncture it is important to contrast the outlook and presentation in our book with studies like Ong and colleagues offer.[7] As important as macroeconomic indicators are in various respects, we are decidedly not focused on them associated with employment, housing status, and the geographic dispersion of racial and ethnic minorities in American cities. These are, to be sure, critical areas of study and analysis, but they are also well-worn areas of assessment, particularly in the form of reports issued by educational and nonprofit organizations. By contrast, our work goes beyond the individual indicators found in the McCone and Kerner reports to include a broader assessment of human relations work in support of local urban environments where access to meaningful employment, quality housing, and useful transportation options are supported by a general respect for groups of different racial, ethnic, and religious backgrounds. We argue that only from this place of general and sustained intergroup respect can the motive to realize the general recommendations of both commission reports be realized.

And it is useful to state what may already be obvious: human relations and similar commissions are not human relations or "HR" in the contemporary personnel sense. Their mission is not to promote a positive organization culture in city governments but, as stated, to work toward the general goal of positive intergroup relations among the citizenry. HRCs are a twentieth-century governing phenomenon steeped largely in the acceptance of human rights such as dignity, fairness, and equity as norms typifying the kind of public outcomes government should endorse. Focus on human rights as an actionable area of policy became particularly tangible following the United Nation's 1948 Universal Declaration of Human Rights. Basic human rights principles include the promotion of equality in all structural forms (including economic, racial, gender, age, and sexual orientation dimensions); the encouragement of broad-based public involvement in government decisions; the eradication of discrimination in the public realm, regardless of the perpetuator's intent or knowledge; government accountability to stakeholders; and a progressive distribution of government resources to help those most in need of economic and social assistance. Not coincidentally, these are the same general values put forward to varying degrees in both the McCone and Kerner Commission reports.

However, connecting values with implementation requires a more specific set of instructions for governments establishing and running HRCs than basic blue-ribbon recommendations or a list of human rights principles. Here the DOJ's guidance is useful because, beyond the basic instructions to promote equality and intergroup understanding, it offers certain operational guidance on how HRC functionality can put human rights principles into practice. One of the most important areas of department guidance is the call to be as specific as possible in delineating HRC powers, including policy enforcement mechanisms, subpoena power, rules for commission partnerships with private organizations, and guidelines for how HRCs relate to other government bodies. As we discover in subsequent chapters, HRCs take on different forms and functions, and these are evolving in the current environment of limited public funds for human relations–related work. Therefore, efforts to make HRCs' scope and mission both detailed and flexible help position these bodies for impact in support of their core objectives.

Any attempt to evaluate HRC effectiveness will require the generation of some type of data, so issues of measurement are critical. The Columbia Law School's Human Rights Institute offers various primers on human rights realization and effect assessment, including case studies the institute has identified as offering promise in measuring impacts. These include impact reviews whereby commission personnel and community partners work collaboratively to identify "positive" and "differential" impacts for specific population groups an HRC serves. Similar to a SWOT analysis in which personnel and other interested observers are asked to evaluate commission programs along an array of indicators (strength, weakness, opportunity, threat), the impact reviews can include elements of racial- or gender-oriented analysis of project outcomes to identify and correct implicit biases in how desired outcomes are determined as well as appropriate data to collect in the assessment process. These analyses are often qualitative or employ basic quantitative measures of percentages, counts of occurrence, or similar measures related to housing discrimination, employment and retention of minorities, and intergroup indicators of trust, perceived commonality, and related items.

These impact assessments are usually material for internal commission and government reports—little has been offered in the way of scholarly insight into the development of these reports or discussion of how the assessments might be made more quantitative or systematic. Note that while we do not argue that quantitative assessments are inherently superior to other approaches, they are useful in the assessment of commission effects in support of their missions for at least two reasons. First, and assuming the Columbia Law School review represents an accurate cross-section of assessment best practices, none of the quantitative assessments recommend the use of more rigorous quantitative approaches to determining causal impacts of policy and programming (e.g., randomly assigned experiments). As such, there is an opportunity to add insight to existing assessment approaches of commissions and their programs using randomized treatment designs and related research designs. Second, and as a related point, bringing the study of HRCs more into the mainstream political science, public administration, and public policy disciplines is made easier if the empirical examination of HRCs uses similar empirical approaches as found in these disciplines. We make a concerted effort throughout this book to use a variety of empirical methods in our analysis of commissions, including qualitative and randomized experimental approaches, with the goal of drawing as complete a picture as possible of what HRCs around the country attempt to accomplish within the contextual frameworks.

As we discuss further in our historical discussion about race relations and HRCs in the following two chapters, many commissions were established in the 1930s and 1940s in response to the influx of African Americans to northern cities. There were, however, a series of commissions established throughout the country in the 1960s and 1970s in response to urban uprisings.[8] The appendix provides a list of the more than 150 HRCs

operating throughout the United States and indicates the general operation type for each. Toward the end of the book we also touch on some of
the future possibilities of increased commission involvement with state
and national human relations organizations, including the International
Association of Official Human Rights Agencies.

Independent of their relationship status with International Association
of Official Human Rights Agencies, several commissions work to enforce
elements of the Fair Housing Act, other HUD policies, and FEPA agencies. These FEPA agencies include, for example, the Alexandria Human
Relations Commission (Virginia); the Human Relations Commission of
Austin, Texas; the Baltimore Community Relations Commission; the District of Columbia Office of Human Rights; the Human Relations Department of Kansas City, Missouri; the New York City Commission on Human
Rights; the Human Relations Department of Orlando, Florida; and the
City of York Human Relations Commission (Pennsylvania). Commissions
enforcing HUD-related fair housing policy include the City of Phoenix
Equal Opportunity Department, the Delaware Division of Human Relations, the Broward County Office of Equal Opportunity, the City of Tampa
Office of Community Relations, the Boston Fair Housing Commission,
and the Vermont Human Rights Commission. Some bodies, such as the
District of Columbia Office of Human Rights, handle both FEPA and
HUD-related duties. But some commissions, like the LAHRC, handle neither of these policy duties. Instead, it and other commissions end up
working almost entirely on intergroup relations–related efforts without a
statute to enforce.

As we demonstrate throughout the book, commissions have certain
advantages in fulfilling their missions but also challenges in both fulfilling these duties and taking on additional responsibilities that may not be
in a commission's current purview but that commissioners, personnel, or
stakeholders would like to see their commission undertake. Arguably, a
book about commissions from the standpoint of enforcing HUD or FEPA
codes would take the analysis in a descriptive direction about policy
enforcement. While a descriptive assessment of code enforcement is
important, we deem it less insightful than a focus on an individual-level
analysis of commissioners, commission staff, and the way the public perceives different aspects of HRC-related work in the communities they

serve. These can include, but are not limited to, housing and employment enforcement but, perhaps more importantly, deal with intergroup relations topics.

Due to the diversity of the Los Angeles population and the publicity surrounding the Watts uprising suggests, the LAHRC serves as the quintessential example of government efforts in addressing intergroup relations, intergroup conflict, and intergroup justice.[9] Therefore, we use the LAHRC as the primary case study through which to evaluate similar agency efforts throughout the United States.

Our book's scope is diverse in terms of both the literature consulted and data analyzed. Drawing on historical documents, government memos, policy papers, interview data (from Los Angeles, Pittsburgh, Cincinnati, and Fort Worth, Texas) and original surveys and survey-embedded experiments of area residents in Los Angeles, Pittsburgh, and Cincinnati conducted specifically for this book, we convey the enormity of the human relations challenges in America's cities while gaining leverage on some of the more promising tools that policy makers and communities might leverage to improve intergroup conditions and related concerns (such as landlord discrimination issues and community–police relations). Each of the four commissions pursue different government missions, and each has varying stature in the organizations and communities they serve. Their geographic diversity and their city's relative histories in dealing with discrimination and intergroup relations issues recommend their inclusion as case studies. That said, there are certainly other commissions that could be featured in the book. Our hope is scholars will examine the work of commissions that were not the subject of our research, attempting to build on the insights we found to further our understanding of HRCs and their community impacts.

Our work offers scholars and other interested observers a window into the very challenging and yet potentially rewarding human relations work occurring at the LAHRC and similar organizations across the country. There is no overarching theory specific to commissions and their work per se, but the organizations' contextual location in local government recommends linkage to broad theories about population change and expectations of government responsiveness, trust in institutions, and a sense of connectedness between residents.[10] In terms of commission attempts to affect change in an inter-institutional environment, Laurence O'Toole and Robert Montjoy's seminal work on implementation from the public administration literature also bears on our efforts.[11]

There is disagreement in the literature as to whether the way people view local government—and their communities more generally—results from personal or macro factors, including historical developments specific to racial and ethnic groups.[12] Clearer is the notion that local population size sets the backdrop for challenges to fostering community unity and trust, with an inverse association between population size and trust in local government.[13] Indeed, the difficulties associated with fostering higher quality of life for larger and more heterogenous population centers may help explain why HRCs are predominantly located in urban areas.

Logically, the more residents are involved in local government decisions, the more we should expect residents to engage with local mechanisms (like commissions) in discerning and dealing with community problems, especially in situations where groups have grievances to express about local political and economic conditions. Janet Abu-Lughod makes a strong case for government responsiveness to those protesting and for the consequences of what might happen if local officials do not engage with stakeholders:

> Where there is ongoing interaction between well-organized protest movements with leaders capable of articulating specific demands for change, and a responsive local government, the more quickly hostilities can be brought to an end. Responsiveness is greater when the local power structure actually includes representatives of the dissatisfied minority group and acknowledge the frustrations underlying the explosion and the legitimacy of the grievances expressed. These possibilities for positive interactions are in turn mediated by . . . the degree to which enhanced paths to political representation and power in a competitive political system exist and can therefore offer constructive ways to bring about desired reforms in local policies without recourse to street violence.[14]

Certainly not all (or even most) groups bearing grievances with local government are engaged in violence or are likely to become violent. But the potential is there. The potential also exists for urban governments to show responsiveness through proactive measures designed to, if not improve economic and social conditions outright, provide a political voice to air discontent on the part of traditionally underrepresented and oppressed groups. For their part, local government officials usually speak positively about resident input in community policymaking decisions.[15] But the problem is that the process by which residents are brought into local decision making varies by bureaucratic willingness to incorporate citizens into the decision process, with such willingness being the outcome of a variety of professional and normative factors.[16] Although HRCs generally represent a hybrid organizational structure with both community members and professional bureaucrats working on behalf of a local agency, we argue that the work and relative success of HRCs are best viewed in the context of bureaucratic responsiveness in addressing community challenges in relatively large (and mostly urban) areas.

Commissions can be used as political tools that elected officials may deploy for rhetorical gain or public relations purposes, but their more common roles are that of community sounding board and, as we discussed above, code enforcer. This is why we consider HRCs as fulfilling at least part of the purpose of government responsiveness that Abu-Lughod outlines.[17] But due largely to their mission as "front facing" government agencies dedicated to improving intergroup relations and combating discrimination, HRCs are dependent on community and bureaucratic cooperation in ways that few other local agency types are. What is more, commissions are perhaps the quintessential example of agencies driven by bureaucratic, not political, values.[18] Especially in cases where HRCs are primarily tasked with improving intergroup relations, bureaucratic creativity and value orientations in determining strategies to meet such an ambiguous goal loom large in organizational efforts. Different from the literature's focus on "creativity" as market-driven, economically focused developments in urban planning, we adopt Patsy Healy's use of "creativity" in urban governance as a process with spiritual or cultural dimensions.[19] We do not suggest that HRCs are explicitly spiritual or cultural, but they can draw on both domains in working toward improved intergroup relations. And, in keeping with Kenneth Meier and Laurence O'Toole's general model of bureaucratic values as the leading instigator of governing decisions, we consider HRC personnel—both professional staff and community volunteer officers—to occupy a creative policy space in which they work to carry out an HRC's mission.[20]

Yet, as we show throughout this book, these creative efforts often result in mixed outcomes, in part because as weaker government agencies that often have limited or no statutory enforcement authority, HRCs are susceptible to ad hoc demands from community stakeholders, inconsistent attention and support from elected officials, and hazy programmatic responsibilities.[21] Add to this an incessant concern about funding, and the creative space that HRCs operate in is both an advantage and a hindrance to realizing long-term goals. And the emphasis here is on the "long term." After all, the strife between different racial and ethnic groups, economic classes, landlords and tenants, and police and community members did not sprout into existence overnight.

Yet the picture here is not all pessimistic. By virtue of their hybrid organization featuring citizen commissioners and bureaucratic staff—coupled with the double-edged sword of mission ambiguity—commissions are generally not part of the standard principal–agent phenomenon that political scientists study.[22] Instead, HRCs operate closer to Meier and O'Toole's theory of bureaucratic representativeness whereby HRC commissioners and bureaucrats undertake action that represent "the values of the public."[23] However, and unlike Wilson's description of "craft" organizations whereby entities are decentralized with sizable bureaucratic autonomy, HRCs face limits in what they can accomplish without direct permission from elected officials (whether in the form of statute or resolution) or from federal mandates aimed at enforcing antidiscrimination laws.[24] But even in cases where HRCs lack any form of authority to subpoena or sanction, there is a public-facing benefit to cities having commissions function in the communities they serve, even if at least parts of their mission may be ambiguous. As the creative space introduced above suggests, HRCs may enjoy a flexibility in their work that invites innovation and fosters some degree of effectiveness.

MULTIPLE COMMISSIONS, MULTIPLE ROLES

By the 1960s and 1970s, most large municipalities and several states had some form of HRC as episodes of urban unrest, community/police clashes, and protests became more common. HRCs were initially recognized as local government responses to intergroup differences and competing

claims for fair treatment, economic improvement, and political enfran-
chisement. Philip Ethington and Christopher West summarize the HRC
role well: "Managing the stresses and incipient conflicts between people
differentiated by race/ethnicity/cultural backgrounds, interests, and access
to wealth and power, while maintaining for all a standard of justice (fairness), is the most basic work of a democracy."[25] To accomplish this enor-
mous task, commissions have historically engaged in wide-ranging activities. Most common are code enforcement, violence prevention, and
community training.[26] In undertaking their main activities, HRCs measure and monitor civil and human rights issues, particularly those that
may be sources of intergroup conflict. HRCs also work to anticipate, prevent, and, if necessary, resolve issues arising from intergroup conflict
before violence results. By involving as many subgroups of the community as possible in their efforts, HRCs work to promote more positive
intergroup relations in their jurisdictions, thereby addressing underlying
issues inherent in civil rights concerns and intergroup conflict.

The way HRCs go about their business is largely determined by the kind
of authority they are given and where they are located in the local
government—decisions that were often made at the time the HRCs were
established but may have also been revised depending on political or
financial considerations. For analytical purposes, we divide HRCs into
three types: quasi-judicial (which includes the HUD and FEPA enforcement functions discussed above), advisory (the power to make recommendations to improve intergroup relations but not to take action enforcing
them), and facilitation (primarily conflict management, assisting or helping to make intergroup relations better or easier). For example, the
Miami–Dade County Commission on Human Rights is what we term a
quasi-judicial entity in that it has statutory power to subpoena and conduct investigations in enforcement of Miami–Dade County's civil and
human rights ordinances. It can also hold public hearings and invoke
fines. This is similar to the statutory powers granted HRCs in Fort Worth
and Pittsburgh. In addition, some HRCs could fall into more than one of
these categories. For example, the Fort Worth and Pittsburgh HRCs also
function as advisory units for city agencies and elected officials. The
LAHRC and Cincinnati HRC, by contrast, have no statutory authority
to act in a judicial capacity and are primarily facilitator units. In this

capacity the LAHRC can only advocate for cooperation between disparate groups divided along neighborhood, class, racial, ethnic, gender, religious, and sexual orientation lines.

As America's troubled history with race relations shows, the work of human relations policy makers in America's major cities is difficult. Part of the problem is that the objectives commissions have to meet can be vague in scope, execution, and effectiveness of evaluation. This is especially true for commissions that lack statutory authority to act in a quasi-judicial manner. Whereas commissions in Pittsburgh and Fort Worth are empowered through local ordinances to investigate issues dealing with discrimination of varying types, the work of commission policy makers and staff in the LAHRC is more challenging. In introducing LAHRC and its programmatic efforts, we pay particular attention to the Los Angeles case and use the Fort Worth, Pittsburgh, and Cincinnati commissions for comparative context.

In a comparative sense, perhaps the LAHRC's greatest advantage is its flexibility. This is because, for commissions enjoying a degree of institutional or quasi-judicial authority, staff may find themselves dealing with the unintended consequence of too specific a set of policy domains or stakeholder expectations. It is difficult for commissions like Pittsburgh and Fort Worth to work on broad community and intergroup relations issues because so much of their budget and staffing obligations are line items designated for HUD or FEPA code enforcement and hearing processes on discrimination cases. Los Angeles, by comparison, has the freedom to undertake a variety of community projects and partnerships because, ironically, its limited institutional authority empowers it to explore public–private collaborations. As such, the relative positions commissions find themselves in, as a product of the institutional structures that create and sustain them, provide comparative advantages in only certain areas. Interestingly, our work with commissions throughout the country has yet to identify an example of an HRC that has the flexibility to function like LAHRC while enjoying the same degree of institutional cachet like those in Pittsburgh and Fort Worth. In other words, there appears to be no single HRC that has the diversity of tools, adequacy of resources, and mandates across the three commission types we identify.

There are also political considerations that impact HRC work. As agencies given broad responsibilities for monitoring interactions and relationships between groups—some of whom may be in intense conflict at times—there can be political pressure brought to bear on commission staff in the form of official and unofficial "guidance" in selecting community projects to support, facilitating intergroup dialogue, and giving public testimony about the state of group relations in a locale. In some instances where progress toward intergroup understanding is slow to materialize, frustration can mount (even among HRC staff). One specific example that an LAHRC staffer related to us during our work for this book involved a heated discussion that occurred between the staffer and community members at an HRC-sponsored event about local neighborhood interactions with the LAPD:

> I was running things at the meeting and a woman came up and started verbally attacking this guy who's a cop, and he's giving testimony. We're talking about having a dialogue here about this, so then she's like you stay out of it, and I'm like, no I'm not going to stay out of it. So I got confrontational and she's like look, this is the problem. She's like what the problem is here is that we're having an exchange of ideas about community violence. You know it's the cops. Oh that's where we're at so, so we take all the responsibility from ourselves so nothing is my fault. Everything is someone else's fault. So then why are we here?

The staffer's frustration was palpable, particularly since part of establishing a constructive dialogue between community members and institutions like the LAPD is for both sides in a dispute to recognize mutual responsibility and accountability in the process of points of conflict. With the rash of racially related police shootings in the United States since 2014, commissions around the country have had to work to balance community concerns about racial disparities in enforcement with police organization duties in providing effective public safety.

Overlaying these discussions is a tense political environment in which elected officials want to be perceived as responsive to minority community concerns while maintaining the confidence of their police forces, businesses, and civic organizations more generally. This places commissions in an especially delicate spot as facilitators of progress in intergroup relations. In the end, the HRCs cannot allow one side of the community–police dialogue to overtake the discussion to the point of obstructing policy reform, community improvement, and better relations and communication between police and residents. Yet, in some instances, the commissions are left with little room to maneuver.

ADDITIONAL IMPORTANT REALITIES

As if the implementation challenges of the job were not already daunting in terms of the political pressures that accompany high profile issues like police–community relations, HRCs face a litany of other political and institutional issues. The most apparent is funding, both in terms of the actual dollar amounts designated for certain purposes and the level of government doing the funding. A recent example featuring the LAHRC involves its reliance on a federal HUD block grant administered through the city's housing department. After the 2008 financial downturn, the commission, which had been funded for decades largely from the City of Los Angeles's general revenue budget, found its city budget line reduced to virtually zero in the wake of steep revenue shortfalls. In order to keep the commission operational in some form, local and state political leaders negotiated a multiyear funding package that kept the HRC going but severely restricted the kinds of projects that it could use the HUD money to fund. While the HRC's shift to the city housing department made some sense given the historic issues minorities have had with securing quality housing, the department's rigid procedures did not mesh well with what the HRC needed to do its job well given its lack of a quasi-judicial role in code and antidiscrimination enforcement.

This is a good example of the irony regarding the LAHRC: its lack of statutory authority gives it flexibility in operations, but its primary funding source over the last decade has restricted the kinds of work that the commission can have reimbursed (a similar set of constraints confronts the Cincinnati commission, as seen in later chapters). Although the Los Angeles commission has a mandate in the city charter to work for the improvement of intergroup relations throughout the city, the HUD restrictions—which essentially limited commission workers to projects in low-income neighborhoods—has meant that any intergroup relations issues more tangentially related to the socioeconomic divide were generally off limits unless the commission could find an alternate way to pay for them. While this is an understandable set of restrictions given HUD's focus, even a cursory look at the history of race relations in America underscores the need for governments to have multiple tools ready to address intergroup conflict. While economic differences play a large role in many sources of conflict, addressing the social-psychological dimensions of group tensions (which often feed on economic disparities but may also be independent of financial deprivation) require more than geomapping of housing availability in neighborhoods, landlord oversight, and the other tasks usually given to city housing authorities and funded through HUD grants.

One example where an intergroup relations issue is generally not within the HUD funding purview in Los Angeles is interfaith dialogue. Although we consider race the central motivator of intergroup conflict in this book given the nation's history, divisions also cleave along alternate sources of group identity, including religion.[27] Although the focus on promoting cooperation among faith groups is a key interest of HRCs, some, like the Los Angeles commission, may be constrained in their ability to focus beyond what housing policy makers have identified as core areas of funding interest. The challenge is not lost on LAHRC commissioners, who are residents appointed by the Los Angeles mayor's office to oversee HRC programming throughout the city. Also apparent are the times when protocols put in place for city housing department staffers more generally may not mesh with the kind of work HRC staff are charged with performing. One of the LAHRC commissioners related to us regarding funding and staff-related challenges:

> You know the HRC is not very well funded. It's not well staffed, and what our staff was able is able to do is pretty amazing. You know I don't even know how they do it, but you know I wish I could do more for them and I wish that you know if we could get more resources for them. But, at this point, we're having trouble even replacing people we lose in these positions, and, oh yeah, we're even having trouble getting things like cell phones for staff. I mean they're spending time on issues like this when

they should be doing the work that's needed. You know, after 2008 I understand everybody had to do their part. I mean we were in a serious economic situation there for a second, and we got for the first time ever shifted from a standalone entity to have been housed under other departments and right now we're under housing that doesn't make any sense to me. Housing has a lot of important work to do, particularly right now, they're focused on homelessness, but we're not their priority and I get it, and I understand that they have a protocol in place for their staff but it doesn't really apply to us—that part of their protocols that staff be at their desks while we have field staff. So HRC staff are being asked to be at their desk. And I get it because those are the protocols in place; they have a hierarchical system of how press information is released which I understand, but when you're dealing with potential unrest or hate crimes or something that's very [interesting to the] media you have to respond immediately, which is what the HRC can do as long as it's not hamstrung.

Importantly, and despite these financial challenges, the LAHRC has developed a reputation for being a facilitator of interfaith dialogues between the Muslim and Jewish communities in part through its support of New Ground, an organization founded to foster constructive dialogue between the Jewish and Muslim communities. Funds had to be procured from other government and private sector accounts to sustain these initiatives, however. But a relative advantage of the Los Angeles commission is that it has become comparatively good at developing partnerships with private organization and academic partners since, quite frankly, it had to be. In this case, the HUD-based funding restrictions fostered a certain degree of bureaucratic creativity among commission staff in meeting programmatic objectives. These partnerships have opened up opportunities to launch initiatives that not only provide insight on community dynamics and intergroup perceptions but also serve as examples of projects that local government may be interested in funding as a later-stage partner. One commission staffer told us during an interview:

If we are successful, then we're getting people who have traditionally been sort of disenfranchised and not connected to a process gauged at creating their own advocacy network, or a system where they feel connected and not feel detached and apathetic. I think that those have been the most successful like when women like the monolingual moms in the northeast of the city who are talking to the police on a consistent basis, when they feel like they have influence and they have influence not only among themselves but in the community. When you feel that success has happened even if the success doesn't lead initially to some wholesale change (which is really ideally what you want to see), all these things take time, but there's a saying: it takes it takes about two or three generations to undo something; it takes about three or four generations to do something. I think that where we're in the media-driven culture is that [people] want to see things happen right away, but the work of human relations takes patience and takes commitment to people over time, and what's happening right now won't bear fruit for a good while.

The Cincinnati commission is much more like the LAHRC, especially in terms of a lack of HUD or FEPA code enforcement powers. It also has had to leverage flexibility to its mission's advantage both in terms of projects and funding. The Pittsburgh and Fort Worth HRCs have also faced funding challenges but of a different kind. Since both commissions are tasked with a quasi-judicial function in city government, the local councils and mayors have worked to protect budget lines to keep the investigatory and enforcement functions of these bodies running (even though both commissions experienced some reduction in force following the 2009 recession). The problem for these commissions, however, has been in finding money to provide for any new initiatives that would help encourage positive intergroup dialogues and related outcomes outside of the commissions' statutory responsibilities. Since the local budget dollars were already earmarked for specific programs on code enforcement and related items, commission staff have encountered pushback to varying degrees when seeking to develop programming similar to what the Los Angeles commission has done. In an interview, a Pittsburgh commission staff member related:

> We want to get to the point of doing more than code enforcement, and making more headway in understanding community member perceptions of government and those around them. Hopefully, we can get there.

There is some support among city council for us to take on an additional research-like role, but we have to balance that with our primary commitment to investigate violations of housing policies and other forms of discrimination. It's definitely a balancing act.

The relative difference in both funding and programmatic flexibility between HRCs is important not as an example of different emphases by these local bodies but in how the difference impacts commission ability to foster positive intergroup relations. The primary goal of commissions of any type is to promote social harmony and justice (or at least encourage an increase of both) to counter the nation's legacy with racial discrimination and oppression. Positive intergroup relations are at the heart of this harmony. The challenge that HRC staffers face, however, is that relative success is not based on a clear-cut or formula-driven process. Neither, for that matter, is the desired outcome easy to assess.

Unlike other local government agencies responsible for issues like public safety, power, and waste removal, the metrics by which positive intergroup perceptions are identified and measured—much less the processes by which they are derived—are amorphous. Although it is likely that most city leaders understand the complexity of group interactions at some level, the caveats and challenges of human relations work are not always at the forefront of how city leaders perceive what HRCs do. Improving basic city services is not a complicated process to understand, but as one of the Los Angeles staffers mentioned to us,

> the work that human relations does requires human capital investment and the outcomes are not always going to be black and white; it's more long term, yeah, it's a very long term. None of our projects are going to be, like, oh we're going to go in there come out next week, and we're going have solved the situation. So I think that's hard to for a legislative official and the community at large to wrap their head around that. It's a long and sometimes tedious process, and . . . you need an investment and you need qualified committed passionate individuals to convene them.

The point made by this person is that the work that HRCs engage in is both complex and delicate, requiring a long-term commitment to funding efforts on social justice issues and a degree of patience with the ambiguity surrounding outcomes related to commission efforts. From a policy analysis standpoint, the code enforcement work of the Fort Worth and Pittsburgh commissions is better suited than the work of the LAHRC for the kind of tangible, results-driven emphasis that budget analysts, elected officials, and government watchdog groups expect to see. Meanwhile, for better or worse, commissions like the Los Angeles case can provide anecdotal reports about successful interventions between community groups, diffusion of potential violence between gangs, and the facilitation of dialogue between community members and law enforcement. Where code enforcement is part of a commission's purview, statistics on the number of complaints filed and successfully resolved may provide a more robust measure of commission effectiveness, but these measures are still a far cry from the assessment of intergroup dynamics that drive the core missions of any HRC. Therefore, just as HRC responsibilities are not one-size-fits-all across jurisdictions, neither are the commissions' capacity to fulfill them.

PLAN FOR THE BOOK

We use the remaining chapters of this book to evaluate how commissions work to fulfill their core missions, including establishing the context in which many commissions must operate. Accordingly, we begin chapter 2 with a historical overview of race and intergroup relations in the United States. For the most part, the story is one of intergroup strife and rebellion.[28] Chapter 3 maps in detail the development of America's HRCs, from the first Race Relations Commission in 1919 to the Human *Rights* Commissions of today. Our discussion of the evolution of HRCs includes attention to the demographic, cultural, and attitudinal changes the country has gone through even as the root causes of intergroup conflict remain much the same.

Featuring interview data collected from human relations policy makers and local community group members in Los Angeles, Cincinnati, Fort Worth, and Pittsburgh, chapter 4 considers each HRC's capacity to implement their founding purpose and specified mandates. Theories of policy implementation and bureaucratic behavior help to explain the actions taken to promote community collaboration while addressing the certain pitfalls that arise from intergroup relations work, including collaborator and staffer burnout, disillusionment, and policy ambiguity.

Expanding into an assessment of intergroup relations and drawing on elements of social identity theory and group contact theory, chapter 5 tests the likelihood of improving intergroup relations via a messaging intervention commonly used by HRCs that emphasizes a superordinate community identity among local residents of different racial and ethnic groups. Specifically, we assess the influence of different group identity cues on perceptions of intergroup commonality using a novel questions-as-treatment survey experiment in Los Angeles County featuring Latino, black, and Anglo subjects.[29]

Building on the previous chapter, chapter 6 illustrates how commissions can use data driven insights from community-based research to improve their facilitation and enforcement efforts and features vignettes from three additional community surveys fielded in Los Angeles, Pittsburgh, and Cincinnati. The Los Angeles survey tests the effect of "Love thy neighbor" messaging. The Pittsburgh survey focuses on perceived discrimination in housing availability and residents' perceptions of the effectiveness of contacting the HRC. Finally, the Cincinnati survey explores residents' perception of community–police relations—a topic of clear interest to HRCs.

We approach chapter 7—the book's final chapter—as both a summary of what was learned in the previous chapters and a series of recommendations for HRCs throughout the United States. The overarching theme of the chapter is that patience and creativity are necessary in engaging in human relations work.

2

THE HISTORY OF INTERGROUP RELATIONS IN AMERICA

One of the first things that we discovered in our research on intergroup relations and the workings of human relations commissions was the dearth of scholarship on the origins and development of HRCs (for the two exceptions, see the 1998 report of Ethington and West and Obermiller and Wagner's 2017 history of the HRC in Cincinnati). The forerunners to HRCs were created in response to race riots in American cities in the early 1940s. Yet, in fact, there had been violent race conflicts/ uprisings in the United States since at least the 1760s. With this point in mind, we use this chapter to provide an historical overview of intergroup relations, focusing on matters of race. In doing so, we give a general overview of the major racial and ethnic groups and their experiences in the country. In the next chapter we transition to a discussion of some of the more structural and economic conditions that precipitated more recent episodes of racial strife, including the efforts of various levels of government to interdict conflict.

Part of our decision to focus primarily on historical matters of race is based on Michael Omi and Howard Winant's conclusion that race is the primary, irreducible factor animating social perception, identities, and relations in America.[1] While some may argue that class, religious, and gender distinctions are equally important in the construction of society, we consider these factors to be secondary to race as a social divider in American history, particularly given Rodney Hero's argument of the existence of two-tiered pluralism in the United States and the lack of substantive equality for racialized subordinate groups.[2] Given this, we argue that not only is a race-centered approach appropriate given the dynamics of identity and group interaction but it also reflects accurately on the motives for establishing HRCs in the first place.

EARLIEST RACIAL AND ETHNIC CONFLICT

Simply stated, the United States has a long history of racial and ethnic tension and conflict. Competition and ill feelings between groups of varying racial, ethnic, national, and religious distinctions has often resulted in civil disorder and mob violence. Racism, commonly understood as discrimination directed against someone of a different race based on the belief that one's own race is superior, has been part of the American landscape since the seventeenth-century European colonization of North America.

Sometimes the conflict is best described as a majority/minority (perhaps more accurately described as dominant/subordinate) issue whereby the dominant group attempts to discipline or suppress a specific subordinate group. This would usually, but not always, occur when the subordinate group resists or rebels against the status quo. Sometimes the conflict is between two or more minority/subordinate groups. Owing to the development of racial hierarchies from colonial America onward, the conflict has most often been racially oriented, but conflict has also extended to class and religion.[3] As Ronald Bayor further explains:

> The underlying element in these conflicts is a sense of threat—a feeling, based on realistic or unrealistic criteria that one's own group is under attack in regard to its interests or values. The basis for a group's concern can stem from a variety of issues—jobs, political power, neighborhood control, foreign policy. Conflicts often develop in a step-by-step fashion as competitive tensions slowly increase. They can also emerge, however, with lightning speed as an explosive issue or event occurs, one that immediately puts groups into contention.[4]

Less prevalent than conflict, and certainly less acknowledged by scholars and the popular press, were the periods of intergroup cooperation.[5] One of the earliest examples of intergroup conflict followed by cooperation began in 1689 between Dutch and English residents in New Amsterdam / New York when Dutch militia led by German-born Jacob Leisler took over Fort James in an attempt to reassert their earlier political influence and economic independence in what had become a British-dominated colony. Leisler subsequently controlled the town for about two years until his militia was forced to step down and Leisler was tried and executed. But tensions continued between the Dutch and English for several years. Then, in 1712, a rebellion of black slaves brought the divided white community together as Dutch and English slave owners organized and fought in unison to successfully suppress the rebellion.[6]

Nativism and racism continued to fuel intergroup tensions during the 1700s, but group violence was limited until the early 1800s with the arrival of large numbers of poor Irish Catholic immigrants. Native-born Protestants generally viewed the newcomers with disdain and suspicion. There were strong differences between the two groups on many issues besides religion, including class, politics, temperance, and so on. Moreover there was competition over employment as many of the native-born perceived the abundance of less-skilled Irish laborers as limiting the opportunities of skilled craftsmen. In Philadelphia and New York, disagreement also occurred over who controlled the schools. The majority-Protestant population moved swiftly to suppress the views of the predominantly Roman Catholic Irish, who were now viewed as a legitimate threat to Protestants' social position.

Fueled by concerns over cultural hegemony, education, and economic opportunity, serious clashes occurred between native-born Protestants and Irish Catholic immigrants in Philadelphia, Boston, and New York. The Philadelphia Nativist Riots of 1844 were especially destructive, with anti-immigrant mobs attacking the Irish in their homes and churches. Before being suppressed by the state militia, the rioters killed at least twenty people, injured one hundred more, and destroyed two Catholic churches and one Catholic convent.[7]

Realizing that outright law breaking was not a viable long-term strategy to deter growing influence from immigrant communities, semisecret local nativist organizations began forming in the 1830s. When asked about their meetings and activities, the members typically responded by saying "I know nothing about it," hence the term the organizations and their members came to be known by: "know nothings." By 1854, after "know nothing" candidates succeeded in winning mayoral contests in several major cities and at least one governorship, the local groups joined together to establish the Native American Party, which espoused an anti-Catholic and anti-immigrant (i.e., anti-Irish) political platform.[8]

Due to abuse from majority Protestants over the years, the Irish developed a "siege mentality" that caused them "to react aggressively to any threat, real or imagined."[9] Accordingly, Irish were frequently confrontational with other minority groups. Mob violence broke out in 1829 and again in 1836 in Cincinnati, when rivalry over jobs and housing resulted in the Irish destroying property and assaulting black residents in the densely populated neighborhood of the First Ward.[10] The most significant outburst of Irish-led group violence was the New York City Draft Riot of 1863, which lasted approximately four days. The rioters were primarily working-class men who resented that their wealthier counterparts were thus spared from the Civil War draft because they could afford to hire a substitute to fight for them. The protests, initially intended to express anger at this avoidance practice, known as commutation, as well as the war draft itself, quickly turned into a race riot with poor white rioters—predominantly Irish immigrants—attacking blacks and their supporters throughout the city. A cause of the working poor's angst was the prospect of thousands of freed slaves entering the job market. By the time public order was finally restored, fifty buildings in the downtown area were destroyed, including multiple churches and the Colored Orphan Asylum. There were at least 125 fatalities (although claims run as high as 1,000 deaths), including 11 black men who were lynched after being beaten.

Of course, not all Irish residents participated in the rioting. There were Irish among the police, firefighters, and militia who worked to bring about and maintain peace. Moreover, the Irish were not alone in their targeting of blacks, as other non-Irish whites also participated. Nativism, class antagonism, racism, proslavery, and pro-Confederate attitudes were all elements contributing to this violent example of racial and ethnic conflict.[11]

AMERICAN INDIANS AND RACISM

Although often treating each other with disdain, as the Irish experience in the last section shows, Europeans tended to coalesce in their treatment of American Indians.[12] European settlers believed that American Indians, the original inhabitants of the new continent known as America, were heathens and savages who needed to be civilized through Christianity and European culture. Even after the American colonies became an independent country, racist attitudes toward Indian people prevailed. Over the course of two hundred years, the United States adopted widely varying Indian policies that fluctuated according to changing perspectives and necessities of Indian supervision.[13] For the most part, the government attempted to force Indians to abandon their cultural identity.

From 1778 to 1871 U.S. relations with individual American Indian tribes/nations were established and conducted primarily through the treaty-making process. These "contracts among nations" recognized and established unique sets of rights, benefits, and conditions for the treaty-making tribes. Now considered "sovereign dependent nations," the tribes agreed to cede millions of acres of their homelands to the United States and accept its protection.[14] The government's policies toward Indians in the second half of the nineteenth century were influenced by the desire to expand westward into territories occupied by tribes. The westward expansion led to broken treaties and military intervention by the U.S. government as well as the expropriation of tribal land that was then made available to American companies and white settlers.

Angered by the government's policies, the Cheyenne, Arapaho, Comanche, and Sioux tribes fought back. Resorting to violence to protect their lands and their tribes' survival, Indians skirmished or battled more than one thousand times with whites in the West between 1861 and 1891. In an attempt to force the Indians onto reservations and end the violence, the federal government responded to these hostilities with costly military campaigns.[15] Notably, there were also Indian individuals who voluntarily assisted private companies and settlers in their migration to western lands. Some tribes continued cooperating with U.S. government officials in exchange for the promise of protection from the hostile whites.

By the 1900s the federal government focused its efforts toward assimilating Indians into American society. The government forced Indian children to attend residential boarding schools that required the students to speak only English and to adopt Euro-American culture and traditions.[16] The government also required all formally recognized tribes to compose and ratify tribal constitutions and establish elected governing councils.[17] Indian men were encouraged to serve in the U.S. military and frequently did serve, including during both world wars.

After World War II ended, the goal of assimilating Indians continued but with a new policy strategy of terminating tribal rights. Termination began with a series of laws intended to dismantle tribal sovereignty along with the relocation of significant numbers of Indians from reservations to urban areas. The most drastic component of the termination laws was the ending of federal recognition of more than one hundred tribes, along with the federal aid that came with that designation. These actions affected more than twelve thousand Indians and removed approximately 2.5 million acres of trust land from protected status allowing it to be sold to non-Indians. Another component granted states jurisdiction over most criminal offenses committed by or against Indians on reservations and on other Indian held lands. Additionally, the government quit funding most of the health care and education programs, utility services, and police and fire departments on Indian reservations. Given the geographic isolation and economic challenges facing many of the reservations, few tribes had the funds to continue these essential services after termination was implemented. Some tribes mounted successful legal challenges to maintain tribal government and the trust relationship with the federal government. In many instances, however, tribes lacked the resources to challenge termination.[18]

The Indian Relocation Act of 1952 was touted by its supporters to address the widespread poverty on reservations by encouraging "voluntary" relocation of residents on reservations to select urban areas. The recruitment of volunteers was highly successful. Participants in the program were offered relocation transportation, fifty dollars for moving expenses, subsistence per diem for both the time of relocation and up to three weeks after arrival, funds to purchase tools or equipment for apprentice workers, and, in some instances, tuition for vocational training. From 1952 to 1972, more than one hundred thousand Indians were relocated to cities. But many of the relocated Indians struggled to adjust to city life as they experienced unemployment, low-end jobs, discrimination, homesickness, and the loss of traditional cultural supports. Approximately 30 percent ultimately returned to their reservations.[19]

Relocation created urban areas filled with Indians from dissimilar tribes. Living in close proximity and in similar circumstances of poverty and discrimination, the relocated individuals increasingly identified ethnically as "Indian" rather than with their tribal affiliations. The urbanization of Indians began to create a sense of pan-tribal identity leading to the creation of urban Indian centers and politically oriented organizations such as the American Indian Movement. Although the American Indian Movement gained national attention from their widely publicized acts of protest against the federal government (e.g., their occupations of Alcatraz Island, the Bureau of Indian Affairs, and Wounded Knee), the conflict that instigated the formation of what would eventually become a national Red Power movement was the ongoing harassment and civil rights violations of Indian residents by local police.[20]

Today more than 80 percent of the Indian population lives in urban areas, primarily in blue-collar neighborhoods. Urban-dwelling Indians still experience discrimination, underemployment, and lower educational attainment compared to other racial or ethnic groups. The circumstances for Indians living on reservations represents extreme differences depending on the reservation's natural resources and proximity to non-Indian populations. The Indians on reservations with oil and gas or with highly popular tourist attractions such as casinos are economically well off, while those on reservations that are more remote or without the resources for economic development are living at or close to the poverty level.[21] What is more, the bifurcated distribution of income among Indians contributes to both intergroup and intragroup tensions.

AFRICAN AMERICANS AND THE LEGACY OF BLACK ENSLAVEMENT

The experience of African Americans in this country is one of enslavement, segregation, lynching, personal discrimination, institutional racism, and violence. Slavery was practiced throughout the American colonies in the seventeenth and eighteenth centuries, beginning 1619, when a Dutch ship brought African slaves to the British colony of Jamestown, Virginia. European settlers turned to African slaves as a cheaper, more plentiful labor source than indentured servants, who were mostly poor white Europeans. Black slaves worked primarily on farms and plantations in the southern region.

After the American Revolution, many colonists—particularly in the North, where slavery was considerably less important to the local economy—began to link the oppression of black slaves to their own oppression by the British and to call for slavery's abolition. However, the new U.S. Constitution tacitly acknowledged the institution of slavery, counting each slave as three-fifths of a person for the purposes of taxation and representation in Congress and guaranteeing the right to repossess any "person held to service or labor" (an obvious euphemism for slavery).

With slavery never being widespread in the North, all of the northern states abolished slavery by 1804, but slavery remained absolutely vital to the South, where the economy continued to depend on the large-scale production of tobacco and later cotton (after the invention of the cotton gin in 1793). The U.S. Congress outlawed the African slave trade in 1808, but the domestic trade flourished and the slave population in the United States nearly tripled over the next fifty years, reaching approximately 4 million by 1860.[22]

Slave owners sought to make their slaves completely dependent on them, and a system of restrictive codes governed life among slaves. Slaves were generally prohibited from learning to read and write, and their behavior and movement were restricted. Masters rewarded obedient slave behavior with favors, while rebellious slaves were brutally punished. Nonetheless, slave rebellions occurred multiple times beginning as early as 1800. The slave insurrection that most terrified white slaveholders was led by Nat Turner in Southampton County, Virginia, in 1831. Over the course of two days, Turner's group, which numbered around seventy-five blacks, murdered approximately sixty whites before armed resistance from local whites and the arrival of state militia forces overwhelmed them. Supporters of slavery pointed to Turner's rebellion as evidence that blacks were barbarians who required an institution such as slavery to discipline them, and fears of similar insurrections led many Southern states to further strengthen their slave codes in order to limit the education, movement, and assembly of slaves. In the North, the increased repression of Southern blacks only fanned the flames of a growing abolitionist movement.[23]

From the 1830s to the 1860s the movement to abolish slavery in America gained strength, led by free blacks such as Frederick Douglass and white supporters such as Harriet Beecher Stowe (author of the bestselling antislavery novel *Uncle Tom's Cabin*) and William Lloyd Garrison (founder and editor of the radical newspaper *The Liberator*). In an effort that became known as the Underground Railroad, abolitionists began helping fugitive slaves escape from Southern plantations to the North via a loose network of safehouses as early as the 1780s. It is difficult to determine exactly how many slaves escaped through the Underground Railroad, but estimates have ranged from 40,000 to 100,000. Historians agree, however, that most of the slaves who managed to make their way to the North came from the border states of Maryland, Kentucky, and Virginia, while fewer attempted escape from the states of the Deep South. The success of the Underground Railroad undoubtedly increased tensions between North and South.[24]

The Missouri Compromise of 1820 admitted Missouri as a slave state and Maine as a free state while also specifying that all new territories above the latitude of Missouri's northern boundary would be prohibited from owning slaves, and territory below that latitude would allow slavery. The compromise was intended to resolve the tensions between the North and the South by striking a balance between free and slave states, but it only delayed the eventual outbreak of violent conflict. The Kansas–Nebraska Act of 1854 (mandating that settlers of a territory would be allowed to choose whether they wanted the institution of slavery in their new state) and the 1858 *Dred Scott* decision by the Supreme Court (involving a slave who unsuccessfully sued for his freedom on the grounds that his master had taken him into free territory), effectively repealed the Missouri Compromise so that all territories were open to slavery. The conflicts that arose in the aftermath of these government actions led to a period of violence between proslavery and abolitionist groups, including John Brown's raid on Harper's Ferry, Virginia, where Brown and a large group of armed abolitionists raided and occupied a federal arsenal resulting in the deaths of ten people before the occupation was ended by an attachment of U.S. Marines. Brown was captured and stood trial for treason where he was found guilty and sentenced to hanging. Public reaction to Brown's execution exposed the massive national split over slavery, with Brown hailed as a martyr in the North and a murderer in the South.

With growing enmity toward slavery among the majority of American voters, Abraham Lincoln won the 1860 election as the first Republican president on a platform pledging to keep slavery out of the territories. In response to Lincoln's win, seven slave states in the Deep South seceded from the United States (usually referred to as the Union during this time period) to form a new nation, the Confederate States of America (usually referred to as the Confederacy). Lincoln and his administration refused to recognize the legitimacy of secession, fearing that, among other things, it would lead to further fragmentation among the remaining states in the Union.

The bloodiest four years in American history began on April 12, 1861, when Confederate soldiers launched an attack on the Union-held Fort Sumter in South Carolina.[25] By the time the war ended in 1865, approximately 620,000 Union and Confederate soldiers were dead. The Emancipation Proclamation, issued by Lincoln in 1863, freed all slaves in the rebellious states of the Confederacy. Initially, he justified his proclamation as a war strategy that was necessary to cripple the Confederacy's war efforts because slaves were being used to support both the Confederate armies on the field and Southern businesses. However, by the end of the war, the proclamation had influenced and prepared many citizens to advocate and accept abolition for slaves in both the North and the South as a matter of human rights. The Thirteenth Amendment, abolishing slavery throughout the country, was ratified on December 6, 1865. Related congressional action followed in 1866 with the passage of the first civil rights act and ratification of the Fourteenth Amendment two years later. This federal action was intended to protect former slaves and other African Americans born free or naturalized in the United States from discrimination by ensuring their equal protection under the laws.[26]

With the end of Reconstruction in the 1870s, the southern response to the Civil War amendments was to implement policies that subjugated African Americans in as many social, political, and economic ways possible. What became known as the Jim Crow laws imposed segregation of races in public places, including educational institutions, and disenfranchised the black vote by imposing poll taxes and literacy tests as a condition for voting. Although African Americans shared common economic realities with poor whites, the generally acknowledged effect of the Jim Crow era was to unite whites as an identity group against blacks.

This racial unity was perhaps no more apparent than in the wave of lynchings perpetrated against African Americans from the 1880s to 1930s. During this time, almost three thousand reported lynchings occurred, and mainly against southern blacks.[27] Members of the Ku Klux Klan, which organized in response to national enforcement acts implemented to ensure compliance with the new constitutional amendments, were the prime instigators. Adding to the challenge posed by the Klan's vigilantism, the Civil Rights Act of 1875 (a second congressional attempt to ensure equal treatment in accommodations), was held unconstitutional by the Supreme Court. The Court based its decision on the reasoning that the Fourteenth Amendment applied only to government-based discrimination. The implication was that discrimination in services provided by private companies or individuals was legal. On top of this, the Compromise of 1877 (which allowed Rutherford B. Hayes to assume the presidency essentially in exchange for the removal of federal troops from the southern states), ended Reconstruction, which effectively ended federal-level civil rights protections for blacks at a time when southern whites felt emboldened to limit black economic and political power.

With federal troops gone and the Civil Rights Act of 1875 effectively set aside by the Supreme Court, southern states adopted both the "separate but equal" mantra and voting rights restrictions throughout the 1880s and 1890s. The "separate but equal" doctrine required blacks to be segregated from whites in virtually all public activities. The exception was for the most visible situations where a clear government service was provided. Public education was the most obvious example of a government service at this time. But Court decisions, including the Slaughterhouse cases and *Plessy v. Ferguson*, favored a quite narrow interpretation of the Fourteenth Amendment's due process clause as it applied to the federal rights of citizens. The eventual result was that the Court held that even segregation in public education was permissible, and, as the Court decided in *Cumming v. Richmond County Board of Education*, local and state governments could generally shirk their responsibilities in providing equal accommodations for blacks.

Eventually, state Democratic parties—the preferred political organization of southern whites given the Republican Party's association with the Union—consolidated power in the South through a combination of disenfranchisement of the black vote, gerrymandering, and outright violence at polling places. Institutionally, Jim Crow segregation was perpetuated through the discriminatory policies of labor and trade unions, banks, and even the teachings in southern Protestant churches. Many southern blacks were forced to make their living through working the land as part of the sharecropping system, which offered little economic opportunity. Other blacks found service-related jobs working for white employers. While all blacks were technically free according to the law, the reality was a significant lack of freedom due to Jim Crow segregation and economic exploitation by whites who continued to own approximately 95 percent of property in the South.[28]

According to Stewart Tolnay, the Jim Crow environment was multidimensional in its oppression of African Americans:

> Exclusion from neighborhoods, towns, and even entire counties restricted the residential options of blacks. Routine restriction of access within neighborhoods and towns—for example, to bathrooms, drinking fountains, restaurants, theaters, and public transportation—constrained blacks to inferior places, services, and facilities. Constant surveillance of blacks in public spaces heightened anxiety and often resulted in harassment while simply conducting the routine activities of life. Discrimination in local institutions such as courts, banks, and schools sharply limited opportunities for justice, the accumulation of wealth, and upward social mobility. Backing up these other forms of oppression was the constant threat of violence at the hands of whites, in the form of lynching, murder, assault, and rape.[29]

THE GREAT MIGRATION AND RED SUMMER

With the start of America's involvement in World War I, the first major threat to the South's social, economic, and political caste system began to take shape as factories in the Northeast and Midwest cities needed workers to fill jobs vacated by those entering the armed forces. By this time factory owners could no longer fill vacancies with European immigrants because of wartime prohibitions on new entrants to the country. With war production accelerating, factory recruiters went to the Mississippi Delta touting the plentiful job opportunities with good wages in the North and West. For example, around 1916, a factory wage in the urban North was typically three times more than what blacks could expect to make working the land in the rural South.[30] This economic opportunity helped spur the long-term migration of blacks from the southern farmlands to Chicago, New York, and other northern cities.

Meanwhile, almost 400,000 blacks either volunteered for or were conscripted into military service during World War I. The U.S. armed forces were segregated throughout the Great War, and the Army was the only branch of the military to allow blacks to serve in anything beyond menial positions. There was a general lack of respect and frequent overt racial prejudice and discrimination toward black soldiers from the majority of their white counterparts, including many who were assigned as officers over the black divisions.[31] Ultimately, more than 1,300 blacks were able to successfully complete their officer training and took over as officers in the all-black units.

The relocation of more than 500,000 blacks from the rural South to cities in the North, Midwest, and West during and just after World War I had a substantial impact on urban life in America. Demographic change resulting from this first wave of migration was extensive: in less than a decade, the black population grew by 66 percent in New York City, 148 percent in Chicago, 500 percent in Philadelphia, and 611 percent in Detroit.[32] Many of the male newcomers found jobs in factories, while others found work in slaughterhouses and foundries where working conditions were notably more strenuous and dangerous. Females had a more difficult time finding work given the intense competition for domestic labor positions.

Aside from competition for employment, housing was scarce in the increasingly crowded cities. While segregation was not legalized in the North, racism and prejudice toward blacks was widespread. After the U.S. Supreme Court declared racially based housing ordinances unconstitutional in 1917, some residential neighborhoods enacted covenants requiring white property owners to agree not to sell to blacks. Rising rents in de facto segregated areas, along with the resurgence of Ku Klux Klan activity, worsened black and white relations across the country. As the "war to end all wars" drew to a conclusion in 1919, the prospect of reintegrating white and black soldiers into the prewar economy further contributed to rising anxiety and intergroup tension.

The summer of 1919 began a period of pronounced interracial strife, including a wave of violent uprisings in more than three dozen cities and towns.[33] During what became known as the "Red Summer," whites often attacked blacks both physically and politically, as the call for racial and economic equality on the part of African Americans was considered akin to the Bolshevism that had just taken hold in Russia.[34] The most serious uprising took place in Chicago.

In 1919 the water and beaches of Lake Michigan in Chicago were unofficially segregated. When a black teenager violated this practice, he was stoned by a group of young whites and subsequently drowned. His death and the refusal of police to arrest anyone for the crime, even though there were multiple eyewitnesses, sparked nearly two weeks of fighting and destruction between groups of black and white Chicagoans on the city's South Side. There were beatings, shootings, and arson attacks killing fifteen whites, twenty-three blacks, and wounding more than five hundred, primarily black residents. An estimated one thousand black families also lost their homes in the fires.[35]

The riot raged against a backdrop of post–World War I tension. African American soldiers had returned home expecting to enjoy the fundamental freedoms they had fought to defend. Instead they faced blatant discrimination and growing racial prejudice. Many whites resented the growing numbers of black southern migrants and aggressively sought to protect their neighborhoods and factory jobs from the newcomers. Black anger over political corruption, a sagging economy and a housing shortage helped fuel the racial maelstrom.

The riot also exposed rampant racism in the ranks of the Chicago police. According to a report by Chicago's Commission on Race Relations, twice as many blacks as whites were arrested during the riot, and little protection was offered to African American neighborhoods.[36] Members of a prominent Irish "athletic club" called Ragen's Colts—who were financially sponsored by a popular local police commissioner, Frank Ragen—organized the groups of heavily armed "hoodlums" who roamed the streets hunting for blacks to hurt or kill with little fear of retribution. Blacks responded with force, making a clear statement that African Americans would no longer be passive victims. Ultimately, the state militia had to intervene to end the violence.

During the rioting, a committee of citizens representing forty-eight social, civic, commercial, and professional organizations met and petitioned the governor to take steps to quiet the existing disorder and appoint a commission to study the situation with the goal of preventing a reoccurrence. Illinois governor Frank Lowden quickly moved to establish an interracial advisory board of private citizens called the Chicago Commission on Race Relations (CCRR). Unfortunately, the CCRR was disbanded following its published report in 1921, and there was no follow-up on its recommendations.[37]

The root causes of the 1919 riots identified by the CCRR, including growing competition for housing and employment between African Americans and poor whites and the exaggerated and biased reporting of media regarding racial incidents, were also present in other major industrial cities. But rather than address these issues through affordable housing construction and attracting new industries, Chicago's reaction was to further segregate African Americans with racially restrictive covenants that prohibited blacks from owning property in select areas. This same policy approach was taken in Atlanta, St. Louis, Detroit, and other places with booming black populations. Needless to say, racial tensions continued to mount during the period between 1921 and the outbreak of World War II.

WORLD WAR II AND THE CIVIL RIGHTS MOVEMENT

Prominent scholars attribute World War II and its aftermath as the primary catalyst for the Civil Rights movement for African Americans.[38] Prior to World War II, most African Americans were low-wage farmers, factory workers, or servants. By the early 1940s, more lucrative war-related work was plentiful, but African Americans were not being hired for the better-paying jobs. They were also initially discouraged from joining the military. After thousands of blacks threatened to march on Washington to demand equal employment rights, President Franklin D. Roosevelt issued Executive Order 8802 on June 25, 1941, which opened national defense jobs and other government jobs to all Americans regardless of race, creed, color, or national origin.

More than a million African Americans enlisted in the armed forces during World War II, and the experience was a major turning point in their lives. Throughout the war, black soldiers often faced as much hostility from their white comrades-in-arms as they did from enemy combatants. At Army training camps in the south, African Americans found themselves in segregated units. Initially black soldiers in the field were usually relegated to menial support positions such as porters, ditch diggers, janitors, and cooks. However, as casualties increased many became infantrymen, airmen, medics, and even officers. All-black or mostly black units such as the 320th Anti-Aircraft Barrage Balloon Battalion, the 761st Tank Battalion, and the Tuskegee Airmen fought their way through Europe and earned reputations as courageous, honorable soldiers. They served heroically, despite suffering segregation and discrimination during their deployment.

Serving overseas gave African American soldiers a new outlook on the world through the opportunity to live in countries where racial segregation was much less pronounced. African American servicemen dedicated themselves to advancing not only the cause of Allied victory in World War II but also the cause of civil rights at home. This dual enterprise to achieve victory over fascism and victory over racism was deemed the "Double V" campaign by the *Pittsburgh Courier*, a prominent black newspaper. African Americans, both in and out of uniform, hoped that their heroic service to the nation would forge a pathway to equal citizenship.[39]

At the end of World War II African Americans were ready to make far-reaching demands to end racism. The campaign for African American rights—better known as the civil rights movement—began with deliberate steps. In the courts the National Association for the Advancement of Colored People successfully attacked restrictive covenants in housing, segregation in interstate transportation, and discrimination in public recreational and educational facilities. In 1954 the U.S. Supreme Court issued one of its most significant rulings in *Brown v. Board of Education*, declaring segregation illegal in public schools.

In 1955 Rosa Parks found a seat on a Montgomery, Alabama, bus after work. Segregation laws at the time stated blacks must sit in designated seats at the back of the bus, and Parks had complied. When a white man got on the bus and couldn't find a seat in the white section at the front of the bus, the bus driver instructed Parks to give up her seat. Parks refused and was arrested. As word of her arrest sparked outrage and support, Parks unwittingly became the "mother of the modern-day civil rights movement." Black community leaders formed the Montgomery Improvement Association (MIA) led by Baptist minister Dr. Martin Luther King Jr. The first action of the MIA was to stage a boycott of the Montgomery bus system, which lasted 381 days. In November of 1956 the Supreme Court ruled segregated seating was unconstitutional.

In the summer of 1957, Central High School in Little Rock, Arkansas, asked for volunteers from all-black high schools to attend the formerly segregated school. When fall classes began, nine black students, known as the Little Rock Nine, arrived at Central High School expecting to attend classes. They were instead met by the Arkansas National Guard (on the order of Arkansas governor Orval Faubus) and a screaming, threatening mob. The Little Rock Nine tried again a couple weeks later and made it inside the school but had to be removed for their safety when violence ensued. President Dwight Eisenhower eventually intervened and ordered federal troops to escort the Little Rock Nine to and from classes at Central High. The students faced continuing harassment, but their efforts brought much-needed attention to the issue of further desegregation in public places and fueled protests on both sides of the issue.

As troubling as they are, these examples of discrimination against African Americans arguably paled in comparison to continuing efforts at voter suppression. Blacks had gained the right to vote way back in 1870 with the passage of the Fifteenth Amendment. However, southern states made it difficult for African Americans to exercise this right. States often required African Americans (and Latinos) to pay a poll tax and take voter literacy tests that were nearly impossible to pass. Recognizing this injustice, the Eisenhower administration pressured Congress to consider new civil rights legislation. Congress bowed to this pressure and passed the Civil Rights Act of 1957, the first major civil rights legislation since Reconstruction. It allowed federal prosecution of anyone who tried to prevent someone from voting. It also created a commission to investigate voter fraud.

Despite legal gains, African Americans still experienced blatant prejudice in their daily lives. In 1960 four black college students took a stand against segregation in Greensboro, North Carolina, by refusing to leave a Woolworth's lunch counter without being served. Over the next several days, others joined their cause. After some were arrested and charged with trespassing, protestors launched a boycott of all segregated lunch counters until the original four students were finally served at the Woolworth's lunch counter where they first stood their ground. Their efforts spearheaded peaceful demonstrations in dozens of cities and helped launch the Student Nonviolent Coordinating Committee to encourage all students to get involved in the civil rights movement.

One of the most remembered events of the civil rights movement, the March on Washington for Jobs and Freedom, took place in August 1963. More than two hundred thousand people, black and white, came together in Washington, D.C., for the peaceful event. Numerous entertainers and celebrities were present that day, but the march's highlight was King's "I Have a Dream" speech, which became a slogan for equality and freedom. On July 2 of the following year, President Lyndon Johnson signed the Civil Rights Act of 1964—legislation initiated by President John F. Kennedy before his assassination. The new law guaranteed equal employment opportunities for all and prohibited unequal voter registration requirements. When President Johnson signed the Voting Rights Act into law on August 6, 1965, he took the Civil Rights Act of 1964 several steps further. The 1965 law banned all voter literacy tests and provided federal examiners in certain voting jurisdictions. It also allowed the attorney general to contest state and local poll taxes. As a result, poll taxes were declared unconstitutional in *Harper v. Virginia State Board of Elections* in 1966.

But despite the legislative and legal rulings that advanced equal rights, the civil rights movement had tragic consequences for two of its leaders. Malcolm X, a former leader in the Nation of Islam and one of the primary instigators of the Black Power movement, was assassinated at a rally in 1965. King was assassinated in 1968. Following King's death, emotionally charged looting and riots in multiple cities put more pressure on the Johnson administration to push through additional civil rights laws. For example, the Fair Housing Act became law on April 11, just days after King's assassination. The act prevented housing discrimination based on race, sex, national origin, and religion. It was also the last legislation enacted during the civil rights era.

ASIAN DISCRIMINATION AND THE INTERNMENT OF JAPANESE AMERICANS

Historically, Asians and Asian Americans have been subjected to discrimination, exclusion, and even internment. China provided the first substantial immigration to the United States from an Asian country, with migration starting soon after the 1849 California gold rush. These first Chinese immigrants provided both services and labor in the gold mines camps and were the primary laborers on the first transcontinental railroad. In spite of their efforts, Chinese workers encountered considerable prejudice, especially from poor whites, as politicians and labor leaders used the Chinese as scapegoats for depressed wage levels.

In 1854 the United States and Japan signed a treaty establishing trade and allowing Americans to reside in designated Japanese cities. But Japan maintained restrictions on the ability of its citizens to immigrate to the America until 1868. By that time, strong anti-Chinese sentiment had developed, and Japanese immigrants were initially welcomed by Americans as an alternative source of cheap labor. Japanese immigration increased significantly after the Chinese Exclusion Act of 1882, which placed an absolute ten-year moratorium on Chinese labor immigration. For the first time, federal law proscribed entry of an ethnic working group on the premise that it endangered the economies of certain localities.

As the numbers of Japanese grew, anti-Chinese sentiment was gradually replaced by anti-Japanese opinions. After the San Francisco earthquake of 1906, the city's school board took the opportunity created by the destruction of many schools to require Japanese students to attend segregated classes. This action was heavily criticized in the Japanese press. President Theodore Roosevelt tried to reverse the policy through informal channels, but the school board refused. Meanwhile, popular support for a federal ban on Japanese immigration, comparable to the Chinese Exclusion Act, grew on the West Coast.

The Japanese government did not want either the continued humiliation of seeing its people segregated in education or to have its nation publicly banned from immigrating. A compromise was reached in the Gentlemen's Agreement of 1907, through which the Japanese government began denying passports to workers who might want to move to the United States. At the same time, de jure (formal) school segregation in San Francisco ended. This status quo remained until the Immigration Act of 1924. The act banned immigration by persons who were ineligible for American citizenship. This included anyone from Japan and was a unilateral abrogation of the Gentlemen's Agreement. Since immigration from Japan had been curtailed substantially in 1907 and ended entirely in 1924, there were virtually no Japanese immigrants on the West Coast who had not spent at least three decades in the country when World War II began.

Prejudice toward Japanese immigrants and Japanese Americans was already widespread in the United States when Japanese military forces bombed American forces stationed at the Pearl Harbor naval base in Hawaii on December 7, 1941. That prejudice turned quickly into bigotry in the days following the bombing. As soon as the United States formally entered World War II, many political leaders and media outlets called for the internment of all individuals of Japanese descent residing in the western portion of the country. In response, in February 1942 President Franklin Roosevelt signed an executive order that authorized U.S. military leaders to detain Japanese Americans in camps, en masse and without due process.

The order forced approximately 110,000 Japanese Americans to dispose of their possessions and leave their homes and businesses in California, Washington, and Oregon. They were sent to live in one of ten "relocation centers" (more commonly known as internment camps) located across the country. Conditions in the relocation centers were similar to prisons: surrounded by barbed wire and guarded by armed soldiers. The housing areas were overcrowded barracks with no running water and little heat. There was minimal privacy and no private bathrooms. The centers did provide medical care and education for the children. As the war progressed, many of the young adults held at the camps were allowed to leave to work or serve in the military.[40] It is important to note that no one from Hawaii, with a population one-third Japanese American, was sent to internment camps. Nor were any Americans of German or Italian ancestry (countries with which the United States was also at war) subjected to government authorized confinement.

The executive internment of Japanese Americans was politically popular and faced no serious opposition from elected officials or the courts. In 1944 the Supreme Court decided *Korematsu v. United States*, upholding the constitutionality of the internment order and authorizing the continued detention of Japanese Americans. When the internment order was officially rescinded in January 1945, after the end of the war, individuals were released from internment but received no compensation for their lost property and mistreatment. More than four decades later President Ronald Reagan signed the Civil Liberties Act of 1988, formally apologizing for internment and authorizing a $20,000 redress payment to each living internment survivor.

THE BRUTALITY OF LATINO DISCRIMINATION

Latinos (also called Hispanics) are persons in the United States who were born or have ancestors from Spain or any country conquered and occupied by Spain (which includes nineteen countries in Central and South America as well as the U.S. commonwealth of Puerto Rico). The U.S. Census Bureau estimated in 2017 the size of the Latino population was nearing 37 million, which is almost 18 percent of the total population. Mexicans and Mexican Americans are by far the largest Latino subgroup, with Puerto Ricans the second largest. As of 2015, Latinos who originate from El Salvador are estimated to be the third largest subgroup. Latinos are technically an ethnic group composed of many races, but the discriminatory treatment of Latinos by government and American society has racialized their status in the United States.[41]

Spaniards and their black slaves, as well as mestizos (mixed race—white European and indigenous Indian), mulattos (mixed race—white European and black African), and other indigenous persons from the area today known as Mexico, were exploring and staying in the southern and southwestern regions of North America long before the first British settlement in Jamestown, Virginia, in 1607. Some of the Spaniards were given official titles to the land they explored by the Spanish monarchy, while others stayed and established ownership by possession. Christopher Columbus claimed the island of Puerto Rico for the Spanish Crown in 1493. The Spanish established a permanent settlement in Puerto Rico in 1508, which remained under Spanish colonial rule until 1886. The oldest continuously inhabited settlement in the continental United States, in St. Augustine, Florida, was founded by the Spanish in 1565. The Spanish, assisted by mixed race and indigenous people from colonial-era Mexico, founded the city of Los Angeles in 1781 as well as other important cities in the West and Southwest around this time.

The discriminatory treatment of Latinos in the United States essentially began in 1848 when the United States defeated Mexico in the Mexican–American War. In the Treaty of Guadalupe Hidalgo, Mexico agreed to cede land to the United States that now includes modern-day Texas, New Mexico, Arizona, California, Utah, Nevada, and parts of Wyoming, Oklahoma, Colorado, and Kansas. The roughly 100,000 Mexicans living on the ceded lands were given one year to decide whether to walk away from their property and return to Mexico or stay in the United States and become citizens.[42] The vast majority (about 90 percent) chose to forego Mexican citizenship and become U.S. citizens in order to remain on their land, where they quickly became a subordinated group that confronted discrimination and violations of their civil and property rights.[43]

The new (Mexican) American citizens were required to register their land and pay property taxes. The deadlines to register and pay were relatively short and firm. Moreover, written proof of land ownership was required. Many of the new citizens simply did not have the knowledge or financial resources to comply. As a result, thousands of Mexican Americans were forced to give up their land and the federal or state governments put it up for sale. Anglo-American settlers quickly moved in and, in many cases, illegally occupied the properties. Once Congress passed the Homestead Act in 1862, these so-called squatters were given legal claim to the dispossessed property. In some instances, the former landowners reacted violently. For example, in New Mexico a small group known as Las Gorras Blancas (The White Hats) would tear down fences and set fire to the interloper's farm buildings in the dark of the night. In Texas, dispossessed landowners were involved in armed conflicts with Texas Rangers. In California, Tiburcio Vásquez, one of the sources for the fictional folk hero Zorro, resorted to banditry. However, most Mexican Americans stoically accepted their fate and went to work for others at very low wages, sometimes on land that they once owned.

By the 1890s the expansion in mining, agriculture, and railroad construction attracted increasing numbers of Mexican laborers. The violence and chaotic economic conditions of the Mexican Revolution (1910–1920) also contributed to the growing number of Mexicans entering the United States. From 1910 to 1928, the number of legal Mexican immigrants grew from around twenty thousand per year to approximately seventy-five thousand per year.[44]

Unlike the concern Americans felt toward immigrants from Asia and Eastern and Southern Europe (who were also arriving in large numbers during this time period), Mexican immigration was tolerated if not encouraged. Many, including policy makers and scientists of the day, supported the now widely debunked theory of eugenics—the idea that racial and ethnic groups have inherent qualities (e.g., intelligence, honesty, physical fitness) and that some groups have better qualities than others.[45] These beliefs connected directly to popular views of different immigrant groups, including Mexican and Mexican Americans. According to historian Julia Young,

> Mexicans were believed to have certain positive qualities that made them "better" labor immigrants than the other groups. They were thought to be docile, taciturn, physically strong, and able to put up with unhealthy and demanding working conditions. Perhaps more importantly, they were perceived as temporary migrants, who were far more likely to return to Mexico than to settle permanently in the United States.[46]

The need for immigrant labor declined drastically with the onset of the Depression in 1929. Mexican immigrants found themselves suddenly without work, and many returned to Mexico voluntarily. However, more than twice as many—including those with U.S. citizenship—were rounded-up and deported under unofficial "repatriation" policies approved by federal, state, and local authorities. An estimated three hundred thousand Mexicans and Mexican Americans were forced out of the United States in the 1930s.[47]

The U.S. government modified its policy toward Mexican immigration once the United States entered World War II. Prompted by the World War II labor shortage, the U.S. made an agreement with Mexico in 1942 to import temporary workers (braceros) to fill labor shortages in agriculture and railroad maintenance/construction. Between 1942 and 1964, when the program was finally terminated, approximately 4.6 million Mexicans came to work in the United States as braceros. This influx of Mexican workers was not particularly welcomed by white Americans. Although the U.S.–Mexico agreement guaranteed a minimum of thirty cents per hour and "humane treatment" for laborers, braceros were frequently "treated" to substandard housing and inflated prices for staples such as food and water.

Discrimination and open hostility from Anglo-Americans were common experiences for Mexican laborers and Mexican American youths. The June 1943 Zoot Suit Riots were a series of violent clashes that occurred in Los Angeles during which mobs of U.S. servicemen, off-duty police officers, and civilians attacked young Mexican Americans and occasionally African Americans or Filipinos who were caught in the wrong place at the wrong time. The riots took their name from the distinctive baggy suits worn by many minority youths during the late 1930s and early 1940s. After the U.S. entry into World War II, the production of civilian clothing containing silk, wool, and other essential fabric was regulated and subject to rationing. Despite these wartime restrictions, many bootleg tailors in Los Angeles, New York, and elsewhere continued to make the popular zoot suits, which used profligate amounts of fabric. Servicemen and many other people, however, saw the oversized suits as a flagrant and unpatriotic waste of resources.

On May 31 a fight between a uniformed servicemen and Mexican American youths resulted in the beating of a U.S. sailor. A few days later about fifty sailors marched through downtown Los Angeles carrying clubs and other crude weapons, attacking anyone wearing a zoot suit. In the following days the racially charged atmosphere in Los Angeles exploded in a number of full-scale riots. Mobs of U.S. servicemen took to the streets and began attacking Mexican Americans and stripping them of their suits, leaving them bloodied and half naked on the sidewalk. Local police officers often watched from the sidelines, then arrested the victims of the beatings. Hundreds more servicemen, off-duty police officers, and civilians joined the fray over the next several days, marching into cafes and movie theaters and beating anyone wearing zoot-suit clothing or hairstyles (duck-tail haircuts were a favorite target and were often cut off). Blacks and Filipinos—even those not clad in zoot suits—were also attacked. By June 7 the rioting had spread outside downtown Los Angeles to Watts, East Los Angeles, and other neighborhoods. Leaders of the Mexican American community implored state and local officials to intervene.[48]

Shortly after midnight on June 8, military officials declared Los Angeles off limits to all military personnel. Officials ordered military police to patrol parts of the city and arrest disorderly military personnel; this, coupled with the travel ban, served to greatly deter the servicemen's riotous actions. The next day the Los Angeles City Council passed a resolution that banned the wearing of zoot suits on Los Angeles streets. The number of attacks dwindled, and the rioting had largely ended by June 10. In the following weeks, however, similar disturbances occurred in other states.

Besides their contributions on the home front, approximately 500,000 Latinos (including 350,000 Mexican Americans and thousands of Mexican nationals) served in the U.S. military abroad during World War II. Latinos were not placed in segregated units like African American soldiers, but, similar to African Americans, Latinos were initially placed in support positions away from combat.[49] Through the course of the war, however, their assignments were upgraded, and Latino combat contributions were formally recognized by the U.S. government. Proportionally, Mexican Americans received more honors and decorations for their service than any other racial or ethnic group. But they did not receive the respect they hoped for, much less deserved, when they returned to the United States.

In western states, Mexican Americans lived under a modified Jim Crow system that limited their movement and hampered their opportunities for social and economic advancement. In southern states, the enforcement of legal segregation in workplaces, housing, and schools was common. Texas instituted rigid segregation, whereas New Mexico protected *nuevomexicanos'* civil rights under its constitution (but tended to separate the races in social settings). Race-based legal distinctions and selective law enforcement were used to enforce segregation in California. Following World War II a small but politically active Mexican American middle class emerged that challenged the practices of "internal colonialism." These activists began to fight the Anglo-dominated power structures by reenergizing *mutualistas* (mutual aid societies) and organizing civil rights organizations to improve living conditions, publicize civil rights issues, and confront segregation practices directly. For instance, the American GI Forum was founded in 1948 by Mexican American veterans in Texas when they were denied medical treatment at Veteran Affairs hospitals and were similarly unsuccessful in obtaining the assistance promised to them under the Servicemen's Readjustment Act of 1944 (better known as the GI Bill).[50] In 1949 the American GI Forum received national attention when it protested the refusal of an Anglo funeral director in Three Rivers, Texas, to hold services in his funeral home (the only one in town) for decorated World War II veteran Felix Longoria, a Mexican American.

Due to Anglo-Americans' fears that unauthorized Mexican immigration was on the upswing, Eisenhower authorized Operation Wetback in 1954: a mass deportation campaign targeting unauthorized Mexican workers. With the help of the Mexican government, which sought the return of Mexican nationals to alleviate a labor shortage, border patrol agents and local officials worked together to capture and deport immigrants. Over the summer of 1954, the program removed by force or by threat more than 1 million Mexicans (including U.S.-born children) from the United States.[51]

AN EASIER TIME: CUBANS AND CUBAN AMERICANS

Until recently Cubans and Cuban Americans have had a much easier time than other racial or ethnic groups, owing to Cold War–era tensions between Cuba and the United States. Cuban immigration is best described as having occurred in waves: prerevolutionary (1868–1898), Golden Exiles (1959–62); Camarioca Freedom Flights (1965–73); the Mariel boatlift (1980); the *balsero* (rafter) crisis (1994); and the post-Soviet exodus (1995–2016). Between 1868 and 1898, prior to the Cuban Revolution, the United States admitted approximately 55,700 Cuban immigrants. Most were either skilled workers in cigar manufacturing or political refugees from the multiple unsuccessful Cuban uprisings trying to win independence from Spain. By the end of the nineteenth century, Cubans had established sizable communities in Key West and Tampa, Florida; New York City; and New Orleans.

The second wave of Cuban immigration occurred as a result of the Cuban Revolution in 1959 when Fidel Castro and his revolutionaries came to power. This wave, lasting from 1959 to 1962, has been referred to as the Golden Exile because most refugees came from the higher strata of Cuban society. They were urban, well-educated, light-skinned, and white-collar professionals. Many fled for political reasons, fearing persecution by the revolutionary government, and they expected to return home as soon as

Castro's government was toppled. One unforgettable event that occurred during this period was Operación Pedro Pan (Operation Peter Pan), which brought more than 14,000 unaccompanied minors to the United States between 1960 and 1962. Sent by their parents to escape the political and economic turmoil of Castro's government, approximately 40–45 percent of the Pedro Pan children were met by family members already living in the United States, and the rest were placed in foster homes, boarding schools, and orphanages located throughout the country.[52]

The Cuban exiles were accepted with open arms by the American government and given various types of assistance, including cash subsidies, English language classes, and the respect that other Latino national-origin groups never received. The Cuban missile crisis in 1962 brought an end to this wave of migration, but by that time the American government had admitted nearly 250,000 exiles, most of whom chose to settle in the southern tip of Florida. A section of Miami that had previously been a majority African American area, later referred to as Little Havana (or Calle Ocho), became the central headquarters, economically, politically, and culturally, for Cuban exiles.

The third wave of Cuban immigration began in the fall of 1965 and ended in the spring of 1973. Wishing to rid his country of political dissidents, Castro decreed that all Cubans with relatives living in the United States would be allowed to leave through the port of Camarioca. He invited exiles to come to Cuba by boat to collect their relatives (because all commercial flights between Cuba and the United States were discontinued after the 1962 Cuban missile crisis). Hundreds of exiles accepted Castro's offer, and in a few short weeks about 5,000 Cubans left Cuba. The Camarioca boatlift ended with an agreement between the American and Cuban governments that resulted in the Freedom Flights, an airlift of twice-daily flights between Cuba and Miami. Nearly 270,000 Cuban refugees were admitted to the United States before Castro ended the exodus in April 1973. This wave of Cuban immigration was composed primarily of small merchants, craftsmen, and skilled and semiskilled workers as well as relatives of middle-class Cubans who had immigrated during the early 1960s.[53]

The American government remained very welcoming to the incoming Cubans. Besides sending planes to pick them up, the government provided low-cost loans and comprehensive assistance from the Cuban Refugee

Center. In 1966 Congress passed the Cuban Adjustment Act, which allowed Cubans to become lawful permanent residents after being physically present in the United States for only one year. These newly arriving "political refugees" were also eligible for various kinds of federal government assistance, such as health and educational benefits, whereas other legal immigrants must have five years of U.S. residency before gaining access.

From the beginning of his regime, Castro often used immigration as "an escape valve" to export political dissidents and excess labor.[54] In April 1980 Castro again announced that Cubans living abroad would be allowed to come get their relatives at the port of El Mariel. During this fourth wave of Cuban immigration, which lasted less than eight months, an estimated 125,000 Cubans were allowed to immigrate to the United States in a massive boatlift that had long-standing consequences for Cubans and Cuban Americans. When the Cuban exiles arrived in Mariel to pick up family members, Cuban officials forced them to also take a small percentage of unrelated persons, some of whom had been inmates in prisons or psychiatric hospitals or identified as prostitutes or homosexuals. A large majority of the Mariel Cubans were young, single, working-class men with little education. Approximately 20 percent were black or mulatto, compared to the overwhelming Anglo-Cubans arriving before 1980. Contrary to media reports, less than 2 percent of the Marielitos (a pejorative label given this group of immigrants) were common criminals.[55]

The Mariel wave of immigrants created divisions between "old" and "new" immigrants in Miami, where most of the Mariel Cubans settled. The year of departure from Cuba became a symbol of social status within the tight-knit Cuban exile community, with those who left after 1980 receiving public scorn. Furthermore, a national Gallup poll conducted one year after the arrival of the Mariel Cubans suggests that American attitudes toward Cubans were also changing. Gallup respondents thought Cubans to be the second least desirable group to have as neighbors, after religious cult members.[56]

With the collapse of the Soviet Union in 1991, Cuba lost its major source of economic and military support. Within three years, the Cuban economy had shrunk by 40 percent, and there was rioting in Havana over the rapid drop in living standards and unmet demands for government reform. To alleviate pressure, Castro declared once more that anyone who wanted to leave Cuba could go. More than 35,000 Cubans took Castro up on his offer with the vast majority deciding to head for the United States. Beginning in August 1994 Cuban *balseros* (rafters) washed up daily along the coast of Florida on board almost every conceivable thing that could float, including wooden rafts, inner tubes, and rowboats.[57]

This fifth wave of Cuban immigration to the United States was obviously a high-risk venture for the individuals involved. It is difficult to estimate the number of *balseros* who lost their lives attempting the perilous journey or were forced to turn back when their means of transportation began to take on seawater. The U.S. Coast Guard reported rescuing more than 21,000 Cubans adrift in the ocean in one month alone.[58] Many of these rescued or intercepted *balseros* were taken to detention in Guantanamo Bay, where lotteries were used to decide who would be allowed to go to the United States. In an effort to curtail the *balseros* crisis, the Clinton administration implemented a significant new policy in 1995 commonly referred to as "wet-foot, dry-foot." Any Cuban refugees intercepted by the U.S. government at sea would be delivered back to Cuba, while those who successfully made their way to U.S. land would be allowed to stay.

The period between 1995 and 2016, labeled the post-Soviet exodus, was the longest and largest wave of Cuban migration, with nearly 650,000 Cubans admitted to the United States. The immigrants of this last wave included primarily laborers and service workers. They traveled by land, air, and sea, both with and without immigrant visas. This last wave ended in in the final days of the Barack Obama administration when the president terminated the "dry-foot" aspect of U.S. immigration policy with Cuba.

Overall, Cubans have been highly successful in adjusting to American life, especially in Miami. The 1959 wave of exiles, who were well above average in educational attainment and professional skills, created a thriving community that would ease the adjustment of later immigrant waves. However, the overall success of Miami's Cubans has led to friction with African Americans, many of whom felt politically marginalized and shut out of economic advancement in the city. This friction resulted in rioting in 1980 in the Overtown District, where the unemployment rate of African Americans was high (approximately 50 percent). The riot was triggered by an incident of police brutality but reflected deep anger at persistent police mistreatment as well as neglect of the black community by Miami's predominantly Cuban American political leaders. In the riot's aftermath, little changed despite promises to fix the underlying causes of the revolt. The Cuban immigrants and their descendants remain a powerful political and cultural force within South Florida.

PUERTO RICANS: A DIVIDED FATE

American soldiers remained in Puerto Rico following the Spanish American War in 1898 when Spain ceded Puerto Rico to the United States in the Treaty of Paris. The United States soon annexed Puerto Rico as an "unincorporated territory" (more accurately characterized as colonization) and promptly dispatched a U.S.-appointed governor to the island. Most of the initial U.S colonial policies were based on patronizing and disparaging views of Puerto Ricans and their former Spanish rulers. The primary policy objective was to "Americanize" the island while also encouraging consent among its residents. One of the more repressive and discriminatory policies imposed on Puerto Ricans was making English the official language of the island and its school system. Their schools' curriculum was rewritten to emphasize American values and history. The governor even Americanized the name of the island, changing it to "Porto Rico." This new spelling was used on all official documents until 1930. At the same time, mainland Protestant churches sent missionaries to proselytize the primarily Catholic island population.

It is important to note that Puerto Ricans were not recognized as citizens of the United States until Congress passed the Jones Act in 1917. Interestingly, many island residents and officials objected to this grant of citizenship. The territory of Puerto Rico was given commonwealth status in 1952, which allows Puerto Ricans to enjoy all the benefits of U.S. citizenship but only when they reside on the mainland. The legal rights of those living on the island are somewhat peculiar. They have no voting representation in Congress and cannot send electors to the Electoral College, but they can be drafted during times of war. Additionally, islanders do not pay taxes on individual income, but they pay business, payroll, and estate taxes to the U.S. government.

Puerto Ricans are allowed to travel freely between the island and the mainland (i.e., without passports or visas), and they are not distinguished from other citizens for taxes and government assistance purposes when they reside stateside. In fact, many Puerto Ricans move between the island and mainland in order to get the "best of both worlds"—culture, identity, and a familiar environment on the island, and material wealth, education, acquisition of skills, and opportunities for their children from temporary residence on the mainland. Many eventually return to live in Puerto Rico, while others chose to live permanently on the mainland. However, the constant circular migration of Puerto Ricans is now an enduring feature of the island's experience.

Poverty and unemployment are perpetual problems in Puerto Rico. Consequently, massive migration occurred between 1945 and 1965, especially to New York City and Chicago, when blue-collar jobs in clothing and textile manufacturing and other industries were plentiful. Spanish Harlem (or El Barrio) in New York City and similar Puerto Rican communities on the East Coast and in Chicago were established during this time. However, these Puerto Rican enclaves never experienced the economic prosperity or political success enjoyed by Cubans in Little Havana (Miami).

After 1965 the decline in manufacturing jobs resulted in higher unemployment and other economic problems for many working-class Americans. El Barrio was one of the hardest hit areas in the 1960s and 1970s as New York City struggled with budget deficits, race riots, urban flight, drug abuse, crime, and poverty. Tenements in El Barrio were crowded, poorly maintained, and frequent targets for arson. For the most part, New York's government was totally unresponsive to the problems in El Barrio and did not even provide adequate basic services such as trash pickup or streetlight maintenance.[59] Similar to the efforts of Mexican American veterans, young Puerto Ricans organized to bring public attention to the problems in their neighborhood. They formed a local chapter of the Young Lords Organization in 1969. The original group formed in Chicago's Puerto Rican neighborhoods to draw attention to local concerns caused by gentrification, excessive use of force by Chicago police, racism, lower social status, and limited job opportunities. The Young Lords of New York City participated in multiple acts of civil disobedience and protests targeting such concerns as trash pickups, lead paint hazards, substandard health services, and more. For outside observers, including those in the media, the actions of the Young Lords were perceived as militant or extreme, but their efforts produced results. Many of the Young Lords' activist campaigns resulted in concrete legislative reforms, improved city services in El Barrio, and careers in media, politics, and public service for many former members.

As the Young Lords expanded their operations to other cities and states, one branch of the organization that was explicitly anticapitalist, pro-union, and procommunist became known as the Puerto Rican Revolutionary Workers Organization. As a result, this branch came under scrutiny and was infiltrated by the FBI. Bureau agents planted seeds of disagreement among the leadership while the extremism of certain factions of the organization led to increased member infighting. Subsequently, the Young Lords membership declined, and the organization was essentially disbanded by 1976.

The status of Puerto Ricans since the 1980 has been aptly characterized by Lisa García Bedolla as "A Divided Fate."[60] Many Puerto Ricans have successfully transitioned into the mainstream of American society with a college education, middle-class jobs, and homes in the suburbs. Meanwhile, others remain locked in El Barrio and other inner-city neighborhoods, with minimal jobs, limited education, and little hope. Approximately 75 percent return regularly to the island in a pattern of circular migration. Economic and political conditions for those living on the island remain essentially unchanged (or worse, due to the devastation caused by Hurricane Maria in 2017).

FEDERALISM AND SHIFTING GOVERNMENT RESPONSIBILITIES IN HUMAN RELATIONS

This cursory look at racial discrimination and oppression throughout American history points to the need for a systemic government response beyond the large-scale efforts at legislative or judicial relief at the federal level. Although the CCRR and the Cincinnati Mayor's Friendly Relations Committee (a World War II–era body) were early examples of local government responses to intergroup relations challenges, these types of bodies were not prevalent across urban centers outside the North and Midwest. Indeed, the need for local government engagement to deal with intergroup relations issues was not widely recognized until the latter half of the twentieth century, and even then federal-level insistence was critical in getting local governments to act.

Local governments were on the frontlines of the intergroup conflict. After a relative respite in the 1950s, civil disorder increased dramatically in the 1960s, when more than three hundred cities experienced civil uprisings in primarily African American neighborhoods.[61] In response to these events, several of America's largest cities and counties established HRCs to help prevent future flash points. Since local and state governments were still considered the primary foci of political power in America, it is logical that incremental efforts to address intergroup tensions began as local experiments in intervention. But it became clear by the late 1950s that there would need to be support and, in some cases, prodding by the federal government to make cities pursue the structural and social changes necessary to promote civil harmony. Of course, and as scholars have shown regarding long-term processes like desegregation, improvement is not linear and progress is not consistent.[62] This was particularly true in the Old South (where virtually all locally elected officials were white[63]). Both the Eisenhower and Kennedy administrations adopted what can best be termed reaction-driven, surgical interventions to restore order and enforce the then-new body of judicial opinions that chipped away at the established *Plessey*-era mentality of "separate but equal."

By contrast, the Johnson administration's muscular use of the Commerce Clause to compel state compliance with federal policy standards, coupled with the passage of the Civil Rights Act and Voting Rights Act and the funding of Great Society programs, stands as a dramatic shift in the state–federal governing dynamic. And although the eradication of material destitution proved more of an intractable problem than acknowledged by 1960s policy makers, the fundamental shift toward making local issues of race, income, poverty, and crime part of the federal assortment of policy responsibilities was clearly accelerated under Johnson.

However, it would be wrong to conclude that the dynamics of minority oppression were merely a matter of lingering resentments from the antebellum South. Across the country, farm subsidies, union wages, labor contract law, and housing regulations were subject to segregation based on race.[64] The result was a growing sentiment on the part of African Americans that their social, economic, and political opportunities were limited largely because of their race—despite whatever economic and social similarities they shared with poor whites and Latinos. This is why David James argues that local–state structures underpinned the norms and codes confronting minorities, particularly African Americans, well into the mid-twentieth century.[65]

As economic, social, and political tensions began to outstrip the ability of local power structures to contain them, calls increased for federal intervention to level the playing field for minorities on items ranging from the right to vote, to economic opportunity, and to access to housing markets. But the robustness of the federal government's involvement in local and state affairs was, at best, inconsistent both in terms of funding and emphasis. This is easily seen in the stark differences in how various administrations preferred to handle the question of racial integration and economic opportunity. But we cannot address either of these issues without also mentioning the urban approach to law enforcement.

Notable was the Johnson era Law Enforcement Assistance Administration, a program designed to increase the federal role in addressing crime, in part, by funneling funds to local police. The crimes of greatest interest to this program, however, were not homicide and robbery but riots and civil unrest.[66] Richard Quinney and John Wildeman, among others, argue that the increased federal investment in the Law Enforcement Assistance Administration during the Nixon administration essentially created a policing strategy of group repression in America's cities.[67] This is generally in line with conflict theorists' expectations that policing has focused too much on using militarized weapons and investigative techniques.[68] These practices likely contributed to the social context that precipitated the 1992 Los Angeles uprising and have traction in the present crisis of law enforcement's dealings with minority populations.

Since at least the 1980s tensions between African Americans, Latinos, and Asians have centered on both competition for scarce local economic resources and shifts in housing market availability (with Asians and Latinos doing somewhat better in transitioning to higher socioeconomic neighborhoods than African Americans).[69] At the same time, the so-called Great Migration of African Americans to northern cities at the turn of the twentieth century and migrations of racial and ethnic groups to areas beyond where they have been traditionally associated (e.g., Latinos moving from the West and Southwest to the South) has contributed to the need to consider strategies to improve intergroup relations across a variety of geographic and population areas.[70]

The comparative urban theory literature, exemplified by Paula McClain's work, provides an analytical lens from which to understand the dynamics of intergroup relations in cities, and we draw on some of this literature in tracing the recent history (i.e., post 1960s) of relations between these racial and ethnic groups.[71] The challenge for America's urban areas is that intergroup tensions, competition, and areas of cooperation have developed as immigrant populations have settled and sought political and economic incorporation.[72]

The main immigrant flows into the United States since the 1960s have been from Mexico and South America, Asia, the Caribbean, and eastern and central Europe, with the largest flow coming from Mexico and South America. Economically, Asian immigrants tend to land higher paying jobs and attain higher levels of education, followed by Caribbean-based immigrants and Latinos. Of course, these groupings are quite broad in terms of the national origins they include. But they are instructive in that they show the underpinnings of immigrant inflows to the United States. These patterns have changed the nation's historical racial dynamic from that of black/white tensions to a plurality of intergroup concerns that now includes Latinos, Asians, and others. The U.S. foreign-born population as a percentage of the nation's total population is around 15 percent according to latest census projections as of this writing. Interestingly, that is approximately the record set during the massive immigrant influx of the late 1800s.[73] By the end of the twenty-first century, immigrants are projected to compose over 20 percent of the U.S. population, and this figure does not include the percentages of second- and third-generation group members who are native-born American citizens.

Since immigrant communities flourish more easily in metropolitan centers, the nation's urban jurisdictions are responsible as the front line for mediating group tensions through HRCs (or by other means). Of course, the dispersion of immigrants is not uniform—most have settled in major urban areas in California, Texas, Florida, and New York. Interestingly, as immigrant communities were expanding in these urban centers, higher-income African Americans began migrating to the suburbs.[74] Those who were not economically mobile stayed in the urban cores, where their group size stagnated relative to growing numbers of Latinos and Asians. A challenge since the civil rights acts of the 1960s—which were written largely in response to African American grievances against entrenched white power—has been for urban governments to balance the competing voices of multiple ethnic and racial groups that often find political influence through growing numbers.

It is important to note that coalition building among marginalized groups is not the norm.[75] Asian/black, Latino/black, and intra-Latino tensions have been documented in America's largest cities for decades, even as cooperation between these groups—often due to the combination of government and local elite cooperation—has also been achieved.[76] Thus, the demographic shifts in America's cities that started in the 1960s—typified by an increased immigrant population and a dwindling but still substantial African American population[77]—created the circumstances for intergroup tension. Some of this rancor was exacerbated by the reality that lower-income African Americans have been found to be the most vulnerable to economic competition from immigrant groups for both private- and public-sector jobs.[78]

As Michael Jones-Correa points out, the intergroup competition in urban areas would likely have been less had it not been for the hollowing out of the manufacturing base in most northern cities beginning in the late 1960s.[79] As the availability of blue-collar jobs diminished, so did economic prospects for many in both the immigrant and African American population. The resulting shift to nonunionized service-sector jobs in urban economies meant both lower wages and less job security during economic downturns throughout the 1970s–1990s. This economic restructuring also had an impact on city government. Although the federal government became a major funder for urban government budgets during the New Deal and Great Society eras, the New Federalism, ushered in by the Richard Nixon and Reagan administrations, shifted the relationship between cities and Washington to one that incorporated state governments as an additional voice in determining how dollars were distributed through the increased reliance on block grant formulas.

Although Reagan reduced federal grants-in-aid to cities, those dollars were eventually replaced by later administrations. However, what was not reversed was the state-centered emphasis on determining how federal dollars were spent on municipalities. Even into the Bill Clinton, George H. W. Bush, and Obama administrations, federal grants for programs affecting city budgets continued to be filtered through state government channels. The problem, of course, was that this provided state governments with the opportunity to redirect federal block grants to other areas of the state budgets that politicians believed required attention. It also opened the door for newly expanding suburbs to compete for dollars with older urban areas.

The 1990s were also a time when government policy approaches began to shift toward the privatization mindset that focused on ways to unload funding responsibilities on private entities—foundations, nonprofit organizations, and corporations. While solving certain short-term financial concerns, the privatization shift, including the development of urban enterprise zones, also exposed city governments to the whims of whatever the private sector believed was worthy of funding, and where.[80] This created the distinct challenge of incongruence between the philosophy behind the public management of urban centers and the agendas of private entities. In some cases, where the two do not find common ground and the city government cannot find local funding sources elsewhere, beneficiaries of the unfunded programs suffer the consequences. This reality was particularly noticeable in funding reductions for services provided by HRCs in these urban centers.

Overcoming intergroup tension is not simply an outcome of urban economic improvement, however. The groups themselves must feel some degree of motive to build a coalition. Raphael Sonenshein's analysis of group relations in Los Angeles suggests three requirements for intergroup coalition building: ideological similarity, overlapping interests, and strong ties among group leaders.[81] Jones-Correa overlaps this troika with a new dimension—different cost calculations to coalition building in urban centers between public and private actors.[82] He argues that elected leaders (especially in city council positions) historically have had little incentive to amass new intergroup coalitions in city government because the short-term needs of one's council district are more important. Jones-Correa is also pessimistic about the role of local service providers in fostering intergroup coalitions in cases where those services were initially instituted to provide for the needs of the African American community (as was the case in Los Angeles following the Watts civil disturbances). But both Sonenshein and Jones-Correa see the potential for intergroup progress through sustained communication and effort made by civil rights groups and grassroots activists representing the interests of their respective communities. If group leaders develop common ground and strong ties, the possibility of those ties extending into organically realized coalitions increases.

Overall, the historical development of race relations in the United States—particularly in terms of how those relations have been shaped by urban development and immigration in the post–World War II era—shines a bright light on the importance of HRCs as a local government response to community challenges. Unlike economic development drivers or social service providers, HRCs exist on a narrow bandwidth that aligns most closely with the civil rights activists.[83] But HRCs are far more than extensions of civil rights organizations and interest groups. They have developed since the mid-twentieth century as part grievance facilitator, part enforcer of social norms (or, more accurately, often-unrealized ideals), and sometimes enforcers of statutory code in preventing discrimination in areas like housing and public services. We explore the role of HRCs in all these dimensions in later chapters.

3

ORIGINS AND DEVELOPMENT OF ORGANIZED HUMAN RELATIONS EFFORTS

The history of intergroup relations in America reveals the pervasiveness of racial prejudice, discrimination, and violence. Human relations commissions in the United States were originally established to specifically address racial violence or uprisings. Today commissions work to address a range of discriminatory actions experienced by a variety of different marginalized groups. Different titles have been given to these commission efforts (e.g., human relations, community relations, human rights) but they all share a common mission: to advance fairness/equality and improve intergroup relations. This chapter traces the origins and development of HRCs up to the twenty-first century.

According to Ethington and West, HRC structures and functions are rooted in specific historical circumstances, so it is important to understand both periods in which HRCs began as well as the transformative eras that informed commission development.[1] They divide the history of HRCs in the United States into distinct time periods, and we adapt these demarcations to organize our summary of HRC origins and development. The time periods we examine are

- 1921–1942: Nongovernmental efforts to improve race relations
- 1943–1971: The "golden age" of human relations organizations
- 1972–2000: The withering of "human relations" and the rise of "human rights"

To provide some context for understanding the actions taken (or not) to correct intergroup problems and the major issues for subordinate groups, we also consider the prevailing outlook(s) of each period with respect to race and intergroup relations.

NONGOVERNMENTAL EFFORTS TO IMPROVE RACE RELATIONS, 1921–1942

Our brief review of U.S. history in chapter 2 explains that race relations were conflictual from the outset of our country. But the typical account of the history of racial discrimination in the United States tends to focus on black slavery and violence targeting African Americans in the South, overlooking some of the worst incidents of racial discrimination and violence that occurred in cities in the North, Midwest and Southern California. African Americans were the most frequent targets, but Latinos and Asians were also victims. Following World War I, African Americans increasingly clashed with whites as blacks became more determined to improve their status in the crowded cities. Yet there were no organized efforts to address these racial conflicts until after the Chicago Race Riots of 1919.

The lack of any organized response to racial discrimination prior to this time could be due to the widespread belief (at least among whites) that nonwhites were culturally and physically inferior and therefore did not deserve equal treatment. Ethington and West specifically point to "the rise of 'scientific' racism" in some of the major works in sociology (George Fitzhugh's *Sociology for the South* [1854] and Henry Hugh's *Treatise on Sociology* [1854]) and natural science (Charles Darwin's, *Origin of the Species* [1859] and *The Descent of Man* [1871]) that were used to advocate (or at least rationalize) the practice of slavery and, later, segregation.[2] Antiracist social scientists openly challenged this popular view of racial hierarchy in their research, including anthropologist Franz Boaz and sociologists W. E. B. DuBois, Ernest Burgess, and Robert Park.

As described in chapter 2, the summer of 1919 was an intense period of racial conflict in many American cities. Following mob violence and considerable destruction in Chicago's South Side and surrounding neighborhoods, Illinois governor Frank Lowden established the first interracial advisory committee composed of thirteen prominent local citizens and called the Chicago Commission on Race Relations (CCRR). Lowden instructed the CCRR to conduct a comprehensive study of relations between whites and blacks in the city, including the causes of the riot, an assessment of the government's response from multiple viewpoints, and recommendations for preventing future uprisings.

Funded entirely by private local donations (most of it coming from the CEO and co-founder of Sears, Roebuck and Company, Julius Rosenwald), the CCRR, with the help of scholars and graduate students from the University of Chicago, conducted an eleven-month investigation of the city's racial situation. The commission divided itself into six subcommittees to research the following areas: racial conflicts/uprisings, black housing, industry, crime, intergroup contacts, and public opinion on race relations. The subcommittees held a series of conferences and informal meetings with substantive experts. They also collected field data and personal testimony from a wide variety of sources. For instance, the Industry Committee collected data on 22,448 African American workers at 192 different work sites and made personal visits to 101 factories. The commission's final report, titled *The Negro in Chicago: A Study of Race Relations and a Race Riot*, is exhaustive and meticulous, at more than 650 pages, and is an impressive example of applied social science even by today's standards.[3]

It is worth noting what the CCRR saw as the root causes of intergroup conflict contributing to the riot because some are the source of intergroup conflict that HRCs deal with today:

- **A massive influx of a new minority population into the local area.** Drawn by wartime employment opportunities and the desire for more personal freedom (i.e., escape from the repression of Jim Crow laws in the South), southern blacks migrated in large numbers to Chicago and other urban areas in the country's northeast and Midwest regions.
- **Combative and prejudiced interracial attitudes.** Whites' prejudice and growing hostility toward African Americans was met with blacks' growing solidarity and determination to protect themselves. It is important to note that CCRR found that African American were also prejudice in their attitudes toward whites, but blacks, unlike whites, rarely had the power or resources to act on their prejudice.

- **Inadequate housing and basic services for minority residents.**
African American residents were forced to live in highly congested
neighborhoods with inferior schools, transportation, parks, and so on.
The severe housing shortages in "black belt" neighborhoods caused spill-
over problems, with black residents moving into nearby ethnic white
neighborhoods.
- **Biased law enforcement.** The police were quick to arrest and use
excessive force with African American residents, while they more frequently dismissed and sometimes facilitated the criminal behaviors of
white residents.
- **Inflammatory media reporting.** Lacking the sources to accurately cover the racial conflicts, Chicago newspapers, both white- and
black-owned, printed unverified reports or rumors of incidents that were
frequently exaggerated and inflammatory in their content.
- **Job competition.** Widespread hard feelings resulted from job
competition (both real and perceived) between white and black (both
skilled and unskilled). Employers' use of black workers as "scabs" to
break or prevent strikes by the (primarily white) labor unions, in particular, put serious strains on race relations. The fact that the unions and
union members were resistant to admitting African Americans exacerbated tensions.

The CCRR's recommendations for resolving or preventing intergroup
conflict were extensive, so here we examine only those that remain relevant today. First, the CCRR prefaced the recommendations with the obvious (but spot-on) warning that there is no "quick remedy" for resolving
intergroup problems. It also acknowledged that the hard feelings and negative tropes or stereotypes between conflicting groups were the result of
multiple sources, including long-term structural causes of intergroup conflict (e.g., the distribution of wealth and national economic trends). These
issues are both difficult to address and, more importantly, beyond the
reach of local remedies.

The CCRR's numerous recommendations to law enforcement, judicial
officers, government administrators, and staff carried the basic message
of treating all groups equally, with an extra emphasis on showing respect
and courtesy to minority residents, including their cultural practices.

Furthermore, the commission advised that anyone who does not follow the equal treatment policy should be quickly dismissed, with legal penalties pursued as needed. It also recommended that all reports of neglect of duty or discriminatory action should be promptly investigated and addressed, with no exceptions.

To all parties (including bureaucrats, social and civic organizations, unions, churches, and private citizens), the CCRR advocated for increased and regular contact with members from different racial, ethnic, and religious groups, including formal meetings and events that focused on learning about the history, culture, and experiences of other groups. The commission called for all citizens to practice racial tolerance by actively opposing the use of force or violence in race relations and by dispassionate, intelligent, and sympathetic consideration by each race of the others' needs and aims.

The commission's advice to the media was basic but nonetheless still relevant today: apply the same standards of accuracy, fairness, and sense of proportion and avoid exaggeration in publishing news about other racial groups, as you would for your own group. Practice greater care and accuracy in reporting interracial incidents. Abandon the practice of writing sensational headlines and articles about race relations.

But the CCRR made its strongest appeal in calling for the establishment of a permanent race-relations body:

> We recommend as of special importance that a permanent local body representing both races be charged with investigating situations likely to produce clashes, with collecting and disseminating information tending to preserve the peace and allay unfounded fears, with bringing sound public sentiment to bear upon the settlement of racial disputes, and with promoting the spirit of interracial tolerance and co-operation.[4]

Although the CCRR report was clearly antiracist and apologetic for the injustices experienced by African American residents, the commission's recommendations were rather conservative. For example, it did not call for expensive public works or housing projects or the integration of neighborhoods. In fact, many of the recommendations that we do not cover here focused on what African Americans needed to do to better accommodate and "fit in" to white society. In many ways, these conclusions reflected the antiracist yet assimilationist approach of Booker T. Washington and the Chicago school of sociology. From both Washington's and the Chicago school's viewpoint, when different racial or ethnic groups come into contact with each other, intergroup conflict is bound to happen. In other words, racial problems are not simply because of majority (white) discrimination toward minority (black) groups. Instead, there exists a natural cycle to race relations, and it proceeds through four stages: competition, conflict, accommodation, and, finally, assimilation.[5] The CCRR's goal (at least from the vantage point of its white members) was to help Chicago get to this final stage as painlessly as possible.

Much to the dismay of many Chicago residents, the CCRR was disbanded upon the completion of its report. There was no formal follow-up on its recommendations or evaluation of any policy success. Yet, according to St. Claire Drake and Horace Cayton, the CCRC's recommendations outlined a plan of action for civic-minded organizations over the next several decades.[6] This may be why Ethington and West characterize Chicago's 1919 riot as the impetus for "human relations" as a field of study and the CCRR as the forerunner to all HRCs in the United States.[7]

Importantly, and despite immense social and economic challenges confronting minorities in most American cities, there were essentially no official, government-led efforts to promote improved intergroup relations between 1921 and 1943. The lone exception was Maryland's Interracial Commission, established in 1927 to consider the "welfare of colored people residing in the State . . . recommend legislation and sponsor movements looking to the welfare of said people, and to the improvement of interracial relations."[8] The commission was initially given no investigative or enforcement powers (and no designated budget for paid staff until 1969). Over the course of decades its name was changed and its scope of authority expanded multiple times. Today, as the Maryland Commission on Civil Rights, the commission works "to ensure opportunity for all through the enforcement of Maryland's laws against discrimination in employment, housing, public accommodations, and state contracts; to provide educational outreach services related to provisions of this law; and to promote and improve civil rights in Maryland."[9] And the commission's expanded mandate includes protection against discrimination based on race, color, religion or creed, sex, age, ancestry or national origin, marital status, physical or mental disability, sexual orientation, and gender identity.

Outside of Maryland, until 1943 the burden of fostering civic harmony among racial and ethnic groups was carried primarily by nongovernmental organizations such as the Urban League, the National Association for the Advancement of Colored People (NAACP), the Young Men's Christian Association, the League of United Latin American Citizens, the National Conference of Christians and Jews, and others. The NAACP's successful antilynching campaign during the 1930s combined widespread publicity about the causes and effects of lynching with a skillful lobbying effort of Congress and the Roosevelt administration to pass a federal antilynching law. Southern senators filibustered, but they could not prevent the formation of a growing national consensus against lynching. By 1938 the number of lynchings had steeply declined.[10]

THE "GOLDEN AGE" OF HUMAN RELATIONS ORGANIZATIONS, 1943–1972

The hands-off and ad hoc approach to race relations by local governments would change beginning with events in the early 1940s. In 1941 President Franklin Roosevelt issued Executive Order No. 8802, which prohibited discrimination on the basis of race, color, creed, or national origin in the government or any defense industry receiving federal monies. The president also created the Fair Employment Practices Committee to investigate violations of the executive order (although the Fair Employment Practices Committee was not given enforcement powers.) The order was issued in response to a threatened march on Washington by the Brotherhood of Sleeping Car Porters, the NAACP, and other minority rights groups to protest racial discrimination in the armed forces and defense industries. Roosevelt's action introduced the federal bureaucracy to the struggle against racial discrimination, even though the order did little to address the inequality in American life between whites and nonwhites.

During World War II, as in the previous world war, there were labor shortages in many factories and industries. In response, black workers from the rural South migrated north looking for employment in such large numbers that cities were incapable of adequately accommodating them. Because African Americans were treated as second-class citizens, they suffered disproportionately from wartime rationing and the overall strains on local cities. Factories offered employment but not housing, and because whites violently defended the borders of their segregated neighborhoods, black residents were forced to "make do" with squalid living arrangements. For example, Detroit's two hundred thousand black residents were crowded into two neighborhoods originally built to accommodate fifty thousand. There, in the sixty square blocks on the city's east side in an area ironically known as Paradise Valley, African Americans lived in tiny subdivided tenements that often housed multiple families.

Black workers faced virulent racism on the job as well. Factories faced habitual slowdowns by bigoted whites who refused to work alongside African Americans. White workers in Detroit's largest munitions factory even halted production to protest the promotion of their African American coworkers. Humiliation and resentment on each side spilled over into all facets of wartime struggles, and by the early 1940s racially motivated street fights were common in many cities. African American veterans acutely felt social inequality. They had hoped that their service in World War II would gain them respect. However, they were continuously harassed, and many veterans faced Jim Crow laws as returning veterans. These inequalities, along with the economic hardships endured by black communities, were instrumental in the inducement of the rioting that occurred throughout the United States toward the end of the war.

Like the uprising in Chicago in 1919, the 1943 riots in Detroit, New York City, and Philadelphia were rooted in racism, poor living conditions, and unequal access to goods and services. The Zoot Suit Riots that took place in Los Angeles that same year masked a deeper social unrest that local governments were unprepared to deal with. Community leaders, including elected officials, throughout the United States were increasingly worried that the rioting would continue and would spread to their cities. Perhaps the one positive outcome of the multiple high-profile race riots was that city and county governments finally responded with the formation of more permanent race-relations committees or commissions. Key examples include

- **Detroit.** Detroit mayor Edward Jeffries established the Mayor's Interracial Committee in the fall of 1943 in response to race rioting that summer. The committee, composed of the heads of six city departments and five lay members, was succeeded by the Commission on Community Relations, which was established by Detroit Common (City) Council ordinance in 1953. This commission, like the Mayor's Interracial Committee, was charged with the responsibility to make recommendations designed to improve governmental services affecting racial relationships, to investigate and seek to correct situations of discrimination and racial tension, and to cooperate in informational programs designed to increase mutual understanding within the community. The city also established the Coordinating Council on Human Relations in 1947 to increase cooperation among local civic groups. Its functions were to develop programs of education and research and to help coordinate the human relations activities of the twenty-two member agencies.
- **Cincinnati.** The Mayor's Friendly Relations Committee (MFRC) in Cincinnati was established in 1943 in direct response to the Detroit riots. According to Phillip Obermiller and Thomas Wagner, "blacks in Cincinnati were just as frustrated with the racial status quo as their counterparts in Detroit."[11] The racial tensions and circumstances were indeed very similar, and many citizens throughout the city were worried. To prevent a racial uprising in Cincinnati, Major James Stewart and local NAACP leaders became proactive. They determined that the mayor would call a meeting of a cross-section of city residents with the purpose of forming a city-sponsored citizens' committee to promote civic unity and racial tolerance. The Cincinnati City Council approved the 109-member MFRC a few weeks later. From the outset, the MFRC was strictly "an advisory body skilled in mediation but having no enforcement powers."[12] Frequent and regular communication, education, research, and calm persuasion were the MFRC's methods in pursuing its racial tolerance and civic unity agenda. The MFRC did not get involved in public protests or other acts of resistance and avoided taking sides as much as possible on racial issues. For these reasons, civil rights organizations and activists frequently expressed frustration with the MFRC. In 1965 the MFRC was renamed the Commission on Community Relations.
- **New York City.** As a result of citywide concerns about race relations following riots in the Harlem borough of New York City in 1943,

Mayor Fiorello H. La Guardia created the Mayor's Committee on Unity by executive order on February 28, 1944. Its purpose was to "make New York City a place where people of all races and religions may work and live side by side in harmony and have mutual respect for each other, and where democracy is a living reality."[13] The committee consisted of four Catholics, four African Americans, four Jews, two labor union representatives, and four white Protestant members. The mayor directed the committee "to study and analyze dangerous trends, and to use their influence to combat them."[14] La Guardia provided the committee with a modest budget (raised from private funds) for a two-year program and provided space in one of the municipal buildings for offices. The committee had no enforcement powers but was able to affect change by relying solely on the persuasive powers of its members. By the mid-1950s, however, it was apparent that the committee could not address the city's discrimination and bias problems. In 1955 Mayor Robert F. Wagner and the city council moved to replace the original committee with a city agency that had more extensive powers and permanent status: the Commission on Intergroup Relations (COIR). COIR was given the power to receive and investigate complaints and to initiate its own investigations into racial, religious, and ethnic group tensions on the basis of race, creed, color, national origin, and ancestry. It was empowered to hold hearings, to report its findings of facts, and to make recommendations to the mayor. COIR was also charged with studying the problems of prejudice, intolerance, bigotry, discrimination, and disorder caused by intergroup tension, and with developing intergroup dialogue. It also coordinated efforts among federal, state, and city agencies to develop courses of instruction on techniques for achieving harmonious intergroup relations within New York City. The first major expansion of COIR's powers came in 1958 with the passage of the Fair Housing Practices. This legislation, which gave COIR the power to investigate and hold hearings on allegations of discrimination in private housing, was the first in the nation to extend protection against discrimination to private housing. COIR was renamed the Commission on Human Rights in 1962. In 1965 the new Human Rights Law of the City of New York greatly expanded the commission's powers of investigation and enforcement and extended its jurisdiction to prosecute discrimination based on race, creed, color, and national origin in employment, public accommodations, housing, and commercial space.

- **County of Los Angeles.** The 1943 Zoot Suit Riots led the Los Angeles County Board of Supervisors to establish the Joint Committee for Interracial Progress in 1946. Its charge was to address community fears regarding racial or ethnic violence by promoting positive race relations. Following national recognition for its effective work, the committee became an official agency of county government in 1948 and was renamed the Los Angeles County Commission on Human Relations. According to Ethington and West, intergroup tensions in Los Angeles County at the time were serious. "Post-war demobilization and the resettlement of returning veterans (of all races), along with the return to civilian life of the interned Japanese issei and nissei, led to widespread flashpoints."[15] For example, in 1947 white students burned an effigy of a black person at John C. Fremont High School in South Central Los Angeles to protest the enrollment of black students. This act of symbolic violence by high school students mobilized a broad-based coalition of organizations to confront intergroup tensions. The Community Relations Conference of Southern California was founded in 1947 to coordinate the efforts of groups working to address racial prejudice and discriminatory action. Membership in the conference, along with several local government agencies (such as the Los Angeles County Commission on Human Relations, the Pasadena Committee on Group Relations, the Claremont Intercultural Council, and the San Fernando Valley Council on Race Relations), included leading civil rights organizations such as the American Civil Liberties Union, Anti-Defamation League of B'nai B'rith, Japanese American Citizens League, National Congress of American Indians, and Los Angeles chapters of both the Urban League and the NAACP.

During the 1940s a new progressive consensus emerged regarding race relations and the necessity for public policy reform to address racial inequalities. This consensus is attributed to the work of Swedish economist Gunnar Myrdal.[16] His book *An American Dilemma: The Negro Problem and Modern Democracy* (1944) painstakingly details the obstacles faced by African Americans and includes a comprehensive analysis of black–white relations. Myrdal's findings shifted responsibility for racial conflict away from the idea of an inevitable process (i.e., the Chicago school's race relations cycle) to the intentional attitudes and actions of the racist white majority. The study concluded that white racism and racial inequality violates the fundamental basis of American democracy, that promoting racial tolerance is desirable but insufficient by itself, and that policy reform to address racial inequality and ensure the fair treatment of all Americans is required if America is ever to become the democracy it claims to be. Mrydal's thesis united and empowered civil rights activists and political leaders until well into the mid-1960s.

By 1950 there were at least fifty municipal or county government-sponsored organizations charged with improving race relations and as many as one thousand additional nongovernmental organizations working to improve intergroup relations.[17] As already stated, rising racial tensions during wartime and the rash of riots in 1943 instigated the formation of some of the earliest race relations committees. But the nationwide proliferation was due partly to the determined efforts of an Illinois-based not-for-profit: the American Council on Race Relations (ACRR), created in 1944.[18]

Besides serving as a clearinghouse of information and experience for existing race relations organizations, the ACRR would send staff out to cities and states to help set up new intergroup organizations or assist in the revamping or expansion of existing programs. The ACRR provided free training programs on race relations for city, county, and state law enforcement agencies.[19] It developed educational literature and programs that were distributed widely, including to public schools and higher educational institutions. The ACRR also initiated a nationwide marketing campaign to increase knowledge about racial groups through radio, newspapers, movies, and other means of mass communication.[20]

It is important to note that many of the government-sponsored organizations were given titles that made no reference to race relations (e.g., the Mayor's Friendly Relations Committee or the Commission on Community Relations). The decision to not use "race relations" in the designations of these entities was partly a move attributable to political tact, necessity, or even timidity. Indeed, few local councils or mayors wanted to advertise the fact that they had race relations problems.

On the positive side, many of the early members involved in these committees were interested in a broader range of questions about intergroup justice. An important push came from activists in the labor movement who wanted class and socioeconomic questions to be considered alongside race. The establishment of regional human relations networks, such as the one in Southern California in the late 1940s, was primarily a matter of coalition-building among labor, religious, civil rights, and ethnic organizations. Adopting the name "Community Relations Conference of Southern California" made sense in this context so as not to exclude the mission of any one of the coalition partners.

During the 1950s the term "human relations" entered greater use for permanent governmental intergroup relations commissions. Ethington and West refer to this period as the "golden age" of human relations due to the existence of a large network of dedicated professionals who shared a relatively consensual vision about their work's focus. The National Association of Intergroup Relations Officials was founded in 1947. Its organizational journal, the *Journal of Intergroup Relations*, published essays on HRC efforts in specific cities and on the larger questions dealing with social justice and inequality in the United States. "It is overwhelmingly clear that everyone understood the core question to be," in the words of a 1958 *Journal of Intergroup Relations* article, "the emergence of social organizations concerned with those problems arising out of relations between racial, religious, and ethnic groups in the United States."[21]

But the early adoption of such broad labels carried a heavy liability. In every case, HRCs and their forerunners were established to deal with racial or ethnic conflict, usually riots. Thus, reducing racial and ethnic conflict, discrimination, and intolerance has always been understood as a basic HRC mission even though all forms of intolerance and injustice (including sex discrimination and unfair wages) have also been germane to HRC efforts. The decision to adopt a broader label to describe commission activities risked allowing the inherent vagueness of "human relations" to touch on almost every conceivable area of social concern.

Thanks to relative agreement on the causes and effects of intergroup conflict, nearly everyone (except perhaps black nationalists and southern segregationists) accepted Myrdal's conclusions as self-evident and adopted the unifying goal of bringing nonwhites into the mainstream of the "American Creed" of equal opportunity. As the civil rights movement gained momentum between 1955 and 1965, the obvious objectives of HRCs fit this progressive consensus model. But apparently no one stopped to establish the boundaries of human relations activities. The cost of this oversight became apparent during the more fractious, radical, and reactionary years of the mid-1960s.

Meanwhile, the federal government's commitment to eliminating inequality was formalized with the passage of the Civil Rights Act in 1964 and the Voting Rights Act in 1965. Numerous government agencies at all levels were created to enforce these laws and provide education programs fostering respect and mutual understanding among all racial, ethnic, and religious groups. Antidiscrimination laws also proliferated at local and state levels. According to Kenneth Saunders and Hyo Eun Bang, there were an estimated thirty state antidiscrimination laws in place by 1961.[22]

While some HRCs remained strictly advisory bodies, such as Cincinnati's commission, the expansion of federal funding meant several commissions were given direct authority in their founding charters to enforce antidiscrimination laws. Some HRCs added enforcement powers in their activities through federal government contracts. For instance, a number of HRCs were designated as Fair Employment Practices Agencies, which gave them authority to enforce state and local antidiscrimination laws related to employment. These agencies would typically contract with the federal government's Equal Employment Opportunity Commission to receive and investigate discrimination complaints brought under applicable federal laws. Some HRCs also became participants in the federal Fair Housing Assistance Program and contracted with the U.S. Department of Housing and Urban Development to investigate and process discrimination in the buying, selling, renting, or advertising of dwellings under the federal Fair Housing Act of 1968.

THE WITHERING OF "HUMAN RELATIONS" AND THE RISE OF "HUMAN RIGHTS," 1972-2000

The 1970s brought considerable change to the mindset and work of HRCs. A new rash of racial uprisings beginning in 1965, war protests on college campuses and at the 1968 Democratic National Convention, and the growth of new group-based movements for equal rights (feminists, Chicano, Puerto Rican, American Indian, Asian American, gay and lesbian, and the disabled) made it increasing difficult to maintain the old coalitions of government agencies and interest groups whose primary goal was improving group relations. The progressive consensus among practitioners and scholars focused on bringing minority groups (primarily African Americans), into the mainstream of American society was essentially replaced by a plurality of viewpoints as to the proper path forward. Some activists and social scientists charged the government with "internal colonization," and they advanced plans of action for the "national liberation" of oppressed groups (see the writings of José Angel Gutiérrez and Stokely Carmichael).[23] Others sided with Karl Marx and focused on ways to take money and power away from the bourgeoisie (in today's terms, the top "1 percent") by replacing capitalism with socialism and eventually communism (see writings of Ronald Takaki).[24] Meanwhile, the different marginalized groups worked separately to identify problems and propose solutions for their individual groups. The passage of the national civil and voting rights legislation, along with new antidiscrimination legislation at the local and state levels, persuaded many, including progressive activists, that the primary obstacles to group-level justice had been removed.

The context for intergroup relations was also shifting as America's demographics underwent change. The Immigration Reform Act of 1965 replaced the old national origins quota system, which favored northern Europeans, with one that emphasized family reunification. In the first five years after the act's passage, immigration to the United States from Asian countries more than quadrupled (under past immigration policies, Asian immigrants had been effectively barred from entry.) Other Cold War–era conflicts during the 1960s and 1970s also brought millions of people fleeing poverty or the hardships of communist regimes in Cuba and eastern Europe. Between 1965 and 1995 more than 18 million legal immigrants entered the United States, which was more than three times the number admitted over the preceding thirty years. In the 1950s more than half of all immigrants were Europeans and just 6 percent were Asians; by the 1990s, however, 31 percent were of Asian descent and only 16 percent were Europeans. The percentages of Latino and African immigrants also jumped significantly. Between 1965 and 2000, the greatest number of immigrants (4.3 million) to the United States came from Mexico.

As the urgency produced by the urban riots of the 1960s receded and all the factors described above grew, some HRCs, particularly those operating primarily as advisory bodies, saw their budgets cut to the point where little activity was possible. But other HRCs thrived in the new environment by relying on the large body of civil rights, fair housing, fair employment, equal education, and minority contracting laws enacted during the heyday of the "golden age."

The commissions that took this route rebranded themselves as human *rights* commissions, thus emphasizing the concrete focus on the actionable aspects of intergroup conflict, relations, and justice. They established relations with the relevant state and federal agencies charged with enforcement of civil rights and fairness legislation, essentially subcontracting with them as local watchdogs. With clear focus and measurable activities (i.e., the number of cases of unfair practices discovered or cited), these enforcement-oriented HRCs thrived (including two that we profile in later chapters).

Overall, the historical evolution of human rights reflects the demographic, cultural, and attitudinal shifts the nation experienced. And commissions were clearly in the middle of this evolution. As the country continues to move through continued immigration and globalization, we foresee commissions needing to expand their efforts to reflect and become more integrated with the communities they serve. In other words, the long-range historical development of HRCs continues to unfold.

4

THE HUMANS WHO MUST RELATE

A s discussed in chapter 1, HRCs have varying policy concerns that focus on their specific missions defined in their charters. According to our typology, commissions generally take on quasi-judicial, advisory, and facilitator functions (or some combination thereof). Perhaps the easiest of these to implement is the quasi-judicial function in that the enforcement of HUD and FEPA statutes provides a relatively straightforward framework under which commissions can operate. Less tangible or regimented is the work associated with a commission's facilitator role, particularly regarding the improvement of intergroup relations (however defined and measured). The advisory function is likely somewhere between these two in terms of ease of implementation although, as with the other two, "ease" may be relative and dependent on what the commission sees as its mission and organizational goals.

In this chapter we consider mission implementation by commissions as a precursor to realizing the impact HRCs and their stakeholders envision for the organizations. The story in this chapter concerns the perceptions that HRC commissioners and staff have of the implementation process—putting organizational goals into measurable action. Montjoy and O'Toole's theory of policy implementation is helpful here in that it sets two specific markers for how implementation should be considered from the perspective of organizational mandates: (1) the specificity of the mandate and (2) the adequacy of resources available for implementing the mandate.[1]

Again, each commission has different types of mandates that relate to their broader function as a quasi-judicial, advisory, or facilitator body. For example, local ordinances for the City of Fort Worth specify that the human relations commission shall have the following duties:

> (a) To advise and consult with the city council and the city manager on matters involving discrimination based on age, race, color, sex, religion, disability, national origin, familial status, sexual orientation, transgender, gender identity or gender expression; (b) to recommend to the city council and the city manager measures designed to eliminate prejudice and discrimination; and (c) to promote and encourage communications between and cooperation of all groups interested in bettering community relations.[2]

The statues go further in defining the Fort Worth HRC's (FWHRC) mission beyond that of a facilitator or advisory role, however. Indeed, the FWHRC is one of the few commissions in the country that has the statutory power to enforce both HUD and FEPA policy. The City of Fort Worth, Texas, Code of Ordinances states:

> It is the intention of city council that the human relations commission's staff supervised by its administrator shall be the agency . . . to receive and investigate all complaints of alleged violations of this division [the Fort Worth City Manager's Office], and that such agency shall attempt to resolve such complaints by informal methods of conference, conciliation and persuasion. If the agency cannot resolve an alleged violation of this division, the administrator of the agency shall be authorized to request that a complaint be filed in municipal court.[3]

The City of Pittsburgh Human Relations Commission has a judicial enforcement mandate similar to Fort Worth's, but Pittsburgh's statutes are even more direct in expectations about the commission's investigatory and judicial powers.

> The Human Relations Commission shall have the power and duty to:
> (a) Initiate, receive, investigate and seek the satisfactory adjustment of complaints charging unlawful practices. . . .

(b) Initiate or receive and investigate other complaints of discrimination against any person because of race, color, religion, ancestry, national origin, place of birth, sex, sexual orientation, familial status, age, handicap or disability . . . and seek the satisfactory adjustments of such complaints. Any complaint filed under this subsection which the Commission believes may constitute a violation of a law of the United States or the Commonwealth may be certified to its Solicitor for such actions as it deems proper. . . .

(c) Hold public hearings, subpoena witnesses and compel their attendance, administer oaths, take the testimony of any person under oath, and in connection therewith require the productions of evidence relating to any matter under investigation of any question before the Commission, make findings of fact, issue orders and publish such findings of fact and orders and do all other things necessary and proper for the enforcement of this Article.[4]

By stark contrast, city documents specify a very different commission mission for the LAHRC:

The commission assists in assuring to all people the opportunity for full and equal participation in the affairs of City government and promotes the general welfare and safety of all residents in the Los Angeles community through activities and programs designed to reduce discrimination, tension, and violence and to advance improved intergroup relations. The Commission supports efforts to create a city free of racism and violence where residents may live and work in an environment of respect, mutual tolerance, and human diversity. The Commission supervises, controls, regulates and manages an Advisory Committee, representative of the religious, racial, economic, industrial, labor and professional groups in the City; investigates and holds public hearings on any matters germane to the Commission in the area of human relations; pursues and coordinates research, community education, and assistance . . .[5]

Note that the "hearings" referenced are more like community meetings; rarely has the LAHRC been able to use subpoena power. And, perhaps as a nod to the reality that the LAHRC has limited (arguably nonexistent) enforcement powers, the Los Angeles City Council and Mayor Eric Garcetti added Ordinance 186134 to the city's administrative code in June 2019. The new ordinance establishes the City Human Rights Commission with the statutory enforcement powers seen in Fort Worth but, curiously, without making any reference to the LAHRC's long-standing role. It appears, then, that the LAHRC will continue to operate on its facilitation track while, as of this writing, the city's new human rights commission will take on discrimination and related enforcement cases. While likely a help to the city's efforts at combating discrimination, the challenges for LAHRC as a facilitation body (which we focus on in this and the following chapters) will remain. We return to mention of this new human rights body in chapter 7.

Cincinnati's HRC has ordinance language similar to the LAHRC's, further underscoring the divide in function type between commissions. The comparison here between commission ordinances is helpful because it works to illustrate the confines in which the HRCs operate according to type, with the Fort Worth and Pittsburgh commissions having clearly defined enforcement roles as quasi-judicial bodies and their Los Angeles and Cincinnati counterparts having primarily the advisory and facilitator responsibilities. Implementation efforts across commission types will differ by nature of the general roles the HRCs fill, but the commissions also exist in a common governmental context in which they are subject to constraints regarding mandates and available resources. Montjoy and O'Toole offer a typology that effectively distills the reality facing HRCs and similar government organizations where the mixture of mandate specificity and available resources vary.[6] And, lest the differences in the ordinances cited above suggest otherwise, mandate specificity is not necessarily an advantage for government organizations. This is because rigid structures might limit opportunities for HRC commissioners and staff to deal creatively with issues of broader interest. Meanwhile, resource availability, or lack thereof, may be a more straightforward limitation on commissions in that initiatives may not get off the ground because of a lack of money or other necessary tools.

Montjoy and O'Toole advance the assumption, which we follow, that members of government organizations generally function as a dominant intra-agency coalition. This means that, in HRC terms, both staff members and commissioners have the same basic value orientation and sense of which activities they want the organization to engage in. We revisit this assumption later in this chapter, but for now the perspective helps link commission circumstances with theoretical understanding of HRCs as organs of local government where everyone is pulling in the same direction. The typology is distillable on a 2 × 2 dimension in which mandates from legislative bodies (e.g., city councils, city managers) are either vague or specific, and resources to accomplish mandates are either provided or not (see table 4.1).

The Type A combination is perhaps the most advantageous for an enterprising commissioner or staff member, as it includes a vague mandate with adequate resources, enabling the undertaking of initiatives deemed useful from a bureaucratic or programming perspective. The Type B circumstance maintains the resource availability from Type A but includes a much stricter mandate. Meanwhile, Type C includes Type A's vagueness but without resource provision, while Type D features both a specific mandate and inadequate resources to accomplish the mandated tasks. It is safe to conclude that the least amount of implementation occurs when HRCs are Type D.

We overlay our discussion of the quasi-judicial, advisory, and facilitator types with the Montjoy and O'Toole's typology to provide perspective on the relative challenges and opportunities commissions have in meeting their mandated operations, looking for opportunities to expand

TABLE 4.1 Montjoy and O'Toole's Theory of Implementation Adapted to HRC Ability to Accomplish Their Mandate

SPECIFICITY OF MANDATE	ADEQUATE RESOURCES	INADEQUATE RESOURCES
Vague	A (Highest opportunity)	C
Specific	B	D (Lowest opportunity)

their mission, or both.[7] The charter and statue information cited previously suggests that the Fort Worth and Pittsburgh commissions operate on stricter mandates as quasi-judicial bodies, while the Los Angeles and Cincinnati commissions have more general mandates as facilitator organizations. All four commissions have responsibility to function in advisory roles for other city agencies and elected officials (including their mayors, city councils, and city managers). There may also be capacity for the Fort Worth and Pittsburgh commissions to perform a facilitator role, if resources are available after existing mandate responsibilities regarding HUD and FEPA enforcement are fulfilled.

But there is virtually no way for the Los Angeles and Cincinnati commissions to operate in the quasi-judicial role (irrespective of available resources) because their respective mandates do not provide for these functions (although LAHRC issued subpoenas in one instance during the 1980s). The result is that each commission, while holding the same general label, functions in distinct ways that create differing opportunity structures for commissioners and commission staffers to fulfill mandates. At the same time, the nature of these mandates and the availability of commission resources limit the scope of work that commissioners and commission staff can perform, in some cases to the palpable frustration of these government professionals.

Drawing on interview data from both commissioners and staffers working in HRCs in Los Angeles, Fort Worth, Pittsburgh, and Cincinnati, we provide links between the perceptions of commission workers regarding their capability to fulfill their HRCs' mandate(s) in the context of varying degrees of specificity and resource availability. The overall picture drawn is one of both gratitude for being able to carry out commission work and a desire for opportunities to grow commission responsibility and activity. The interview comments of HRC staff we feature below were collected in various stages: May 2016 in Los Angeles, March 2017 in Pittsburgh, February 2019 in Fort Worth, and March 2019 in Cincinnati.

As mentioned in chapter 1, both bureaucratic creativity and value orientations are critical to the consideration of commission work. This is especially true for HRCs confronting the Types C and D realities of inadequate or no resource provision. To complete assigned tasks of varying specificity, these types of HRCs have to be as creative as possible in finding ways to advance the commission mission. Patsy Healey identifies a series of qualities that support what she terms "the creative modes of urban governance."[8] These include, among other things,

> diverse and mutually aware networks and coalitions,. . . open, transparent and fluid stakeholder selection processes, open-minded, inclusive, informative, and inventive discourses, facilitative and experimental practices,. . . laws, formal competences and resource flow principles which value local initiative and encourage experiment, appreciation of diversity,. . . identity and open negotiation of values and ethics,. . . encouragement of open-minded tolerance and sensitivity.[9]

Commissions should be well-positioned to exercise creativity according to Healy's criteria, which assumes open-minded orientations and an emphasis on facilitation and experimentation. But just how HRCs can effectively harness creativity to drive innovations in their missions will still largely be up to the specific dynamics at work in the local political and bureaucratic contexts in which commissions operate. After all, commissions remain accountable to higher-level appointed and elected bodies within the local governance unit from which they operate while confronting the mandate and resource challenges just discussed.

Healey says as much in her more general appraisal of local governing creativity, but she also suggests that the creative modes she identifies should be offered the chance to thrive.[10] But if creativity is not given such an opportunity, does this mean that commission work will be in peril? The answer likely depends on the nature of the mandate and resources that commissions may access. Interestingly, the literature on workplace creativity pays a lot of attention to creativity in private enterprise, which is not wholly appropriate for the implementation of mandates in the public sector. Torill Strand offers a series of metaphors for how to think about organizational creativity.[11] For HRCs, the most appropriate metaphor appears to be "creativity as reconstruction," which Strand describes as

> a reconstruction that affects ways of seeing the world, ways of making the world and the ways of the world themselves. The metaphor suggests a radical remaking of people's common sense, and may help to illustrate

how shifts within contemporary working life are closely related to the ways in which the global and the local unavoidably interact. This metaphor helps portray the creative ways of contemporary professional work and learning.[12]

The commission mandates cited previously are clear that, no matter the specific function they perform regarding HUD or FEPA enforcement, political advising, and intergroup facilitation, the commissions exist to foster a remaking of how members of the public interact with each other. Such a remaking conjures elements of organizationally driven innovation, although scholars have traditionally assumed that public bureaucracy is immune to innovative motives.[13] In contrast, Mark Matthews and colleagues suggest that public sector innovation and creativity can indeed thrive.[14] They identify three types of public sector innovation that overlap with commission mandates, including conceptual innovation as a way to challenge existing assumptions, administrative innovation in dealing with how mandates get implemented, and systemic innovation focusing on different ways of interacting with other organizations.

Yet success at public innovation—both generally and in support of commission mandates—requires not only buy-in from local political leaders but resources and orientations specific to those carrying out the commission mission. These include, among other things, motivation and initiative.[15] Charles Landry also suggests the need for maintaining focus on local conditions, representation of diverse viewpoints, and the recognition by higher levels of government that localized approaches to problem solving are best determined by local leaders.[16]

It is this focus on "the local" that may be the best opportunity for commissions to successfully harness creative forces to either successfully fulfill its existing mandate, branch out into other areas of service in human relations, or both. The challenges of mandate implementation that Montjoy and O'Toole identify are but one part of this story.[17] Indeed, while mandates and resources are often subject to political consideration or control by elected officials or their hand-picked organization managers, Meier and O'Toole eloquently argue

The reciprocal nature of the bureaucrat-politician relationship, the greater expertise possessed by the bureaucracy in both political and technical terms, the time constraints on political, the relative longevity of bureaucratic actors, and the general bluntness of political tools of control all suggest severe limits for overhead democracy. As Robert Dahl[18] notes, the primary control on administrative behavior is the inner check—the values held by the bureaucrat.[19]

Meier and O'Toole assessed the effect of politician and bureaucratically held values on Latino student performance across 1,043 Texas school districts over a nine-year period. Their general finding is that the influence of teacher (i.e., local bureaucrat) values trumped the influence of the further-removed elected officials in improving student performance. The case of HRC influence is much different in terms of measurable impacts, in large part because the performance metrics in question are not as rigorous as student grades, test scores, and graduation rates. Still, the general logic holds: local bureaucrats, both in the form of HRC commissioners (who do not enjoy great prestige in their appointed positions) and staff members have the ability to bend the arc of commission work in the values-based direction they prefer, even if attempts at innovation and creativity remain somewhat stifled. The rest of this chapter focuses on the perceptions these bureaucrats have of their relative influence in affecting changes within their commissions in support of their understanding of the HRC mission. These bureaucrats are, of course, mindful that they operate under the mandate and resource constraints introduced at the chapter's start.

LOS ANGELES: FINANCIAL AND MENTAL RESOURCE CHALLENGES

The enduring legacy of the 1965 Watts uprising served as a predecessor to the urban unrest that would characterize the late 1960s. The role the Watts episode played in encouraging the McCone Commission's recommendations for the City of Los Angeles to establish an HRC separate from the existing Los Angeles County commission leads us to consider the LAHRC as perhaps the country's quintessential commission (at least in fulfilling the facilitator role). It is appropriate, therefore, to begin our interview section with the perspectives of Lorraine Bradley, a longtime LAHRC commissioner and the daughter of former Los Angeles mayor Tom Bradley. Mayor Bradley, the longest-serving mayor in the city's history, was instrumental in the LAHRC's development; he left office shortly after the 1992 city uprising following the acquittal of four LAPD officers involved in the March 1991 beating of Rodney King.

One of the recurring themes in our interview with Ms. Bradley was an emphasis on just how starved the LAHRC has been for resources, not just in responding to new mandates but in fulfilling its basic charge of improving intergroup relations in Los Angeles.

> When daddy wanted to do this at the beginning and they had no budget and there wasn't even a commission, it was just simply some people getting together and doing this job. One of our members was responsible for bringing the coffee cups and stuff so they could have coffee for the meetings. But you know, he spent his whole career with the police department and had worked on similar initiatives there, so it was a natural transition to have a city commission as far as he was concerned. . . . It was all about connecting with the people as far as he was concerned, which is one of the reasons I think they kept electing him mayor. He was promoting the city and letting citizens know that somebody down there in city hall cares about what you have to say.[20]

Bradley also summed up her view of human relations, at least in terms of how it is conducted by LAHRC. "Most of human relations is listening to people. I can't make everything right for you in human relations, but I can at least listen to you and take your ideas and try to incorporate them to make things better. It sounds trite, I know, but it's all about service."

We also interviewed several current HRC staff members, who asked that their names not be mentioned. One staffer was instrumental in the development of what became known as the Watts Gang Task Force—a group of community, city, and LAPD representatives that meets weekly to discuss the latest community dynamics in Watts and how each constituency can work together more effectively to address community issues before they become conflagrations. This staffer has substantial experience working with the community and sees relationship building as essential to the work performed. Importantly, the staffer's efforts at LAHRC began through a program developed by Mayor Bradley.

> I was fortunate enough to actually be part of the summer employment initiative that was created by Mayor Tom Bradley. A lot of people look at us and see a government body and they're intimidated. My approach is a little bit different because I pretty much came from the same environment as a lot of the people I serve. I started my career in Nickerson Gardens [one of the four public housing projects in Watts], and I was there for a little bit under five years. And so one of my strengths is building relationships with individuals. Because I was there for so long, I know the people, I know the young people, I know the parents, I know the grandparents. That's why I was hired. There was an ad in the paper looking for someone that the people in the community could relate to. And so I was able to introduce my city colleagues and coworkers to the key players in the community, the shopkeepers, the people who have the potential to say yea or nay if the taskforce is going to be functioning or not because it could have easily broken down.

The staffer's commitment is clear, even while expressing agreement with Ms. Bradley that the LAHRC is under-resourced in fulfilling its most basic mandates as set forth by city ordinance. The staffer also sees LAHRC as having too little in the way of organizational flexibility to expand from its current emphasis on facilitation of community group forums like the Watts Gang Task Force. Still, the staffer related that he sees commission work in terms of a personal promise to city residents. "I want to make sure that my promise to the city is that we will never have another civil unrest because we have a physical body here."

At the same time, there might be the potential for LAHRC staffers and commissioners to extend the commission's mandate through some creative thinking about how it works with much larger and better-funded city divisions, including the LAPD. "LAPD calls us in for trainings and to help when there are tensions that need attention and they want our input, and that's a positive sign."

Yet to the LAHRC's great frustration, city budgets reflect a strong commitment to funding core law enforcement functions, with little offered in support of LAHRC facilitation initiatives. As mentioned in chapter 1, LAHRC once enjoyed a much larger staff than it presently has, and it was somewhat recently folded into the city's Housing and Community Investment Department (HCID) as part of a reorganization (even though the commission lacks enforcement powers). Theoretically, LAHRC's proximity to city offices relating to housing and community development and code enforcement should serve as opportunities for creative exercises in expanding LAHRC's mandate, even in the face of restricted or limited resources. And while LAHRC has become more integrated into the collective, interdepartmental discourse of HCID, our staff and commissioner interviews suggest that this proximity has not generally offered an unfettered opportunity for LAHRC to move outside its existing lane as a community facilitator.

Part of the reason for this, at least from the perspective of the commission staff, is that, as a "latecomer" to working with the departments that formed HCID (which had already spent considerable time collaborating under predecessor city departments), LAHRC was considered a bureaucratic and resource rival. At the same time, LAHRC staffers shared concern that their value set was not consonant with broader HCID emphasis on planning, development, and code enforcement and that the lack of a shared value orientation across departments creates difficulty for LAHRC to do work in ways beyond its current facilitator role. The irony here is that the staffers' long-standing professional responsibilities as group facilitators may have contributed to mental silos whereby staffers will pan code enforcement and related responsibilities even if the opportunity to expand the commission mandate under HCID becomes available.

But perhaps an even greater challenge for LAHRC is that the work of intergroup facilitation takes a substantial toll on commission staffers. As another of the staffers mentioned in our interviews, the goals that are part of the facilitation process are inherently long term and the sought-after outcomes are not inherently quantitative.

> What do I look for when I look for success isn't so much about the numbers or quantifying things so the bean counters can say things are good? When I think we are successful is when we have people who have been

traditionally sort of disenfranchised and not connected to the process are stimulated about creating their own advocacy network, or a system where they feel connected and not feel detached or apathetic. . . . These things take time, and there's a saying that it takes two or three generations to do something right. The problem is that we want to see something right away, but the work of human relations takes patience and takes commitment of people over time, and what's happening now is that people think things must bear fruit right away or it's worthless.

And, as we touched on previously, the work LAHRC is mandated to pursue is not the most natural fit for HCID's other departments. This staffer goes a bit further, though, pitting LAHRC's facilitation efforts in disadvantaged communities against some of the same economic and housing development interests that HCID works with to ensure quality, if not entirely affordable, housing.

Then there is the bigger context of things that happen here. Housing is big. We're part of the housing department, but the commission is a bit of sideshow because the housing issues themselves are dealt with by other offices in the department. But we have to go out and make people feel okay about losing their homes and all to developers. So you've got these two competing interests, and that includes the people who want to preserve poverty for some political agenda. What they're preaching is stay in poverty, stay poor, no development. Then there are the developers. And the politicians who want to tear down the old and put up a lot of bright shiny stuff, and they want to get the poverty and the homeless out of the area and make it attractive for young professional people.

But a mismatch among bureaucratic values across offices, mandate vagueness, and resource constraints are not the only issues facing LAHRC staffers. Also part of the challenge are actions by community members. As the same staffer relates, commission attempts at community facilitation can sometimes run into roadblocks by citizens themselves. Perhaps the most obvious path to obstruction is for community members to attempt to turn commission facilitations into one-sided protest statements.

The result is a stymieing of constructive dialogue and common goal development between community, police, government, business, and religious sectors.

> They came and were attacking people and doing chants and disrupting, and this is not what we want. I said well I guess you have some internal work to do and we have some internal work to do, but don't lose touch with us if you want to have a meeting to actually talk about things without shouting because it just can't be that you're coming here to disrupt and attack. It gets nothing done. That tactic used by Black Lives Matter is a temporal template that will be outdated. . . . I mean, it brings some level of consciousness, but let me tell you, if you ask me, anyone who views that movement objectively thinks it's a joke. So you go to every meeting and you disrupt. I'm never going to get anywhere with this. It is a waste of time when people come to meetings and they want to attack you and they're not there to listen.

The same staffer used actions by Black Lives Matter activists as an example not in terms of questioning the overall policy points that Black Lives Matter raises but, rather, the general tactic of disruption that the organization utilizes. Yet the staffer did more in our interview than lob critiques at activists—by turning the analytical focus personal. The staffer's concern about job performance is clear and is a strong indication of the toll that human relations—especially of the facilitation variety that LAHRC engages in—takes on one's sense of professional (and personal) well-being. The following quote reveals much about commission work on both the professional and personal levels.

> So what I've been doing for the last three weeks is sort of therapy on myself and looking at my own shortcomings and asking the hard questions of myself that hopefully leads to some sort of change that can point me toward the right. And that means in the office I want to develop a better communication protocol and sort of figure out a better way forward and then to be more engaged. But I also have to be realistic about the people around me and what they are capable of. There are all these questions I'm asking of myself now because I want to have a better

quality of life. I don't want to feel like I'm spinning out of control. I don't want to feel like I'm anxious or want to feel nervous or anxiety or all of those things I was just feeling so much of before. I just want to feel like I can enjoy my life and do some good work.

We sensed that the staffer's dissatisfaction with performance—which necessitated the "change" to point "toward the right"—was a direct result of what the staffer considered a lack of progress in successfully mediating differences between the local communities that LAHRC serves, the LAPD, and the disparate racial, ethnic, and religious groups whose proximate tensions have the potential to erupt into violence. But the essence of the staffer's quote goes beyond a bad day at the office. The notion of "spinning out of control" is a call to recognize the real mental and emotional strain that commission work can have on even the most experienced and well-trained professionals. We do not know if the changes in protocol the commissioner staffer mentioned were ever implemented or whether any changes made an appreciable impact on LAHRC work. But there is reason to expect that whatever changes the staffer can oversee will be hampered by a lack of resources available to the commission.

At the same time, this staffer might also be prone to sensitivity over the commission's general standing in relation to other city departments and personal work performance. The staffer might internally sense being "out of control" while looking very much "in control" and competent to observers. Indeed, there is no indication that the staffer behaved unprofessionally in any way on the job. Instead, the reference to being "out of control" is largely the staffer's internal appraisal of his job performance and feelings and personal frustrations about not being able to make more of a perceptible impact on the intergroup relations projects handled for the commission. As we said in chapter 1, progress—especially in terms of improving intergroup relations—is not a linear process. What we see now is that the staffers charged with undertaking the facilitation work may take the work "home" with them to such an extent that a sizable psychological toll is exacted.

I'm asking the hard questions of myself right now, and I don't like the answers half the time and I'm not happy. I mean, the answer is that life and other things are complex, so it's not easy to get to the bottom of things. The reality is also that human relations work is undervalued. . . . Not only that, but you never get a sense of completion. My work always leaves me a little frustrated because I never quite see a final stage outcome. I mean you want dialogue and all of that, but you never see the end, and that's the kind of moment you'd like to see—the finished product.

This sentiment extended to several of the LAHRC commissioners we interviewed. Generally, the commissioners' concerns were a partial restatement of what Ms. Bradley offered in her interview concerning the lack of resources dedicated to commission pursuits. Commissioners were also vocal about the lack of demonstrable progress on some of the commission's key projects, especially the ongoing efforts to improve community and police relations in some of the poorest areas of the city. There was also concern that segments of the community appear to have captured the facilitation process as "regulars," impeding intergroup relations progress in the process. In the words of one commissioner:

I want to believe that the people in the city matter enough that the city will invest in people to care for them and walk with them in the tough times. Really be advocates for people whose voices are seldom heard. But they're just going to get the same people because they're not drilling down. It's like, don't call your contact community organizations only. Really branch out and work with the grass roots. Have a meeting with them and say this is real. We're so tired of the usual suspects. We get the same people from the valley. We get the same from the west. We get the same people when we go to the south. When we do that, we'll continue to be disappointed about who shows up to the meetings and what gets accomplished.

Changing the dynamics inherent in public meetings, including the sometimes challenging presence of "regulars," will likely require creativity. And, other things equal, exercising creativity should align with the kind of mandate vagueness the LAHRC has. But when asked specifically about ways staffers might exercise creativity in dealing with challenging meeting dynamics in their facilitations or in pointing to examples of creativity in their work more generally, they were somewhat stumped in offering specifics. The reason may be that the work of facilitating meetings between opposing groups is an ongoing creative activity in its own right, especially when having to make the kind of extemporaneous decisions inherent in keeping people calm and focused in what can easily turn into an adversarial environment. Commission staffers who primarily work in facilitation may be so enmeshed in a creative process as part of their work that they do not perceive the systematic aspects of their work clearly enough to effectively articulate what their creative work looks like. Indeed, and recalling the list of key creativity "ingredients" mentioned above, it is striking that the kind of interpersonal skill set and flexibility often displayed by LAHRC staffers in their work is not clearly delineated. This is likely because the facilitation work is highly specialized and undertaken by so few bureaucrats, comparatively speaking, that it has not yet rated examination in the relevant literature.

What, then, of the bureaucratic values that Meier and O'Toole speak of? This is a somewhat challenging question to address if only because of the desirability bias involved. After all, directly asking anyone in government whether they value groups getting along across the city, abhor racism and discrimination, and want to see more emphasis placed on the kind of work that LAHRC performs will result in uniform agreement to all three questions. The interviews with all LAHRC personnel—commissioners and staffers—suggest that they are all on the same page in terms of the commission's overall mission to bring as many diverse voices together as possible in order to better human relations throughout Los Angeles.

In some ways it appears that the commissioners defer to staffers in terms of how the facilitations are structured and prioritized. Still, the commissioners were clearly independent thinkers offering input into ways the commission's mission might be better realized (especially regarding garnering a friendly ear on the city council or in the Mayor's Office as a way to increase budget lines). When we posed the general question to the commissioners about areas where they feel LAHRC might benefit from a focus on creativity, a couple blurted out almost in unison, "Can we get a printing press?"

But this does not mean that value differences are missing between the commissioners, staffers, and elected officials. If anything, the staffer and commissioner interviews suggest that city officials at the highest levels have a general preference to readily fund LAPD initiatives, even when these initiatives could be better accomplished through facilitation work led by the commission. Obviously, the LAPD has a wholly separate mission from the LAHRC, but, perhaps due to the department's growing emphasis on the community policing model following the city's 1992 uprising, community- and intergroup-oriented projects are often funded through the LAPD. As a result, commission personnel play more of a supporting role at LAPD-led functions. And, while a small event, the symbolism of moving the LAHRC from City Hall in late 2016 to make room for additional LAPD offices in that building (the LAPD already has sprawling facilities around the city hall complex) suggests that city administrations might value the bottom-line outcomes that the commission strives for but are not willing to empower the LAHRC with the kind of mandate and resource commitment that might address some of the aforementioned staffer and commissioner concerns.

Taken together, then, it would seem that the LAHRC's combination of nonspecific mandate and limited resources hinders a group of dedicated professionals who are given a challenging task that takes a clear toll on staffers. Creativity is inherently part of the commission's facilitation process and could fill the pages of a separate volume documenting the staffer efforts to help different racial, ethnic, gender, and religious groups see each other as having more in commonalities than differences. But the mandate and resource challenges are not limited to LAHRC. Even commissions with clear judicial mandates, and the federal resources to go along to enforce them, have challenges.

PITTSBURGH: WORKING THE LONG GAME

Our interviews with staffers and commissioners on the Pittsburgh commission, which is charged with enforcing HUD nondiscrimination statues throughout the city, uncovered the opposite problem as confronts the LAHRC. Since the Pittsburgh commission operates under specific mandates, it makes branching out into other areas of intergroup relations work just as challenging as having a broad charge. One of the Pittsburgh staffers summed up the view of the commission's problem in terms of both a general lack of community awareness about the commission and difficulty in finding a way to balance a new set of responsibilities.

> I think the issue is that we're not hearing from the communities that are being discriminated against. . . . I think we have a problem marketing ourselves so to speak as a government agency. We also have to think about how our mission as a commission fits with the rest of what we do because we have certain things we do well now and that we are obligated to do by statue. But if you ask whether we want to be at the table to talk about community–police relations, and to discuss larger issues with religious discrimination and other, related items, yes, we'd be right there. But we really have to think through what's next because I don't see the commission abandoning its existing mission to do something that is exclusively related to intergroup issues, important as they are.

Here the issue is not a lack of desire to explore creative ways to address larger human relations concerns across Pittsburgh but, instead, a challenge of figuring out where money will need to come from to support an expanded commission footprint. According to this same staffer:

> We're an investigative body that enforces HUD policies in relation to the Fair Housing Act. But we would like to do more in the areas of discrimination. Religion comes to mind, given what's happened. But our money comes from different sources. To perform our HUD enforcement work, we have HUD money, and we get some from general revenue, but we must do better in getting grants to support intergroup relations work. There's so much tension in our community now caused by racial, ethnic, and religious differences. Now is the time we should engage in community outreach, but we're not able to do as much as we'd like because we lack the financial resources.

The two Pittsburgh commissioners we interviewed shared the staffer's views, and both identified the need for better education and outreach on intergroup issues as what they wish the commission could be devoting more time to. Of course, one might suggest that part of engaging in bureaucratic creativity is looking for ways to accomplish tasks without financial support. Our sense is that this approach might work well in "one-off" situations where the commission can leverage investment from public–private partnerships and volunteer labor to implement programs. As useful as this approach might be, however, a sustained effort to address discrimination across religious and racial or ethnic lines (as the staffer identified) will require a more sustained approach. This is where foundation grants might also be a path to increasing commission work, although it is unclear what the alternative plan would be if a grant does not materialize or when one expires. A sustained funding approach is critical but can be elusive.

At the same time, securing additional commission resources from the city's general fund—which is the most likely and readily available financial source for an expanded commission footprint—will require a concurrent expansion of the commission's mandate, which, in the Pittsburgh case, must come from city council. It is here that we may potentially see friction between what local commission bureaucrats value and envision for the Pittsburgh HRC and what elected officials are willing to empower the commission to do (so long as financial support is provided). Providing that the Pittsburgh commission effectively discharges its existing HUD-related responsibilities first, and does not expect the city council to fund the new programs, there appears to be little in the way of impediment from the city's elected leaders to the commission looking for ad hoc ways to creatively expand its mandate into more of the facilitation-type work that the LAHRC undertakes. Whether this means that the elected officials hold different values from the commissioners and commission is unknown, although it is likely that, as we mentioned regarding the Los Angeles case, there is no hesitation in giving verbal assent to the idea that group-based discrimination should be eradicated, better intergroup relations promoted, and so on. The value difference may instead come in terms of appropriating funds for the direct and sustained support of these services.

We know at this point that commissions have key strengths and weaknesses when it comes to fulfilling their mandates. In the case of Pittsburgh, it is not so much the existing HUD enforcement mandate that is the issue but an expansion into more of the facilitation work that the LAHRC performs. Meanwhile, the LAHRC struggles with making the best of a very broad mandate (without any enforcement powers) and with less-than-ideal resource levels. The frustration among the LAHRC staffers and commissioners centers on the lack resources, with at least one of the staffers expressing deep, personal frustration at not making progress on intergroup issues in the city. The Pittsburgh interviewees did not express the same degree of personal frustration but seemed to chafe at the limitations placed on their actions or, more specifically, the lack of resources to support expanding their commission's mandate.

One of the key functions that commissioners in Pittsburgh and Fort Worth play in discharging their existing mandates is serving as a hearing panel for property owners and employers accused of violating nondiscrimination laws. Sometimes the commission staff and commissioners have a different viewpoint. A FWHRC staffer explains how it is possible for the commissioners and staffers to differ on perceived code violations and which group ends up making final determination on a housing discrimination code case:

> We had a case that we believed—staff believed—that it was cause. It went to a hearing panel, and the HRC [commissioners] said we don't believe that it's cause. So they [the commissioners] overturned what we recommended because ours is a recommendation. The parties may elect to skip the HRC and go directly to district court, but more often than not, the way the Fair Housing law reads, you're supposed to try to conciliate from the beginning to the end, including after you may find reasonable cause. So according to federal law, commissions with the quasi-judicial function are empowered to find ways to settle disputes without going to court, and it appears that, generally speaking, there is a desire on the part of the defendant to settle the case. And I will tell you, more often than not, if we get to that reasonable cause, they settle. We end up with a conciliation agreement, which has to provide some substantial public interest relief and relief for the complainant. So there may be a monetary relief in that conciliation agreement that ranges, and then there's also we may make them go through training, we may make them create a policy.

In this example, because a majority of commissioners did not find cause with respect to the housing complaint, the ability of the staff to negotiate between the renters and the property owner was curtailed and the dispute ended up in district court with the outcome unknown at the time of our interviews. This incident highlights the disruption of the enforcement process, which may occur when there is disagreement or differences in perspective among commissioners or between commissioners and staff.

The quasi-judicial commissions like Fort Worth and Pittsburgh also work with defendants to ensure that previous violations are not repeated, in part by helping property owners and employers modify their accommodation policies and related items. It is here that the commissions' enforcement work may be the most creative. This same FWHRC staffer related the following example:

> Let's say it's a reasonable accommodation case, we may make them, as part of the conciliation agreement, create a reasonable accommodation policy and distribute it to their tenants. We can make all their staff go through training. We may make them post posters. . . . We actually had a case about a year ago where we said after we do all this, we're so concerned that we're going to bring the city's code compliance back in to verify that you've made these fixes that had to do with doors and locks and safety, and there were so many other issues that combined with this housing complaint that brought them in and make them go through mini-steps and then we monitor.

Sometimes the enforcement work can involve dealing with some of the most difficult aspects of the tenant–landlord or employee–employer relationships: eviction and firing. Commissioners and staffers must exercise great care to help resolve situations before they escalate, potentially posing direct threats to a person's safety and quality of life. Again, the commissions' pursuit of conciliation agreements and bringing creativity and certain values to the process are key. The same staffer continued in providing an explanation of the commission's efforts on this front.

> So part of the conciliation agreement was that an individual was about to be evicted, and we were able to work out that they're not evicted and they wanted to stay another year, and we make sure that they can stay. If they want to move out, we make sure it's a neutral reference when they

go to look for other housing. . . . More often than not, you're going to find that if it's a reasonable cause, it tends to settle even at that last stage, even after the cause has been found because going forward they know that we have all this information. It's in their best interest. But the complainant usually doesn't want to drag this out either. Our goal with HUD is to close these cases within 100 days, but sometimes these cases can go longer just because of the complexity of the cases. It's generally similar with employment cases. We want those resolved quickly because you're talking perhaps about a family's sole breadwinner.

But, although the FWHRC is closer to its Pittsburgh counterpart in mandate type and resourcing, the Fort Worth commissioners and staff we interviewed seemed more concerned with the difference between what the commission would like to do and what the city's elected officials would allow. The FWHRC perhaps demonstrates the clearest difference in values between HRC personnel and elected officials of the three commissions thus far considered. As one FWHRC staffer lamented, "It's a challenge. If you look at any board or commission appointed by a city council—they're advisory. So they can make recommendations, they can push those forward, but in the end it's the elected body that decides 'Are we going to accept these recommendations? Are we going to implement these recommendations?' They [the commissioners] don't have authority beyond the city council."

To be clear, the lack of authority discussed here deals with the commission's advisory function—outside of the HUD and FEPA purviews—to advise or request that the council adopt ordinances that promote the improvement of intergroup relations and marginalized communities around Fort Worth. Like Pittsburgh's commission, the FWHRC operates from at least one position of defined mandate and resource strength: its enforcement function. But both the Pittsburgh and Fort Worth commissions have essentially the same limitations as the LAHRC in any advisory or facilitator work they undertake. The FWHRC staffer noted that the HRC commissioners are

supposed to be the voice of the community. They're supposed to be the ones bringing those concerns forward, and then we try to look for creative ways to address them, to bring those to the attention of city council. But sometimes it's also how strong the individual members of that commission are at the time. You might have a group that they're not as aggressive as at other times. And I've been around it long enough to see the back and forth and back and forth, and sometimes it takes years to get where their final goal is.

This last comment suggests a new layer of complication. How do HRCs effectively operate when the local political environment does not appear to support, or at least prioritize, the social justice– and inclusion-oriented intent that is the foundation HRCs? More explicitly, HRCs were established to improve race relations and ensure better treatment for marginalized residents. Some would characterize this founding purpose as change-oriented and as promoting a progressive government ideology. However, the dominant ideology among elected officials in some cities, especially in the middle of the country, is predominantly conservative. By and large, these leaders may be less interested in changing or upsetting the status quo or may hold negative opinions on the importance of addressing the concerns of marginalized groups. Both appear to be the case in the City of Fort Worth. An example is the decision of the city council not to join the lawsuit against Senate Bill 4 (SB4), the so-called Sanctuary City law.

SB4, signed into Texas law on May 7, 2017, makes it a Class A misdemeanor for officials in local governments, public colleges, and universities to refuse to work with the federal government on immigration enforcement. The fines established for not complying with the requests of U.S. Immigration and Customs Enforcement or U.S. Homeland Security range from $1,000 to $25,000, depending on the length of the infraction. The law also authorizes local police officers to check the immigration status of persons detained. SB4 is a source of major concern for many members of the Fort Worth community, both citizens and noncitizens. But obviously, the law has a greater negative impact on immigrant residents. In fact, although crimes against immigrants have increased across the city, the Fort Worth Police Department also saw a significant drop in victims reporting crimes following SB4's passage.[21]

In late June 2017, in response to the fears of immigrant residents and their U.S.-born family and friends, the FWHRC sent a strongly worded recommendation to the mayor and city council members urging the city to join Dallas, Houston, San Antonio, Austin, and several other Texas towns in their lawsuit opposing SB4's constitutionality. The FWHRC never received a response from the mayor or city council members, except for an acknowledgment of receiving the recommendation. According to one of the FWHRC commissioners we interviewed,

> Some of us tried to speak with the mayor in person about SB4. She was never available according to her secretary, and she did not return my phone calls. At the reception for [name removed for confidentiality], I could tell she was trying to avoid me. We all went to the council work-shop on SB4 and later at the open meeting where they discussed and voted on whether to join the lawsuit, and they never called on us. They never even mentioned the letter they received from us. Even though there were hundreds of supporters [for joining the lawsuit] at the meeting and outside, they voted against us.

At the August 2017 council meeting, against the recommendations of the FWHRC and the Fort Worth chief of police, the mayor and council members voted 4–5 not to join the lawsuit against SB4. This made Fort Worth the only major city in Texas not to join. There is an additional layer of complexity in Fort Worth to the mandate/resource/values/creativity template outlined at the beginning of the chapter. Unlike commission staffers, many of whom have some degree of civil service protection and specialized training to perform their work as career bureaucrats, HRC commissioners are volunteers appointed for fixed terms and typically have limited knowledge much less any training in human relations. Even though most terms are renewable, commissioner slots usually are filled by mayoral appointment, meaning they are part of a larger political consideration dependent on election outcomes. The FWHRC staffer's earlier reference to varying levels of aggressiveness by past commissions is both a reflection of the interpersonal dynamic at work among members of the commission with city elected officials or city staff and potentially a case where the agendas (and overarching values) of elected officials, commissioners, and commission staffers do not align.

Our point here is not that local bureaucrats do not maintain the kind of latitude that Meier and O'Toole suggest but that the strategy and success of bureaucratic effort may be a function of the long game for commissions in their advisory role (much as in their facilitatory work). A second FWHRC staffer offered a prime example:

> We tried to pass sexual orientation, and it took us over five years. And we tried and it failed. And we tried again, and it failed. And then we finally succeeded in 2000. So in 2000 we added sexual orientation for our local employment, housing, and public accommodation, and then in 2009, we added transgender, gender identity, and gender expression. And both of those did not happen overnight. It was not an initial, "oh, let's make this recommendation" and it was just completely accepted. It took a lot of relationship building between the commission and the council to bring their concerns back and forth. It took community involvement to be a part of that process also. For us to get the transgender, gender identity, and gender expression, the Rainbow Lounge incident [an LGBT bar raided by the Fort Worth Police and the Texas Alcoholic Beverage Commission where several patrons were seriously injured] was a big catalyst for that. We had already been discussing it, but that helped push that proposed change to add that protected basis. . . . Through the work a task force, and the work of the commission, and community involvement, especially the LGBT community leaders, we were able to get those protected bases added, but it certainly wasn't easy. I think the meeting in which we added sexual orientation was the longest in city council history.

The significance of high-profile events and community involvement to the operation and accomplishments of HRCs is evident in the above account. Another more recent incident for the FWHRC further emphasizes the point about how political values between HRCs and elected officials may diverge, even among HRC commissioners themselves. The issue centered on the 2015 appointment of a commissioner who did not support the values reflected in the FWHRC mission and objectives.

The appointee was a former city council member in a town directly adjacent to Fort Worth. He was also a prolific Facebook user. Given his social media profile, the appointee's racist and anti-immigrant views were known to many in the community by 2015. His posts included negative comments about transgender persons, Muslims, and immigrants.[22] One FWHRC commissioner described the 2015 appointee this way: "I could tell years ago he was not open minded." Another former commissioner, when asked about her sudden resignation from the FWHRC in 2016, expressed concern to a local newspaper reporter about her fellow commissioner's Facebook posts and said the person's comments during meetings "didn't align with the commission's mission, which includes eliminating prejudice and discrimination."[23] One of the commissioners we interviewed said:

> It was difficult for the commission to take actions when problems were brought to us because he hardly ever agreed with anything the rest of us wanted to do. I expressed my concerns about his hostile behavior and comments at meetings directly to [a member of city staff] and she told me he was appointed to represent conservative, pro-Trump viewpoints. I kinda thought that was a strange response because our commission is supposed to be nonpartisan.

When the City of Fort Worth received a complaint from residents about the commissioner's Facebook page in 2017, the city investigated and found his posts were political in nature but "did not violate any city rules."[24] None of the commissioners we spoke with knew whether the mayor was aware of the complaint. However, the commissioner was reappointed for a second two-year term. For the next eighteen months, the FWHRC struggled in its decision making in arriving at consensus over certain programmatic efforts because of the attitude of this particular commissioner toward any FWHRC initiatives that might be considered progressive or "pro-immigrant." The resignations of two commissioners who were not replaced (thereby making quorum and procedural votes harder to achieve), enabled this commissioner to continue efforts at blocking FWHRC efforts.

The challenge inherent in this example for the FWHRC commissions and staff is that the city's guidelines or criteria for board and commission positions are limited. Interestingly, no mention of qualifications, expected behavior, and so on, and certainly no mention of social media policy is made in city documents. Beyond conflict of interest, the only written expectation is that "those who serve in these positions conduct themselves in a civil manner," which leaves considerable room for interpretation.[25] Given the stark misalignment between this particular commissioner and FWHRC values, the other commissioners could have recommended to the city council to have the problematic commissioner removed. Yet without more explicit policy guidelines, the FWHRC was reluctant to take action. This changed in July 2019, when a professor at a local university began tweeting screenshots of the commissioner's Facebook posts. With more than 1,200 followers on Twitter, the professor's tweets raised a local awareness of the commissioner's Facebook content. Interviewed by a local newspaper, the professor said

> she was appalled to see [the commissioner's name] public profile, calling his posts "racist, sexist, transphobic, and anti-immigrant. . . . As an officer of the city serving on a commission dedicated to eliminating prejudice and discrimination, [the commissioner's name] posts are completely out of line with the mission of the Human Relations Commission. . . . The city wishes to promote the message of 'y'all means all,' yet a member of its commission leading on issues of inclusion is posting derogatory and discriminatory messages on his public social media."[26]

This professor initiated a petition calling for the commissioner's removal and within a few days more than five hundred people had signed. The mayor asked the commissioner for his resignation, but he refused to resign. The removal petition was presented to the FWHRC at a special meeting called in late July. There are usually only a few people besides commissioners and city staff at HRC meetings, but that night the room was filled with local residents. Besides the professor, five people spoke in favor of removal. The offending commissioner did not attend the meeting, and no one present spoke on his behalf. The FWHRC vote was unanimous to recommend to the city council for his removal. At the August regular meeting of the Fort Worth City Council, the council accepted the FWHRC's recommendation and voted to remove the commissioner. The council also agreed to review their criteria for members selected to boards and commissions and asked staff to investigate the social media policy for those serving on boards and commissions for other local governments.

While this episode ended with a resignation, this does not mean the challenge of implementing a commission mission of inclusion and other "progressive" political efforts is met. If anything, the ideological incongruence between commissioner appointees and the inherent mission of HRCs will likely remain a problem requiring more careful vetting of commissioners and perhaps another layer of creativity by commissions in navigating the ideological proclivities of elected officials running municipal governments in "red state" America.

In broader terms, if creativity can be measured in terms of programming, both the Los Angeles and Fort Worth commissions offer strong examples. Just after our Los Angeles interviews, the LAHRC embarked on the first in a series of community dinners designed to enable a sense of shared concern between members of different social, racial, ethnic, and religious groups in the city. Meanwhile, FWHRC has established a series of community programs that leverage commissioner contacts throughout the city as well as entertainment media to drive home important points about intergroup relations, gender issues, and related topics. The first FWHRC staffer we interviewed offered the following perspective:

> In the work we do, you find passion on both sides. For us, because they [the commission] are an advisory board, we try to use their influence in those communities. So, we've done conferences, we did a disability conference. We also have this program started, we're now in our seventh year, which is our Movies that Matter program. And we introduce very difficult topics to discuss through this program. We've discussed everything from human trafficking, immigration, to race discrimination, color discrimination.

CINCINNATI: SEARCHING FOR PROMISE

Both the LAHRC and FWHRC have also empaneled ad hoc committees and task forces to study and make advisory recommendations through the commission to city council about a range of intergroup relations issues. This leaves the Cincinnati Commission on Human Relations (CCHR) as the last of the four to be addressed. As stated near this chapter's beginning, the Cincinnati commission enjoys the same broad faciliatory and advisory mandate as the LAHRC but has none of the quasi-judicial responsibilities of the Fort Worth or Pittsburgh commissions. Interestingly, and different from the LAHRC, the CCHR, likely owing to the reverberations from the city's well-publicized 2001 uprising over police conduct in killing several unarmed African Americans in a series of altercations, is expected to report to Cincinnati Police Department (CPD) any information—even unsubstantiated rumors—of community unrest. As a former CCHR staffer told us, "The police code says that the commission is responsible for reporting any rumors of unrest or when tensions could lead to mass protests. So we have to essentially notify the police."

While certainly raising the commission's bureaucratic profile within the city government, the problems associated with CPD's expectation are clear. Although CPD might be well intentioned in looking to address any community complaints about its work before a situation escalates into physical violence or property damage, the expectation of reporting any and all information heard from the community to the CPD places the CCHR in a position whereby trust will be harder to build with segments of the community. As we saw with the LAHRC, facilitation work is challenging enough without an added dimension of distrust. But the former CCHR staffer we interviewed essentially indicated that the commissioners and staff made the best of circumstances, often by redoubling focus on groups marginalized along religious and sexuality lines: "We would work to do a lot of programming and dialogue and work to improve conditions and victim protection from anti-gay attacks and other situations where people are being harmed, and we're pushing back on anti-Semitism."

Like the LAHRC, however, the CCHR has trouble expanding its mandate to include anything resembling quasi-judicial enforcement. And, like its Los Angeles counterpart, the CCHR struggled to make sense of whether the commission's community work was having an impact. According to the staffer, "there was never enough continuity in the agreements that structured the commission to get an assessment of anything, any data to tell us if what we were doing was effective."

Another CCHR staffer suggested that the best the commission could hope to do was to alert vulnerable communities as to the city CHR's existence, even if the commission's actual capacity to assist was limited.

My assessment is that we would work in proximity with communities that were being harmed or targeted to figure out what support they needed, 'cause there's no systemic remedy that we could offer. It's important to make sure that we're at least in relationship with the communities the need us. With immigrant communities, with folks with disabilities, folks experiencing homelessness. Enquiring about what concerns they do have and trying to work a program.

Yet, somewhat unlike the LAHRC staffers, the CCHR staffers seem much more eager to engage city council in pushing for ordinance-codified reforms for marginalized groups. This might owe to differences in the bureaucratic lanes between the CHR and Cincinnati City Council versus the structure of Los Angeles city government (certainly, the size difference between the two governments would suggest the CHR has easier access to council staffers). There might also be a difference in personnel temperament in pushing for specific changes on council. Regardless, CHR staffers and commissioners made tenacious and creative use of their advisory power to push for council action, as this second staffer indicated:

We have made some impact, like on some legislation that went before council. I will say that the longer I was there, we did try to develop some more proactive statements. So, in 2014, I think, there was an indigenous group that used to gather every Columbus Day. But they would ask us to request a proclamation from the Mayor's Office to recognize the third Monday in October as Indigenous People's Day. And somewhere along the line I got wind of some legislation that was passed in another city just abolishing Columbus Day. So, I asked my boss, "Can we do that?" I mean, city council's like right up the street. And he's like "yeah, figure it out." So, there's sort of this question of whether we're allowed to pass policy, but one of things that we knew that we had to do was at least consult local indigenous folks on whether or not they think this is important. So we started an indigenous people's working group and started talking about what is the history and knowledge of indigenous folks in this area. So we met for like over a year as a working group and drafted legislation that eventually failed. We figured out what the appropriate committee, presented it before the committee, and it went to the floor and it failed 5–4 [in Cincinnati City Council]. The 5 was five abstentions, which was literally unprecedented. . . . There's speculation for why it failed the way that it failed, but it also hit Breitbart and a lot of conservative news outlets. But that experience was one of helping us understand how we could do more proactive work. So, we saw a need, saw what another city was doing, we consulted the population that would be impacted, worked with them to build out the legislation. It failed, but we stayed in communication and it just passed last year.

HRCS ARE THE SAME, BUT DIFFERENT

This chapter provides a sense of the work that HRCs do from the perspective of the commissioners and staffers themselves. What each commission featured here seems to have in common is a general alignment in value orientation to improve intergroup relations and reduce discrimination (the Fort Worth episode notwithstanding). Each commission also takes its role as a local advisory voice for elected officials and community members seriously, even if a commission's primary function is of a quasi-judicial nature. Generally speaking, we should not expect anything less from professionals and interested community volunteers who self-select into this line of work. However, beyond common values and advisory efforts, the similarities between the commissions breaks down by virtue of the local ordinances governing commission existence. Indeed, all four commissions implement aspects of their codified missions within specific and different mandate and resource contexts.

And, interestingly, none of the cases evince an ideal whereby commissions function across the various domains critical to human relations issues without engaging in tradeoffs. From a pure implementation standpoint, the quasi-judicial commissions have the most linear job to perform in that they enforce HUD or FEPA codes and have the mandated power and resources to do this job independent from local political control. But staffers and commissioners in both Pittsburgh and Fort Worth were quick to offer their desire to expand into the kind of facilitation work that is both the hallmark and core frustration point for their Los Angeles and Cincinnati counterparts. The constraints each commission operates under necessitates the levels of creativity and dedication we found across HRCs in our study.

In addition to the examples of creativity seen among the interviewees in this chapter, human relations practitioners may effectively draw on data-driven insights to help work through at least some of the more challenging aspects of their work—especially the promotion of positive intergroup relations and the reduction of discrimination. Chapter 5 is the first of two chapters dedicated to examining ways that commissions can leverage data-driven insights about group identity.

5

EXPERIMENTING WITH THE DYNAMICS OF INTERGROUP IDENTITY

Given what commissioners and staffers expressed about the challenges surrounding the facilitation role that HRCs undertake—and the general lack of resources for this kind of intergroup work across commissions—we focus the next two chapters on identifying and testing strategies for promoting positive human relations–based outcomes. This chapter features Los Angeles as a case study with the desired positive outcome being perceptions of greater commonality among residents of different racial or ethnic groups. The insights generated from this exercise are applicable to essentially any locale with similarly diverse racial and ethnic populations. Although the LAHRC has greater relative flexibility in addressing intergroup issues because of its lack of code enforcement responsibility, other commissions should be able to adopt similar strategies based on what we outline below. Our analysis is informed by LAHRC efforts to address community tensions and historical conflict. As referenced in prior chapters, perhaps the most famous of historical tensions was the Watts uprising of August 1965.

On August 11, 2015, the fiftieth anniversary of the Watts riots in South Los Angeles, the LAHRC sponsored a series of community-wide educational events on Watts and the circumstances surrounding the riots. The LAHRC believed that these commemorative events to heighten awareness or knowledge of past challenges (and the efforts made to overcome them) that the Watts turmoil typified, along with facilitating intergroup contact with communication that emphasizes a collective or shared Los Angeles identity, would "bring people together," thereby improving intergroup relations.[1] Patricia Villasenor, the LAHRC director at the time, best articulated an overview of this approach during an interview with us: "I really believe that knowledge is power, and I think part of that is when people have the knowledge of their community and of the operational functions of government, [then] they have the power to come together and say no or yes to current conditions they live with."[2] Another staffer related to us: "The big challenge is getting people to see that they have things uniting them. We have to work to make them see it, and it's tough. People are so quick to blame others and all that, so we try and get back to the basics with them and talk about things like community and local needs. It's all very basic, but we try to make it work."

What this staffer refers to is the act of focusing people on the notion that they share a collective identity that transcends racial, ethnic, religious, and other divisions. Some political science and social psychology research supports the assumption that encouraging reflection on a collective or superordinate identity can have positive effects in generating increased perceptions of intergroup similarity and reduced bias.[3] The positive benefits are less clear with dual identity—when recognition and respect of the person's subgroup (minority) identity is simultaneously activated with the collective identity.[4] And some scholars have found increased intergroup conflict when there is heightened identity awareness.[5] Also complicating matters is that none of the prior research on identity perceptions and intergroup outcomes deals specifically with commission-related work, and most existing research focuses primarily on white and black individuals. We wanted to address these weaknesses in the literature with our study in Los Angeles.

Despite the fact that HRCs work as part of government institutions, many of the commissions' core missions—particularly the promotion of positive intergroup relations—are closely tied to the social identity tradition in social psychology. Specifically, social identity theory suggests that people gain a sense of self by identifying with a social group.[6] While people hold multiple social identities, one group identity is likely to be more salient but not necessarily all the time.[7] This sets the stage for potential conflicts as people align their sense of self with a group of others deemed alike (i.e., an in-group), and react to threats perceived by those considered different (i.e., an out-group).[8] These in-group and out-group perceptions are central to the difficulties that commissions confront in their daily work. At the same time, however, since identity is largely a socially constructed reality, there is reason to expect that efforts to encourage people to realign their identity perceptions, even temporarily, might have a positive impact on intergroup perceptions, thereby making commission efforts to improve intergroup relations more successful.

In this chapter we use theories from social psychology, including common in-group identity, dual identity, and intergroup contact theories, to help illustrate that identity is a variable construct that can change considerably given exposure to certain stimuli.[9] What is more, such change can significantly impact perceived commonality with out-group members.

SOCIAL GROUP IDENTITY AND INTERGROUP BIAS

When people categorize other people into groups, they tend to minimize the differences between members of the same group (often ignoring such differences when making decisions or forming impressions), and they tend to exaggerate differences between groups.[10] Interestingly, people are also found to have better memories when it comes to information about the ways in-group members are similar to themselves and out-group members are dissimilar.[11] In terms of behavioral outcomes, people are simply more welcoming and more cooperative toward members of their own group than they are toward those of an out-group.[12] Yet, from the standpoint of commissions working to improve intergroup relations, there is reason to believe that these group identities are malleable. According to John Dovidio and colleagues, "Social categorization is a dynamic process, however, and people possess many group identities and are capable of focusing on different social categories. By modifying the individual subject's goals, perceptions of past experiences, and experiences, one has the opportunity to alter the level of group inclusiveness that will be primary or most influential in a given situation."[13]

With this in mind, we discuss some of the theoretical approaches that scholars have used to understand the foundational motives behind group coalescence and, more importantly with respect to commission work, possible ways to encourage seeing group identities as at least somewhat similar. Samuel Gaertner and John Dovidio's common ingroup identity model

(CIIM) emphasizes recategorization whereby members of different groups are encouraged to conceive of themselves as a single, more inclusive super-ordinate group (rather than as completely separate ones).[14] Further, the CIIM hypotheses that intergroup prejudice is reduced when people recat-egorize one another so that the in-group and out-group(s) are subsumed into a collective or superordinate category. Changing group boundaries in this way allows some of the cognitive and behavioral processes that con-tributed to intergroup biases initially to be redirected toward the devel-opment of more positive intergroup relations. Importantly, the CIIM has been supported by both laboratory experiments and field studies and in different cultures.[15]

But the CIIM is not a panacea for constructive intergroup relations. This is often because the majority group in question potentially benefits more than minorities when separate group categories are diminished or abandoned in favor of a common collective identity. Indeed, for minori-ties, it simply may not be politically or psychologically feasible to give up important identities.[16] Another practical concern is that minority groups could lose special protections or benefits when being rolled into a larger group construct.

DUAL IDENTITY

The dual identity model claims that it is possible to reap the benefits of a common in-group identity (through recategorization) while maintaining distinctive subgroup identities during contact. A dual identity approach, which is similar if not the same as multiculturalism, is especially valuable when one group (the majority) is larger than the other (the minority). This is because minority group members may resist a collective identity if accepting that identity means that their own distinctiveness will be lost. Group diversity is recognized when everyone has dual identities, all within a shared social framework.[17]

Note that we steer away from the basic CIIM and the problematic nature of a naïve superordinate identity cue used in isolation as part of our Los Angeles study (e.g., "we are all Angelenos"). We instead focus on testing aspects of the dual identity model in ways that might promote a sense of intergroup commonality while testing "on the ground" messages that LAHRC analysts have told us are key in their work. HRC staffers made clear during their interviews with us that promoting positive intergroup relations is a core programmatic interest and that this promotion is often done through messages aimed at convincing people with disparate group identities and perspectives that they share more as local residents than they have as differences. We term this broader or superordinate sense of sharing a "collective identity." One of the challenges commissions face in doing this work, of course, is that there have been no systematic tests of whether the strategies that HRC staffers use have their intended effects on residents.

To gain insight on this question, we conducted a survey-embedded experiment with three randomized treatment cues or stimuli modified from the group identity cues used by John Transue.[18] The three treatments are versions of dual identity model constructs that all include a baseline reminder of subjects' Los Angeles identity. Table 5.1 includes the treatment cue wording. The first treatment uses an identity cue that encourages focus on a collective Angeleno identity while not threatening subgroup identities. The collective cue also simultaneously contrasts the superordinate identity with a political out-group: elected officials.

Public perception of political leaders from a social identity perspective is a developing area in the literature that presents promise for a broader understanding of how differentiating subgroup perceptions of common problems along racial and ethnic lines from those of government leaders strengthens perceptions of intergroup commonality among local residents.[19] The intent of a collective cue is to draw subgroup members together to address common local concerns in a collective way. Contrasting local residents and elected officials from the standpoint of addressing local problems is also a hallmark of the LAHRC's programmatic efforts. As an HRC staffer offered during an interview, "We try to make everyone feel like what they experience as local residents matters just as much as some councilman's view, or the police chief's opinion. Because it does. We can't get everyone on the same page if we don't have ways for residents to know that their views are important and will be heard and taken seriously in the process—that their word matters as much as the politicians."

TABLE 5.1 Treatment Group Assignments, Variable Wording, and Number of Subjects

TREATMENT GROUP ASSIGNMENTS	WORDING	NUMBER OF SUBJECTS ASSIGNED
Collective identity cue	"Los Angeles residents—no matter their race, ethnicity, or religion—may see community problems in ways that elected officials do not. This should be taken into account in any study of problems facing Los Angeles."	116 Anglos 135 Latinos 34 African Americans
Subgroup distinctiveness cue	"Los Angeles area residents of certain racial, ethnic, or religious backgrounds may see community problems differently than others. This should be taken into account in any study of problems facing Los Angeles."	94 Anglos 127 Latinos 37 African Americans
Combined cue	Collective identity AND subgroup distinctiveness cues	102 Anglos 135 Latinos 42 African Americans
Control (no cues)		102 Anglos 134 Latinos 46 African Americans
	POLITICAL COMMUNITY	**SCALE**
	"Thinking about things like government services, political power, and representation, how much does your racial or ethnic group have in common with other groups in Los Angeles today? Would you say your group has a lot in common, some in common, little in common, or nothing at all in common with [African Americans, Asians, Whites, Latinos]?"	4 = A lot in common 3 = Some in common 2 = Little in common 1 = Nothing at all in common

INTERGROUP CONTACT CONTROL	SCALE
"About how many of your friends/ coworkers have a difference race or ethnicity than yours?"	5 = >20 4 = 10–20 3 = 4–9 2 = 1–3 1 = None

KNOWLEDGE OF WATTS	SCALE
"How familiar are you with the circumstances and issues surrounding the 1965 Watts Riots"	5 = Extremely 4 = Very 3 = Moderately 2 = Slightly 1 = Not at all

DEMOGRAPHIC CONTROLS	CODING
Subject gender	Female = 1
Subject party ID	Republican = 1, Democrat = 1
Subject age	18–72, continuous
Subject education	1 = College educated
Subject annual income	1 = <$50,000

The focus on contrasting peoples' experiences versus those of elected officials in the treatments is based on a larger, citywide initiative in Los Angeles. This initiative aims at identifying where policymaker assumptions about city services and outreach may be missing the boat in terms of what community members actually perceive about their local government. At the same time, the resident/official contrast is also an opportunity to provide an alternate conceptualization of Manuela Barreto and Naomi Ellemer's design, where subjects were shown varying levels of respect for their chosen identities.[20] In our design, respect for subjects' identity is provided through the notion that resident perceptions of community problems—no matter resident race or ethnicity—are said to warrant consideration by elected officials.

We contrast the collective identity cue with a more traditional "subgroup distinctiveness" cue that pits racial, ethnic, and religious identities against reference to a common "community." This is done mainly as a validity check on respondent's answers as we do not expect a subgroup distinctiveness cue to increase perceptions of intergroup commonality. Finally, we test the combined effect of both cues on subjects as our third randomly assigned treatment. Again, we expect that emphasizing collective identity among Los Angeles residents that contrasts with the perspectives of elected officials will increase perceived commonality between groups.

INTERGROUP CONTACT AND KNOWLEDGE

In addition to the effects from group identity constructs, actual intergroup contact and relative knowledge about the history and plights of other local racial and ethnic groups in Los Angeles may impact how people perceive each other. Population growth and changing demographics in the United States has increased the importance of intergroup relations as residents—especially those in urban areas—interact with people from increasingly diverse backgrounds. However, the growth in intergroup contact can have both positive and negative outcomes.[21] An important theory of the conditions that are most likely to produce positive outcomes is Gordon Allport's intergroup contact theory, which hypothesizes that properly managed contact between racial and ethnic groups should reduce prejudice and lead to better interactions.[22] The original idea of earlier theorists was that intergroup contact facilitated learning about other groups (outgroups), and this new knowledge in turn reduced prejudice toward outgroup members.

But Allport also proposed that equal status, common goals, intergroup cooperation, personal or one-on-one exchanges, and institutional support were all necessary conditions for positive effects from contact. Others argue that positive intergroup contact is more likely to occur when the exchange occurs voluntarily.[23] Still, there is no guarantee intergroup contact always results in positive outcomes.[24]

The influence of contact on intergroup relations has been the subject of numerous studies (especially in social psychology) since the 1940s. A meta-analysis of 515 studies on intergroup contact with more than 250,000 subjects shows "intergroup contact typically reduces prejudice" and may result in other positive changes in intergroup attitudes, including greater trust, empathy, and forgiveness for past transgressions.[25] Importantly, the conditions Allport identified to facilitate positive outcomes between racial and ethnic groups are not required.[26] This is critical because, at least in terms of intergroup relations in American cities, the sharing of common goals, equal status, and institutional support and the absence of intergroup competition are not likely to be in alignment at any one time. Additionally, knowledge of other racial and ethnic groups' culture and history is found to have moderating effects on intergroup contact and resulting attitudes of intergroup commonality and cooperation.

At the same time, research in social psychology, history, and political science suggest the importance of past events on both individual and group attitudes and behavior.[27] Laboratory experiments indicate that "when events that happen to a community are remembered, discussed or challenged individuals can recognize their part in them, can divide or distance themselves from them, can feel passionately supportive about or passionately reject what was/is at stake."[28] Furthermore, "a group's representation of its history will condition its sense of what it was, is, can and should be, and is central to the construction of its identity, norms, and values."[29]

The work in political science examining the influence of past events on intergroup relationships focuses primarily on international or subnational conflict, but some research examines the relationship of historical events with individuals' policy preferences.[30] Michael Dawson, for example, suggests that the historical memory of black slavery strengthens a sense of linked fate among African Americans and leads to policy preferences that favor group interests over individual interests.[31] Similarly Gabriel Sanchez and Eduardo Vargas find that past discrimination is an important dimension of group consciousness among all racial and ethnic groups but with considerable variability in effect size.[32]

The potential influence that knowledge of local intergroup history has on Los Angeles County residents influenced us to examine responses from Latinos and Anglos in our survey experiment. Latinos are 48 percent and Anglos 27 percent of the total county population (African Americans comprise 9 percent, while Asians are about 15 percent). As Los Angeles County's two largest ethnic groups, Anglos and Latinos play major roles in contemporary community intergroup initiatives.

Latinos' numeric representation in the Los Angeles population expanded precipitously after 1970, which helps explain why there was no Latino involvement in the Watts uprising.[33] Watts was a segregated African American neighborhood in 1965. It was the actions of city officials, particularly Anglo police officers, that sparked the rioting of African American residents.[34] Not surprisingly, African American residents thought Anglo authorities did a "bad job" handling the situation, attributed the violence to frustration over specific grievances, and expected the riots would make Anglos more sympathetic to "Negro problems."[35] In sharp contrast, Anglos living in Los Angeles County thought authorities handled the situation well, had little sympathy for the grievances identified by Watts residents, and believed the riots had increased the "gap between the races." Later research suggested Anglo residents' perception of the Watts riots was predicted by their prior belief in discrimination against blacks in Los Angeles and their prior support for civil rights, which suggests knowledge of the riots will not necessarily lead to increased Anglo perceptions of commonality with African Americans.[36]

Given the likely well-formed levels of knowledge of local intergroup history regarding Watts among African Americans, increased intergroup history knowledge should have a more variable impact on Latino perceptions of intergroup commonality. At the same time, situating our survey experiment in the larger, community-wide context of LAHRC's efforts to raise awareness of the uprising's fiftieth anniversary in 2015 should make it equally as likely for African American, Anglo, and Latino subjects to be aware of this historical event as part of a natural experiment of sorts—one whose resonance may be most noticeable among Los Angeles County's two largest ethnic groups.

While Latinos were not directly part of the 1965 Watts uprising, they were involved in the city's 1992 unrest, where, again, abuse by local law enforcement precipitated the public outcry. Latinos' linked fate and increased experiences with police abuse overall (which Anglos will generally not share) suggests that Latinos' relative levels of knowledge of the

1965 Watts uprising will have a stronger impact on Latino intergroup perceptions relative to Anglos.

DATA AND METHODS

Our data come from a twenty-minute, survey-embedded, questions-as-treatment experiment conducted with an online sample of 1,100 Los Angeles County adults by Qualtrics Inc., a research firm, from August 3 to 10, 2015. For those unfamiliar with this type of research approach, a survey-embedded experiment looks and functions in much the same way as a traditional survey featuring a series of questions and corresponding response options, but there is a survey component that researchers determine ahead of time will be presented to some respondents at random and not others at a specific time in the survey flow.[37] The embedded "experiment" in this case are three question statements (i.e., treatments) that are randomly assigned to three groups of respondents who will receive them during the course of taking the survey. A fourth group of respondents, also randomly determined, is not assigned a treatment statement, and they serve as the control group for our experiment. The random assignments are made by the survey software used to collect the responses. Respondents are not aware that they are selected to receive a specific treatment. The purpose of this research design approach is to test for any effect that exposure to the statement/treatment has on respondents' answers following the statement/treatment. The use of random assignment of treatments allows researchers to have confidence that any differences in how respondents answer follow-on survey questions are attributable to the assigned treatments themselves. In the case of our Los Angeles study, the treatments include different ways of characterizing group identity. The goal is to see if exposing respondents to these different characterizations at random impacts their reported impressions of other identity groups that we ask about later in the survey. Note that we use the same research design approach in chapter 6.

Before moving to an analysis of the assigned treatments and other covariates, we briefly summarize basic characteristics of our Los Angeles respondents according to a series of demographic, partisan, and local issue–oriented descriptions. The respondent sample is composed of 63 percent females. Thirty-two percent of subjects identify as white, 13 percent as African American, 11 percent as Asian, and 43 percent—by far the largest ethnic group in the sample—as Latino. The mean age of our subjects is forty-one. Sixty-three percent say they are currently employed, 53 percent say they are married or living with a partner, and almost 56 percent say they own their current residence. Thirty-four percent are college graduates, while 30 percent report to be Roman Catholic, 6 percent say they are Jewish, and 4 percent claim a Muslim identity.

In terms of partisanship, Democrats far outnumber Republicans, 51 to 17 percent, respectively. Finally, 52 percent of subjects are city of Los Angeles residents, with 48 percent residing in Los Angeles County. Although not a representative sample (see our additional discussion below), the partisanship, religion, racial, and ethnic percentages are close to what the U.S. Census and other sources project for Los Angeles County.[38]

We used a questions-as-treatment protocol where the different statements that were randomly assigned appeared near the beginning of the survey for those in the three treatment groups, placed just after the sample quota-generating questions relating to subject's race/ethnicity, sex, and geographic location. A post hoc analysis of difference between the treatment and control responses to the dependent variable (respondent's perception of intergroup commonality) shows the experiment to have a power of .90, which is enough statistical power in the design to detect effect differences between the treatments.

Again, data about respondent assignment to treatment groups, including response distribution for the dependent variable, is located in Table 5.1. In terms of the number of respondents across racial and ethnic groups, the twenty-minute Qualtrics-administered survey included African American ($n = 159$), Latino ($n = 531$), and Anglo ($n = 414$) adult subjects residing in Los Angeles County who were at least eighteen years of age. The survey instrument was available in both English and Spanish. Different from most other studies in the literature that focus on one or two of these groups, our design features a three-way group comparison of perceived commonality.[39] The utility of this inclusive approach is reflected in the growing size of the Latino community in American cities, but it maintains comparative focus on Anglos the socially and politically dominant group and African Americans who were the first racial minority group to be incorporated into the power structure of Los Angeles politics.

Our sample was drawn from an online panel of respondents maintained by Qualtrics where subject selection for survey participation matches as closely as possible the demographic characteristics and size of all three groups in Los Angeles County (which also resulted in the African American subject pool being considerably smaller).[40] The use of online opt-in "convenience" samples has become popular in political science research leveraging survey-embedded experiments, and Kevin Mullinix and colleagues report "considerably similarity" in treatment effects across twenty separate research design pairings where probability and online convenience samples were compared. They further point out, with the growing rate of nonresponse to surveys and polls using probability samples, that the assumed operational validity of probability samples falls into increasing doubt.[41]

Still, in terms of external validity, there are tradeoffs made when using an Internet sample such as Qualtrics. This mainly has to do with the degree of discrepancy between the sample and U.S. Census targets for an area. It is encouraging that a recent study by Miliaikeala Heen and colleagues shows Qualtrics (i.e., the panel service we used to procure survey respondents) to have the lowest average difference in panel characteristics versus the census among the major competing panel services, while Taylor Boas and colleagues conclude that Qualtrics is the most representative versus competitors (including Facebook) in recruiting online samples.[42]

Comparing our respondent sample with the U.S. Census Bureau's population estimates for Los Angeles County indicates that the Qualtrics sample is very close to census estimates for age, education, and income but moderately more female (data not shown).[43] The continued drawback, however, is that the convenience sample may still differ from a population on dimensions that are unmeasured. However, from an applied perspective, and given LAHRC's broad, intergroup focus across such a diverse geographic and population area, findings of a direct and statistically significant treatment effect in our experiment on messaging that aligns with existing LAHRC programming provides it and similar organizations with guidance that residents respond favorably to the theme of intergroup commonality (thereby encouraging replication and extension of this and similar studies with additional samples of varying type).

That said, even if the current sample is externally valid to the Los Angeles area in terms of LAHRC goals, there is the question of whether findings related to Los Angeles generalize to the rest of the country. We suggest that our findings should transfer to urban settings where Anglos are in a numerical minority and where there are multiple racial and ethnic groups composing a minority majority. Our analysis has perhaps less relatability in more racially homogenous locales (i.e., those that look much less like Los Angeles) or even those cities, like Fort Worth, where there is considerable ideological heterogeneity among political and policy leaders. As such, we speak with greater clarity to commissions and similar bodies in more racially diverse, and likely urban, settings while recognizing that HRCs across the country will always need to make locally informed (and creative) adjustments in whatever "on the ground" strategies they employ.

Our questions-as-treatment experiment was embedded toward the beginning of the survey. The experiment included treatment cues in the form of statements that were randomly assigned for subjects to read just prior to the outcome question of interest on the survey. A control group of subjects did not receive the treatment cue prior to the outcome question being asked.

The first treatment emphasizes a collective identity by distinguishing between the superiority of residents' perceptions of community problems versus those of elected officials; this treatment is related to the type of superordinate identity cues that Transue tested.[44] The collective identity cue in the survey read: "Los Angeles area residents—no matter their race, ethnicity, or religion—may see community problems in ways that elected officials do not. This should be taken into account in any study of problems facing Los Angeles."

The second treatment emphasizes subgroup distinctiveness in the perceptions of community problems. The subgroup distinctive cue in the survey read: "Los Angeles–area residents of certain racial, ethnic, or religious backgrounds may see community problems differently than others. This should be taken into account in any study of problems facing Los Angeles."

The third treatment combines the prior two cue statements, thereby acknowledging the superiority of residents' perceptions of community problems over those of elected officials while recognizing subgroup differences in problem perception (the cue statements were ordered at random by the Qualtrics software for display to subjects). The combined identity cue in the survey read: "Los Angeles area residents—no matter their race, ethnicity, or religion—may see community problems in ways that elected officials do not. Still, residents of certain racial, ethnic, or religious backgrounds may see community problems differently than others. This should be taken into account in any study of problems facing Los Angeles."

Finally, a control group of respondents received no identity treatment cue statement prior to the outcome variable being asked in the survey.

The dependent or outcome variable is a measure of intergroup commonality taken from a posttreatment survey question that read: "Thinking about things like government services, political power, and representation, how much does your racial or ethnic group have in common with other groups in Los Angeles today?" Respondents answered the question for each group that did not reflect their self-reported race/ethnicity. Although we did not have Asian subjects in our survey experiment, we included commonality perception outcomes for them as a point of comparison between responses from the Latino, African American, and Anglo respondents.

In terms of attrition across the assigned groups (i.e., respondents who were exposed to the treatment but then stopped answering survey questions, which thereby excluded them from our analysis): there were twenty-four in the superordinate identity group, thirty-six in the subgroup distinctive group, twenty-nine in the combined identity group, and thirty-one in the control group. Importantly, there was no evidence that the attrition was nonrandom (based on a comparison of all racial or ethnic and gender covariate information collected at the beginning of the survey for each subject).

In addition to our direct treatment effects, we include the two other covariates of interest: intergroup contact and knowledge of local racial history. Taking our cue from prior explanations of Allport's theory as a proxy for intergroup contact, we ask: "About how many of your friends/ coworkers have a different race or ethnicity than yours?"[45] Our proxy for racial group history focuses on relative, self-perceived awareness of the best-known racial uprising in Los Angeles history: the 1965 Watts uprising. The Watts proxy is useful for more than reference to an uprising, however. Different from the 1992 Los Angeles uprising, which was precipitated by the acquittal of LAPD officers indicted for the Rodney King beating in March 1991, the 1965 Watts event reflected an unprecedented racial response to long-standing police mistreatment of the African American community, and fallout from Watts helped precipitate formation of the LAHRC itself.

Therefore, one's relative knowledge about the Watts uprising should reflect a general appreciation for the region's overall state of race relations. Our question asked, "How familiar are you with the circumstances and issues surrounding the 1965 Watts Riots?" Our models, including demographic control variables reported later in the chapter, included the following: age, sex (1 = female), partisan affiliation (Republican and Democrat), education level, and income level. Tables A.1–A.5 in the appendix include the full statistical results from this chapter's analysis.

TREATMENT EFFECTS: PERCEIVING
INTERGROUP SIMILARITY

Again, post hoc analysis of the differences between the treatment and control responses for the dependent variable—intergroup commonality— shows the experiment's statistical power (i.e., the ability for the analysis to distinguish statistically significant effects) at .90 ($p < .01$). Additionally, a qualitative review of subjects' answers to an open-ended question included on the survey questionnaire suggests that subjects were not aware of the purpose of the randomized treatment statements, and regressions on the treatment variables indicate treatment assignment was not predicted by subjects' sex, race, income, age, income, or partisanship (results not shown).[46]

We move now to an assessment of treatment effects on respondents in terms of the survey's intergroup perception measures. The question measures respondent perception of how much in common people feel they have with those in other ethnic and racial groups and reads as follows: "Thinking about things like government services, political power, and representation, how much does your racial or ethnic group have in common with other groups in Los Angeles today? Would you say your group has a lot in common, some in common, little in common, or nothing at all in common with [African Americans, Asian Americans, Anglos, Latinos]?"[47] Given the strong LAHRC emphasis on convincing residents of different identities that they have a mutual or common stake in the health of their neighborhoods and communities, the intergroup commonality perception measure is a good place to start in testing the effectiveness of LAHRC strategies for improving intergroup relations. And the use of random assignment in our design enables us to disentangle the direction of effect in encouraging intergroup commonality perception.

In examining the frequency distribution of the dependent variables among our subjects in figures 5.1–5.3, we see that a plurality of Anglos feel some degree of perceived political commonality with African Americans, Asians, and Latinos, with a clear majority of Anglos saying they have either "some" or "a lot" in common (politically) with the other racial and ethnic groups. Latino subject perceptions displayed in figures 5.2 show the same general response pattern (although the combined percentages of those saying they perceive "some" or "a lot" politically in common with other groups are slightly lower than among whites). Still, the overall response distribution suggests that our subjects are willing to view ethnic and racial out-group as sharing political interests and needs. Meanwhile, African American respondents in figure 5.3 reveal a clearer pattern of perceived political commonality toward Latinos, although they also view Anglos and Asians as having a general degree of commonality. In other words, none of the three groups of subjects expressed an overly strong sense that they do not find political commonality with other racial and ethnic groups. In some ways, then, this makes the confirmations of

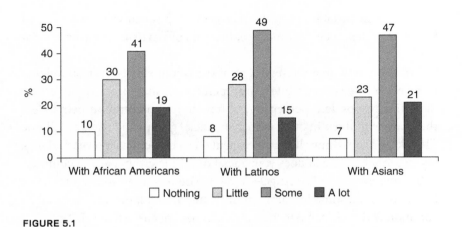

FIGURE 5.1

Anglo Perceived Commonality, *n* = 419

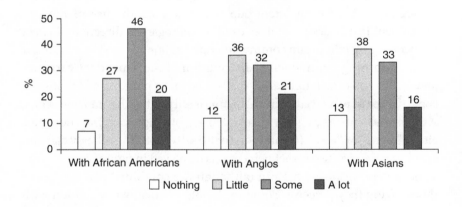

FIGURE 5.2

Latino Perceived Commonality, *n* = 533

our initial research expectation more difficult in that there may be a "ceiling" effect whereby the assigned treatment cues are unable to move subjects to increased levels of perceived commonality.

Figure 5.4 shows the percentage breakdown for subjects' self-reported levels of cooperative contact—their number of friends and coworkers with

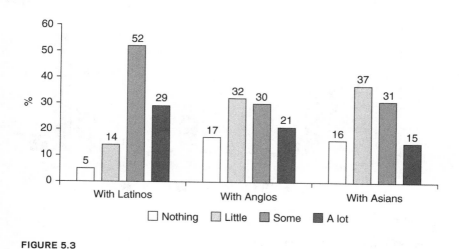

FIGURE 5.3

African American Perceived Commonality, $n = 155$

a different racial or ethnic identity. The distributions between Anglos and Latinos are relatively even, with only about 2 percent of both subject cohorts self-reporting more than twenty friends and coworkers in different groups. Around 5 percent of Latinos said they had no friends or coworkers from other groups, while 7 percent of Anglos said the same. Among African Americans, just under 5 percent said they had no friends and coworkers from other groups, while just over 6 percent had more than twenty friends and coworkers in different groups.

Finally, figure 5.5 shows the percentage breakdown of familiarity with the Watts riots by subject cohort. The major difference is that a substantially higher percentage of Latino subjects say they have no knowledge of the issues surrounding the Watts uprising (almost 28 percent) versus Anglos (slightly more than 11 percent). Still, more than a third of Anglos say they have either slight or no knowledge of the Watts issue. Interestingly, the familiarity pattern whites have of Watts is basically mirrored by African American respondents (just over 10 percent say they have no familiarity).

Our initial statistical analysis is based on a simple difference of means measure in response across the three treatment and control groups. Using

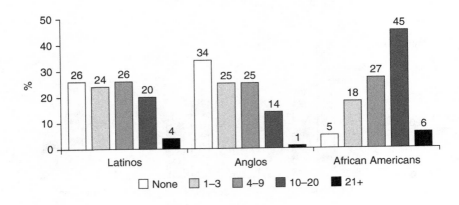

FIGURE 5.4

Friends/Coworkers of Different Races

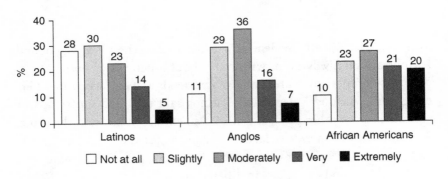

FIGURE 5.5

Knowledge of Watts Uprising

the Tukey HSD critical value for statistical differences in means after ANOVA on the 1–4 group commonality ordinal measure, we can detect which of the treatments affected respondents beyond what we would expect to occur by chance. Recall that our expectation is that those respondents exposed to the collective identity cue will show a significant increase in perceiving commonalty across groups, while exposure to the subgroup distinctive cue should move respondents toward their in-group identities—thereby lowering intergroup commonality perceptions. Finally, given our sense that collective identity cue will have a strong impact on subjects, the combined treatment is expected to move people toward increased intergroup commonality.

ANGLO PERCEPTIONS

In examining treatment effects, note that higher scale values equal increased commonality perceptions. Beginning first with how white subjects say they perceive commonality with African Americans, Anglos assigned the collective identity cue showed the highest commonality score, 3.39, on the 1–4 scale (see table A.2 in the appendix). This is contrasted with the Anglo control group's commonality score of 2.36 (a difference significant at $p < .01$) and helps to confirm our expectation about this cue's effect. Meanwhile, the collective identity mean perception is also statistically distinguishable from the other two treatment means. Specifically, the subgroup distinctive treatment mean of 2.50 and the combined treatment mean of 2.41 are both significantly different from the collective identity mean, while neither the subgroup nor combined means differ significantly from the control or each other. The lower means for the subgroup and combined treatments generally confirm expectations, at least regarding Anglo perceptions of commonality with African Americans, but they undermine expectations for the combined treatment, as outlined above.

Transitioning to Anglo perception of commonality with Asians, we notice a similar pattern as with white views of African Americans. In continued support of expectations about collective identity, Anglos exposed to the collective identity treatment have a mean perception of commonality with Asians of 3.30 (on the 1–4 scale), which is statistically different from the control group mean of 2.59 ($p < .01$). And in a repeat of the pattern found for Anglo perceptions of African Americans, the collective identity treatment is significantly different from the subgroup distinctive mean (2.75) and the combined treatment (2.70) ($p < .01$), while the subgroup and combined treatment means are not significantly different from each other. Again, the combined treatment shows the lowest mean agreement of the three treatments on the commonality scale (i.e., not including the control group). This finding among Latino subjects continues to undermine our expectation about the combined identity treatment.

Next we assess Anglo perception commonality with Latinos across the four assigned groups. Interestingly, although the results pattern is similar to what we find for Anglo perceptions of African Americans and Asians, the group mean differences are clustered more tightly. In further support of the effect pattern detected thus far, the collective identity treatment mean of 2.97 is statistically different from the control group mean of 2.49 ($p < .01$). However, the collective treatment mean is not statistically distinguishable from the subgroup distinctive mean of 2.69. The lower mean for the subgroup treatment supports our expectation as outlined above while also suggesting that the impacts from these intergroup treatments are delicate, with subjects perhaps on the fence between sensing intergroup similarity or moving closer to their in-group ethnic identities. Of course, and in comparison to Anglo perceptions of similarity with Asians and African Americans discussed previously, it might also be that Anglos among our Los Angeles respondents are somewhat more reluctant to admit commonality with Latinos.

LATINO PERCEPTIONS

Transitioning now to focus on perceptions of intergroup commonality among our Latino subjects, we focus on how Latinos view African Americans. As we saw for the Anglo respondents, the collective identity cue produces the highest level of agreement on our 1–4 scale, with a mean of 3.10 versus 2.67 for the control group ($p < .01$). This supports our expectation for the collective identity effect among Latinos, suggesting that the treatment produces similar sentiments in these subjects as they did among Anglos in our subject pool. The means for the subgroup distinctive and combined treatments also fall into the same pattern we observed for Anglos, with the subgroup distinctive group mean of 2.75 and the combined mean of 2.65 both statistically distinguishable from the collective identity mean ($p < .01$). This finding continues support for our expectation in terms of moving subjects more toward their racial subgroups, while it is becoming apparent that the combined identity treatment's impact in increasing group commonality perceptions is hindered by the use of competing messages about group identity.

In terms of Latino perceptions of group commonality with Asians, we see the collective identity cue's continued impact—increasing the perception of commonality mean to 3.05 on the 1–4 scale versus the control group mean of 2.33 ($p < .01$). The subgroup distinctive mean of 2.37 and the combined treatment of 2.33 are both in line with our previous results and are both statistically different from the collective identity mean ($p < .01$).

Finally, in terms of how Latino subjects' perceptions of Anglo are affected by treatment assignment, the collective identity treatment pushes the mean perception to 3.23, which is significantly different from the control group mean of 2.49 ($p < .01$). The subgroup distinctive mean of 2.45 and the combined mean of 2.31 continue their effect pattern across the mean comparisons reported here, and both treatments are statistically distinguishable from the collective treatment ($p < .01$).

AFRICAN AMERICAN PERCEPTIONS

The third respondent group is African Americans. It is here that the relatively high level of commonality that African American subjects report having with Latinos undermines the collective identity treatment's mean effect of 3.06 versus the control of 3.11, a difference that is not statistically significant. At the same time, the differences between the subgroup distinctive mean of 2.94 and the combined mean of 3.07 also fail to reach statistical significance for African American's perceptions of Latinos.

The outcome is different in terms of African American perceptions of Asians, where the collective identity mean of 3.21 on the 1–4 scale is significantly higher than the control mean of 2.39 ($p < .01$). The subgroup distinctive mean of 2.06 is also the lowest of the four, and although it is not significantly different from the control, it is significantly different from its collective counterpart ($p < .01$), suggesting that emphasis on subgroup differences is strong enough to push African Americans away from perceived commonality with Asians. Meanwhile, the combined identity mean of 2.29 sits just below the control value and is significantly different from its collective identity counterpart.

The effect pattern is similar for African American's perceptions of Anglos, with the collective identity's treatment boosting perceived political commonality to 3.41 versus the control mean of 2.40 ($p < .01$). Similar to the perceptions of Asians, the subgroup distinctive mean of 2.22 was not significantly different from the mean, while the combined identity mean of 2.26 is also distinguishable from the collective treatment.

Overall, then, and in robust confirmation our expectations, the collective identity cue has a consistent and robust impact on Latino, African American, and Anglo perceptions of intergroup political commonality (African American's perception of Latinos excepted). Among other things, this may reflect the nature of cognitive reflection on social identity more broadly—it does not take much for people to either widen or constrict their views of those with whom they share common political interests (at least in this instance). Another intriguing aspect of these findings is that the treatment statements contrast between identity groups and elected officials—something that comes directly from LAHRC efforts to empower community members—and is particularly powerful when used as part of the collective identity treatment. This is encouraging news for the commission staffers' strategy, as explained to us during our interviews, and recommends a continuation of this approach in the field. That said, the almost equally robust effects found for the subgroup distinctive treatment, where the intergroup contrast between racial, ethnic, and religious groups was highlighted, suggest that HRC staffers continue to ply their trade in an environment in which the negative aspects of intergroup difference can easily come to the fore at any time.

This assessment is bolstered by the rather poor performance of the combined identity treatment across our difference of means comparisons. Across all comparisons save African American perceptions of Latinos, those exposed to both the collective and subgroup distinctive statements had the lowest means of the three treatments (only the control group mean was lower across groups). And although the differences between the subgroup distinctive and combined treatments were not statistically significant, the effect pattern's consistency regarding the lower mean for the combined treatment suggests that, of the two competing identity statements in this version of the treatment, inclusion of the subgroup sentiment overpowers the influence found for the collective identity treatment. At the least, this should be a word of caution to HRC practitioners in that their fieldwork efforts might be undermined by a surge of in-group-related perceptions.

CONTACT AND KNOWLEDGE EFFECTS

We now turn to a broadening of our analysis of treatment effects that includes measures of intergroup contact and knowledge of intergroup history as part of a regression framework in modeling perceived intergroup commonality. We use a series of binary logit models (similar to OLS [ordinary least squares] regression, except that the outcome measure is binary instead of continuous). The models contain the three treatment variables, measures for intergroup contact, knowledge of the Watts uprisings, and the various demographic and partisanship controls mentioned above. Although the original outcome variables for perceived intergroup commonalty were on 1–4 ordinal scales (as seen in the difference of means tests just reported), we collapsed these into 0–1 measures for ease of interpretation in the logit models (note that the substantive outcomes between the ordinal and binary outcome measures are the same—results not shown). To gauge effects from our independent variables on the outcome, we report differences in predicted probabilities as the independent variable moves from its minimum to maximum value, holding all other variables at their means (see tables A.3–A.5 in the appendix).

These probabilities, which are also featured in chapter 6, range from 0 to .99 and are a common way to assess the effect magnitude for logit model variables on the outcome. The reported percentage increase or decrease for each variable is in comparison to the variable category (or categories) not referenced. For example, if we report that "women have a 15 percent increase in perceiving commonality," this percentage increase is in comparison to men. The reported baselines in the appendix are the probability of the outcome occurring hold all variables in the model at their means.

As seen throughout the difference of means tests, of the three treatments, exposure to the collective identity treatment is, again, a significant factor in increasing the likelihood of Anglos perceiving political commonality with Latinos. In this case, the probability of Anglos saying they perceive closeness increases by 13 percent for those exposed to the collective identity treatment. Interestingly, and in terms of influence from intergroup contact, we find that Anglos with more racially diverse friend and family networks do not show a significant probability increase of perceiving commonality with Latinos.

Meanwhile, and concerning covariate effects in the model, Anglo women show a significant decrease in probability of perceiving political commonalty by 12 percent. And an increase in self-reported knowledge of the Watts uprising increases the likelihood of white subjects perceiving commonality with Latinos by 16 percent ($p < .05$ in a one-tailed test). This latter finding is intriguing given that neither Anglos nor Latinos were the predominant racial groups involved in the 1965 event.

Moving to Anglos subjects' perceptions of closeness with African Americans, we see that, again, random exposure to the collective identity treatment increases perceived political commonality by 41 percent, but, unlike for perceptions of Latinos, none of the covariates are statistically significant in the model. This is not the case in terms of Anglo perceptions of political commonality with Asians. There the collective identity treatment increases the likelihood that Anglos perceive commonality with Asians by 24 percent. At the same time, Republican identifiers among the Anglo subjects have a 14 percent decrease in likelihood of perceiving commonality with Asians, while women have a 13 percent decrease in likelihood (similar to their reaction to commonality with African Americans).

Across the Anglo covariate models, it is clear that the collective identity treatment is effective, while the other two treatments show no impact on perceived commonality with Asians, Latinos, and African Americans. This helps support our expectations about the importance of a superordinate statement about group similarity, and it also generally undermines the influence from the other two identity cue types (although there was some evidence for the divisive effect of the subgroup-oriented treatment in the difference of means tests).

Regarding the contact and knowledge expectations, it is noteworthy that, for Anglos at least, contact makes no statistical difference in perceiving political commonality with Latinos, African Americans, and Asians but only at a marginal level of significance. The same is generally true of self-identified knowledge of the Watts uprising, but, ironically, the statistical difference is for how Anglos perceived Latinos, not African Americans. The lack of effect for the Watts variable might be due to the strong effect from the collective identity treatment, which crowded out significance for all other covariates.

The vast majority of the LAHRC's effort is focused on perceived differences between Latinos and African Americans. As such, how our Latino subjects are affected by the contact and knowledge questions is perhaps an even more important indicator for commission work than the Anglo response. Moving to Latinos' perceptions of closeness with African Americans, subjects exposed to the collective identity treatment cue show a 19 percent increase in probability of perceiving political closeness, which continues the effect pattern for this collective treatment.

In terms of Latinos' perceptions of political closeness with Asians Americans, the collective identity treatment increases the likelihood of perceiving commonality by 27 percent. In terms of other covariate effects in this model, Latino women show a decrease in probability of perceiving commonality by 15 percent. Finally, the last model features Latinos' perceptions of commonality with Anglos. The collective identity treatment increases the probability of Latino subjects perceiving commonality with whites by 28 percent. Finally, both the Republican and gender covariates are again significant in the model, with Republican Latinos increasing the probability of feeling close to Anglos by 20 percent, female Latinos showing a decrease in sensing commonality by 12 percent, and Latinos making less than $50,000 annual income having a decrease in perceived commonality of by 13 percent.

The last set of control models concerns African American's perceptions of Anglos, Latinos, and Asians. Here we see that, as with the difference of means reported earlier in the chapter, the collective identity treatment does not have an impact on a perceived outcome when it comes to Latinos, but it increases perceived commonality with Asians by 35 percent and with Anglos by 41 percent. As before, we credit this to the already high level of perceived political similarity that African American respondents report having for Latinos. In terms of covariates, however, both the intergroup contact and knowledge of Watts measures increase perceived commonality with Latinos. Contact increases commonality by 29 percent while knowledge does the same by 30 percent. Interestingly, African Americans who are college graduates have a decrease in perceived commonality with Latinos of 18 percent, while those with incomes under $50,000 show a decrease of 9 percent. Finally, and in terms of perceived commonality with Asians, African American women have a 21 percent increase in perceiving commonality.

DISCUSSION

Although the specific direction of influence from specific covariates may be somewhat difficult to explain adequately, the covariate model findings are important in that they show the consistency of the collective identity cue's effect, even when controlling for economic and political variables across the three racial and ethnic groups. These variables help to represent the larger structural context in which minorities find themselves and suggest that commission messaging efforts promoting CIIM may cut across macro-level differences between racial and ethnic groups. The results show strong support for the CIIM theory among Latinos and Anglos, with mixed support among African Americans. Specifically, cueing a collective identity has significant positive impact on the attitudes of both Anglos and Latinos toward other racial and ethnic groups, while African Americans show responsiveness to the cue in evaluating Asians and Anglos.

Interestingly, the magnitude of the collective effect varies considerably. The cue has the largest effect on the probability of African Americans perceiving commonality with Anglos (42 percent), followed closely by Anglos perceiving commonality with African Americans (41 percent). The smallest effect is on Anglos' attitudes toward Latinos (14 percent). There is less variation in the effects of collective priming on Latino perceptions, and the magnitude of the predicted changes are all less than the largest effect predicted for Anglos. This finding appears to refute Elze Ufkes and colleagues' finding that majority-group individuals are more receptive to superordinate priming than minority group individuals.[48] However, it could be that Anglos in Los Angeles County retain a dominant group mindset (despite being in the numeric minority), meaning they view Anglo culture and concerns as more prototypical than others.

By contrast, Latinos, who are now the plurality of Los Angeles County residents, retain a subordinate group mentality.[49] An alternate explanation is that Latino identity is more contested and complicated than Anglo identity for reasons of nativity, legal status, language skills, and so on, making Latinos less receptive to collective identity cues.[50] As previously noted, some research also suggests that Latinos have a lower sense of linked fate than Anglos, which could moderate the size of the cue effect.[51]

There is seemingly no confirmation of intergroup contact theory in our results except for African American commonality with Latinos. Regarding the exception, relative contact does what the collective identity cue could not. For both Anglos and Latinos, however, the coefficients for the intergroup contact variable are positive across the models, but none reach statistical significance except increased African American contact with Latinos. The general lack of effect across models could be due to limitations in our data. Because there were no questions in the survey that directly assess the amount of intergroup contact (i.e., the length of time spent with people of a different race or ethnicity than the subject) or the nature of that contact (e.g., whether that contact was frequent or infrequent, voluntary or involuntary, friendly or hostile), we chose to use a proxy measure: "About how many of your friends/coworkers have a different race or ethnicity than yours?" In hindsight, there is the potential for imprecision in this question. For example, due to the wording, we do not know the extent to which our subjects' intergroup communication is with friends versus coworkers. Although coworkers may be friends, and vice versa, that is not always the case, and our data do not allow us to account for this distinction. Our findings serve to underscore the complicated nature of intergroup communication, an issue Thomas Pettigrew and colleagues identify.[52]

■ ■ ■

The primary finding of our analysis—that priming residents with a sense of collective identity increases perceptions of their commonality with outgroups—should encourage commissions that include in-group identity cues in their local work to continue to do so (as in the LAHRC case). To be clear, increased perceptions of intergroup commonality are not tantamount to improved intergroup relations between racial and ethnic groups in American cities. But improved perceptions between in-group and out-group members are arguably a key part of any reform mechanism that local HRCs can leverage, particularly since perceptions of intergroup commonality are thought to be precursors to coalition building.[53]

We have presented evidence that effects from messaging stimuli premised on the CIIM spark increased perceptions of intergroup commonality among Anglo and Latino subjects. This study extends the work of Transue, which focuses on the effect of superordinate (what we have termed "collective" in this chapter) identity cues on Anglos' policy opinions, and of Kevin Wallsten and Tatishe Nteta, which examines superordinate cues pitting elites against the public (similar to our design but without reference to elite partisanship and race).[54] Our work also supplements the often anecdotal assessments of successful intergroup relationship building from HRC personnel in their local mediations between conflicting racial and ethnic groups. Human relations practitioners can leverage the evidence in our survey experiment to initiate or continue messaging strategies, with the caveat that racial and ethnic group perceptions, like messaging effects, may be ephemeral.

Perception improvement between members of different racial and ethnic groups is the basic, first-order goal of these cues among the LAHRC and likely other, similar organizations. In this regard, the collective identity cue appears generally efficacious among the Los Angeles respondents and represents evidence for LAHRC staff to build on in their existing efforts. Still, and although our study was conducted with subjects in their local milieu, we are also mindful of Leonie Huddy's contention that priming effects from identity cues (similar to what our survey experiment accomplished) do not always lead to positive or productive intergroup outcomes.[55] Therefore, and because it is always possible for people to reject attempts to have their identities seem broadly similar with those around them (especially in racially and ethnically diverse settings), scholars and policy makers should continue to monitor intergroup responsiveness to the superordinate/collective-oriented cues for any changes in effects that new circumstances may affect.

These findings strongly suggest that what the LAHRC already tries to do in the field—encourage a sense of collective identity among residents with different racial and ethnic identities—has a positive impact on the sense of intergroup commonality that respondents in our experiment told us they feel. The creation and continued government support of a commission, operating with these identified relationships in mind, will likely promote goodwill among groups and minimize intergroup conflict. At the same time, effects from the collective identity cue, although consistently robust in our models, are also likely delicate in terms of effectiveness across a wide array of applications in which commissions might wish to use them. This appraisal is based on the consistent lack of impact from the combined treatment that featured both the collective and subgroup distinctive cues. We interpret this lack of effect for pairing both identity statements in the same treatment in line with something scholars have understood for decades: it is relatively easy to stoke intergroup difference and suspicions of out-group members.

It is encouraging that pitting Los Angeles residents against elected officials in a survey experiment moves area respondents toward increased perceptions of similarity, but this is also subject to caveats regarding countervailing forces that pull racial and ethnic groups toward retrenchment within their typical in-group enclaves. Our findings are also susceptible to the obvious critique that what commission staffers are able to encourage residents to think about in terms of collective identity "on the ground" may be more limited than what can be accomplished in a survey experiment—even one conducted on local residents.

The dynamic in which collective and subgroup distinctive motives compete for influence over individual perceptions of others suggests that the in-group retains a default advantage. After all, if improving intergroup relations were simply a matter of promulgating the idea that people from different racial and ethnic groups are similar, commissions throughout the country would have a fairly easy task to accomplish. Still, these findings are encouraging for the insight they provide on a potentially effective mechanism that brings local residents together by underscoring a contrast with elected leaders. The contributions of cooperative contact and knowledge of group struggles in overcoming systemic racism are also useful for HRCs as they continue their efforts.

It will be important for scholars to move beyond the group perception outcomes to better assess how commission approaches to improving intergroup relations affect political behavior, institutional perceptions, stress, and neighborhood cohesion. Focus on these broader outcomes will provide a more nuanced understanding of whether and to what extent identity cues tested here have wider applicability in shaping attitudes and behavior. For now, however, we can conclude that commissions (even ones as limited in powers and money as the LAHRC) can use strategies that appear to have a positive effect on intergroup relations by emphasizing collective identity cues and, to a lesser extent, increasing intergroup knowledge. Intergroup contact is complicated, so commissions must proceed with caution. Facilitating meetings for communication may not always work unless there are already cooperative relationships, knowledge, and understanding between the different group participants (in other words, the conditions identified by Allport). In these troubled times, the creation and continued government support of HRCs, operating with these identified relationships in mind, will promote goodwill among groups and help to minimize intergroup conflict.

Caveats aside, these treatment effects are heartening, and they spur us to consider additional ways in which identity-based messages might contribute to HRC efforts. As a follow-up to this initial test, we use chapter 6 to evaluate effects from a religiously themed messaging experiment in Los Angeles, a Pittsburgh-based experiment featuring a racial discrimination prime to test for residents' perceptions of interactions with their landlords (among other outcomes), and a survey-embedded experiment in Cincinnati that focuses on community trust in the city's police force. Given the breadth of issues that commissions across the country cover, this topical expansion in the following chapter complements well the findings presented in this one.

6

REPORTING AND RESPONDING
TO COMMUNITY

We have learned two key things from chapters 4 and 5. First, HRCs are under-resourced, even if they have a judicial enforcement function. This is mainly because commissions see the need to be as involved as possible in the various components of human relations work. They do not simply wish to function as code enforcers, even if enforcement is their commission's primary responsibility. Second, to perform the facilitation role well, commissions need to understand what helps to motivate the perceptions of those in the communities they serve. For example, the previous chapter presents robust evidence that the LAHRCs' method of emphasizing a superordinate (i.e., common) identity in its mediation work is an effective motivator for different racial and ethnic groups to see out-groups as sharing political commonality. Although an isolated test in a survey-embedded experiment of Angelenos, the finding is actually just the kind of insight that commissions working to improve their facilitation role need. After all, it is more than arguable that improving intergroup relations is as much an exercise in shaping perceptions as it is working on the tangible economic, housing, and political conditions that residents encounter.

Moreover, it would be wrong to assume that understanding what shapes resident perceptions about other groups is only important for commission facilitation work. Indeed, both the enforcement and advisory functions that commissions perform can be helped by understanding resident perceptions. Although HUD, FEPA, and other related enforcement responsibilities of HRCs have clear procedural requirements the actual act of reporting problems or instances of discrimination to a commission requires a person to be motivated enough to express grievances. Recall from chapter 4 that Pittsburgh commission staffers were concerned that there is potentially not enough reporting of housing discrimination taking place in the city. This concern suggests that figuring out what encourages people to make an issue known to the proper enforcement authority and then leveraging this knowledge to encourage people to make timely reports is very much a perception-oriented issue.

This chapter explores additional ways for HRCs to understand and shape the perceptions of the people they serve. In doing so, we argue that commissions can use data-driven insights from community-based research to improve their facilitation and enforcement efforts and at the same time potentially increase both public and government reliance on commissions in their advisory capacity to help shape local government policy.

Still, there is a more utility-based reason for HRCs to focus on community perception-driven questions and data: cost-effectiveness. Assuming there are funding constraints for commission work not related to code enforcement, a perception-based focus to facilitation work represents a way for commissions to gain insight into their communities that is more systematic than piecing together anecdotal accounts of interactions with residents in meetings or on the street during turbulent events. Additionally, data collection of the sort used in this chapter does not require substantial resources to generate. To illustrate, we report on three separate data-driven perception studies focusing on three major areas of concern for the commissions in this book: (1) community perceptions of police and local government, (2) levels of trust between religious groups, and (3) the underreporting of problems with landlords—one of the key HUD-related issues that commissions in Fort Worth, Pittsburgh, and elsewhere monitor.

Each of the three studies employed a survey with embedded questions-as-treatment in a randomized experimental design (just like the experimental design used in the previous chapter). Using a survey-embedded experiment is desirable both for its direct assessment of cause and effect on respondents' answers and for the relative simplicity with which the survey experiment can be deployed using Internet survey or social media software. Our hope is that other HRCs will draw on the examples provided here to aid their future data-collection efforts, addressing specific concerns of local interest to them. We begin our examination with the Cincinnati case study regarding community perceptions of the city's police force.

CINCINNATI'S COLLABORATIVE AGREEMENT

The Cincinnati case pertains more to what might occur when HRCs are less involved in helping communities work through issues with local governments and police forces than when a commission is robustly empowered and engaged. As discussed in chapter 3, the Cincinnati Human Relations Commission (CHRC) was established in 1943, partially out of concern that the racial uprisings in Detroit might spread to other midwestern cities. By 2000 the CHRC was facing calls for dissolution from various political and community stakeholders who questioned its usefulness and criticized it for "being virtually unknown and unseen."[1]

Recall that the CHRC was not invested with quasi-judicial enforcement powers as part of its mandate. At the same time, its advisory and facilitation-based functions garnered a reputation for being spotty in terms of perceived usefulness and effectiveness. As we have seen, particularly concerning the LAHRC, such a perception is certainly not a complete or accurate assessment of a commission's impact, but a less-than-stellar perception does not help when attempting to justify additional political and financial support from city hall. Ironically, just as the Cincinnati government was weighing what to do with the CHRC, the city found itself in the midst of an unprecedented racial uprising that drew national headlines and brought the challenging state of community–police relations to the fore.

As discussed in chapter 2, multiple cities across the United States have experienced large-scale protests and sporadic violence during the past three years over perceptions of police misconduct and excessive use of force.[2] Cincinnati has a much longer history of racially charged tensions between the community and police, dating back to the Irish and African American riots over available jobs in the 1820s. But socially, politically, economically, and legally, the policing incidents that precipitated the 2001 civil uprising continue to impact African Americans' quality of life in the Queen City.

Various members of the African American community suffered violent (and unwarranted) treatment from the Cincinnati Police Department (CPD) dating to documented reports at least as far back as the mid-1990s. Between 1996 and 2001 CPD actions resulted in the deaths of fifteen African American citizens, none of whom used firearms in their altercations with police. The highest profile of these cases were the deaths of Roger Owensby Jr. and Jeffrey Irons in 2000. Both were in police custody for unrelated altercations. The acquittal or mistrial of CPD officers involved in these citizens' deaths, along with the fatal shooting of an unarmed teenager, Timothy Thomas, are generally considered the precipitating factors in the April 2001 uprising. All of this would seem to support the notion that Cincinnati, like similar cities, would benefit from a robustly engaged human relations commission, but for reasons that are both related to the commission's mandate and the perceptions of local elected officials, the CHRC played a much smaller role both before and after the 2001 uprising than it might have otherwise.

Obermiller and Wagner, in their detailed historical analysis of CHRC, also lay bare the general fallout related to the 2001 civil unrest, which was the nation's largest civil disturbance since the Los Angeles uprising of 1992:

> A number of injuries were reported but there were no deaths attributed to the disturbance; nine hundred people were arrested. . . . Damage to private property was estimated at more than $3 million and direct costs to the city at nearly $2 million. A subsequent boycott of the city resulted in an estimated $10 million loss for the region's entertainment and convention businesses.
>
> The riots were triggered by the police shooting of Timothy Thomas, an unarmed black man, on April 7, 2001. The deaths of two black men at the hands of the police in the months before the shooting of Thomas had already raised tensions between the black community and Cincinnati Police (CPD). In the six years before Thomas's death, moreover, fifteen black men had been killed in encounters with the CPD . . . [although] only three of the deaths . . . were strictly due to police action. . . .

The 2001 riots were centered in Over-the-Rhine, a predominantly black and formerly urban Appalachian neighborhood just north of the city's business district.[3]

The Cincinnati City Council's deliberations on what to do with the CHRC just prior to the riots were rife with indecision. Proponents of the commission's work argued that its facilitation function was critical during times of unrest, while critics continued to harp on the notion that commission initiatives were too low-profile and difficult to assess for effectiveness (these are, again, common criticisms of commissions without a quasi-judicial mandate). Eventually the council came to a resolution on the commission's future, but funding levels remained suboptimal, and no mandate expansion was provided. A new commission director and former CPD officer, Cecil Thomas, took over CHRC operations in 2000 and immediately began retooling commission functions to focus more on community–police issues. He told Obermiller and Wagner:

> I began my work to really begin to rebuild the structure and I needed to, at the time, fashion it around police-community relations, youth and things that were going on with them. . . . The tensions were high between citizens and police. My role as head of the commission was to find ways to reduce that tension. I kept going to city council, saying to them, you've got to give me more resources to get people into the community to let people vent their frustrations.[4]

Thomas is credited with leveraging what the commission called community relations monitors—coaches, community leaders, recreation center employees, in other words, those with established frontline contact with residents—to help quell tensions following the 2001 uprising. The community relations monitors were one of several facilitation programs launched either through or in collaboration with the CHRC post-2001. But gaining consistent funding from the city council and public questioning of CHRC effectiveness and purpose were again problems by late in the decade. The commission was spared draconian cuts by the city council only because commission staffers effectively convinced elected officials that CHRC presence on the streets was essential to, as Cheryl Meadows, Thomas's successor explained, "put out fires and spike rumors."[5] Also recall from chapter 4 that the commission has been incorporated into what are, essentially, intelligence collection efforts on behalf of the CPD, with commission staffers required to notify the police of rumors or other information related to potential civil unrest.

Yet because of lingering questions about CHRC's relevance, its limited mandate, and its lack of independent commission status relative to city government, the commission was relegated to the role of spectator in the 2001 federal lawsuit brought against the city and CPD by the Cincinnati Black United Front (CBUF) (a grassroots organization founded in 2000 in response to growing discontent with CPD treatment of the city's black residents) and the American Civil Liberties Union of Ohio Foundation. The result of the suit was a signed statement of intent, termed the Collaborative Agreement, to find solutions for ongoing issues related to community–police relations between the plaintiffs and defendants, enforced by the U.S. District Court for the Southern District of Ohio.

Legally, it would have been impossible for the CHRC to sue the city (given that the commission is a city entity) even though commission staffers and community monitors likely shared concerns similar to the CBUF and American Civil Liberties Union of Ohio Foundation about CPD and the state of community–police relations more generally. But, given the commission's overall mission and focus, it is ironic that the CHRC is not directly party to the legal agreement designed to bring relief to community strife over police conduct. In fact, thinking about the facilitation and advisory roles that commissions play, several of the Collaborative Agreement's stated goals look much like outcomes one would expect to be encouraged by a human relations commission.

First Goal: Police officers and community members will become proactive partners in community problem solving.

Second Goal: Build relationships of respect, cooperation, and trust within and between police and communities.

Third Goal: Improve education, oversight monitoring, hiring practices, and accountability of CPD.

Fourth Goal: Ensure fair, equitable, and courteous treatment for all.

Fifth Goal: Create methods to establish the public's understanding of police policies and procedures and recognition of exception service in an effort to foster support of the police.[6]

Among other things, the agreement implemented an approach to dealing with crime that focuses as much on community involvement as it does on police response to the issue. To that end, the city adopted a new policy called "community problem-oriented policing" that focused on identifying, analyzing, and implementing planned responses to address underlying or contributing problems that lead to law breaking, and then evaluating their effectiveness. The agreement also stipulated that the city and CPD would make data on arrest records, vehicle and pedestrian stops, and use of force (among other outcomes) publicly and regularly available across Cincinnati's fifty-two neighborhoods. Evaluation of process was also a key component of the agreement, with provisions made to assess improvement between community and police relations throughout the city.

The Collaborative Agreement also called for increased civilian oversight of the CPD through the creation of a new agency: The Citizen Complaint Authority (CCA). The CCA, created in April 2002, is an independent civilian oversight agency made up of a team of professional investigators and an independent board of citizens appointed by the mayor. The CCA has both administrative and investigative powers to adjudicate cases of police abuse, although attempts have been made in recent years to adjust its mission and mandate scope to exclude certain cases under its purview.

As might be expected with such an ambitious undertaking, implementation of the agreement and its various initiatives has succeeded in some areas and fallen short in others, according to professional monitors tasked in 2017 with reviewing progress. One of the biggest areas of evaluator concern was in the structure and accessibility of various forms of performance data related to CPD operations (including juvenile versus adult arrests). This is an issue that the city, CPD, CBUF, and other interested entities continue to work to resolve (with uneven results and intragovernment finger-pointing between city and county law enforcement). The

2017 evaluators also expressed concern about reported specificity on the internal procedures to determine if individual CPD officers engaged in conduct detrimental to realizing bias-free policing. These are important critiques in need of attention, but the evaluators struck a more positive and historically reflective note in their report's introduction:

> There is no alternative to a Collaborative Agreement in some form. We have experienced the difficulties the police and public faced before the agreement. And we routinely see the difficulties faced by other communities who have not developed their own agreements. In Cincinnati, over the last 15 years, crime declined. This may or may not be due to the Collaborative Agreement: it is impossible to tell. Still, while crime has been declining, police have arrested fewer and fewer people, and they have used less and less force against members of the public. Again, there are many factors that have caused these drops. Nevertheless, the Collaborative Agreement provided a framework for understanding that the police can be effective, lawful, and fair. We do not have to choose between safety and fairness.[7]

If past attempts to reform public institutions like police forces are any indication, initiatives set forth in the Collaborative Agreement will continue along varying trajectories of success. But one concern for members of the CBUF and related entities is that court-ordered enforcement of the Collaborative Agreement ended in 2008. The reasons for the sunset provision after six years are not clear, but the implication is that all of the data reporting, policing reform, problem solving, bias-correction among officers, and complaint procedures outlined in the agreement are now enforced by political will rather than legal force. This does not mean that the agreement's basic provisions are in danger of complete abandonment. Going this route would constitute a gross political miscalculation on the part of the city's elected officials (and would likely trigger a new federal lawsuit). But the speed and thoroughness by which agreement provisions that the 2017 evaluators flagged for improvement are arguably in range of being undermined by the lack of judicial oversight.

What this means for the CBUF and Cincinnati's minority communities is that they must look beyond city hall and CPD headquarters for ways to prevent the conditions that precipitated the 2001 uprising from again taking hold on the city's streets. And arguably the best prevention mechanism is enhanced and consistent dialogue between the community and CPD so that both constituencies understand the other's concerns and needs. In 2017 the CCA commissioned a survey of over two dozen local criminal justice professionals and community leaders with a history of involvement in the Collaborative Agreement process (coauthor Brian Calfano assisted with data collection and an analysis). The recommendations from these respondents to an open-ended question asking how to improve community–police relations were telling for the kind of organizational structure they recommend:

> Need to respect each position—to get back to having police assigned to neighborhoods and to have open dialogue about race relations and how to protect neighborhoods. . . . Training on how to de-escalate issues that are driven by emotions rather than by the actual crime or incident itself. . . . More community engagement between the parties. . . . Need to get CPD and residents talking to one another. CPD being in the community really listening to the community about what the issues are in their neighborhoods and understanding what the community perspective is about CPD. . . . For police officers: it's relationship building when interacting with people from different ethnic backgrounds. . . . [Police] have to be able to understand and acknowledge and work through their biases. For citizens, it's our responsibility to understand what the role of the police is and to understand the sacrifices they make. Not many of us would run towards gunfire. Not many of us would put our lives on the line. Some citizens don't understand or respect that.

These responses are telling in they suggest dialogue as a common expectation to improve community–police relations, and dialogue is clearly the core part of HRC facilitation efforts. The CHRC—especially given its historical use of community relations monitors to learn what community residents perceive about the police, the city, and related institutions—may be in the best position to step into a supporting role to implement these professional recommendations. To be sure, and similar to the Los Angeles commission's frustration over the open-ended nature of intergroup progress based on facilitation efforts without a code enforcement function, any effort by the CHRC under its current facilitation mandate alone will not, by itself, sustain or improve community–police relations. Concrete policies must be devised and implemented by city hall and CPD that continue the Collaborative Agreement reforms.

Unless politicians and communities decide to terminate the use of commissions with a primary facilitator role that lacks enforcement—which has been a real possibility for the Cincinnati commission over the last two decades—there must be a way forward for faciliatory-based HRCs to better contribute to the overall improvement of both intergroup and community–police relations. Recall that we when we analyzed possible areas for the LAHRC to build on its facilitation programming using superordinate/common identity messaging, respondents showed significant positive response across groups in our survey experiments. We see a similar path for the CHRC, at least in principle, and expect the kind of cue used in our chapter 5 study to have enough generalizability to be effective in places like Cincinnati. Given this, we turn our focus to assess other types of cues that impact items of immediate concern to the CBUF, CPD, and the other collaborative agreement constituencies. Specifically, we examine how memories of discrimination among community members affect their perceptions of CPD, city government, and community–police relations.

THE CINCINNATI COMMUNITY'S PERCEPTIONS OF POLICE AND LOCAL GOVERNMENT

As with the Los Angeles case, the empirical emphasis on what people perceive about their lives, those they encounter, and their local institutions may go far in informing human relations work as it involves facilitation. What's more, effective facilitation efforts may then lay the foundation for a more credible advisory function for commissions (at least in the eyes of elected officials). In the CHRC case, the best way for the commission to increase its relevancy is clearly to focus on concerns related to community–police relations. This is different from the intergroup relations focus in Los Angeles, and even from the CHRC staffer's experiences with LGBT and indigenous people's issues discussed in chapter 4. Although both of these marginalized groups deserve the best efforts of human relations practitioners, the resource and political climate confronting the CHRC suggests that the issue of core focus in the short term should be understanding what helps motivate residents' perceptions of the police, their city government, and overall community–police relations.

The problem for any city in Cincinnati's position is that a decline in public support for local policing could ultimately result in a significant drop in public safety. Both government officials and crime experts broadly agree that community support for, and cooperation with, their local police is critical for law enforcement efforts to successfully reduce crime.[8] As government officials act to improve police–community relations, they would benefit from having more information about the factors that explain public perceptions of local law enforcement and from expanding the commission's role in helping to facilitate discussion between community members and police. At the same time, the public can benefit from additional knowledge about predominant views about local institutions (including the police), as held by fellow residents, again, ideally with commission participation as part of the package.

For local political and community leaders, information about perceptions is critical because, while extant research indicates people generally support the police and are satisfied with the way police perform their duties, it also demonstrates that not all segments of society hold equally positive opinions.[9] Studies consistently show that attitudes toward the police vary widely by race, with African Americans being less trusting and more critical of police conduct than whites.[10] Moreover, the majority of existing studies focus on civilians' trust in law enforcement, while evaluations of performance (if it is even included in the study) is often less emphasized.[11] Ultimately, the findings are mixed regarding the factors that explain variation in attitudes toward the police, with some finding that the influence of race disappears when other factors are accounted for.[12]

To advance local understanding of community perceptions of CPD, we partnered with the CBUF to conduct an Internet-based survey of local residents on a variety of topics relating to CPD and other local institutions. We obtained survey responses from 1,078 qualifying respondents living in the Cincinnati area. This included 470 self-reported African Americans and 608 self-reported non–African Americans. Survey questions ranged from perceptions about CPD, city institutions, and community–police relations in Greater Cincinnati as well as demographic items.

Using a chain-referral sampling technique, respondents were invited to participate in the survey if they lived in the Cincinnati area and were at least eighteen years of age. Chain-referral does not use a random sample of the population, so there is no standard response rate to report. This approach is also cost-effective for commissions with small budgets for facilitation-oriented research in that fielding a chain-referral survey costs a fraction to implement over what a probability sample version would cost. Of course, an obvious methodological drawback is the impossibility of directly inferring that the survey sample's characteristics mirror those of the general population of interest within specific statistical bounds.

Our counter to this critique, however, is threefold. First, and most obviously, if a funder wishes to endow a commission with the tens of thousands of dollars needed to successfully field a survey using a probability sample, such a survey design would be fine to pursue. In the absence of this funding, which is the assumed norm across commissions nationwide, the status quo cannot be to forgo any data-driven approach to understanding community perceptions. This means that nonprobability samples must be used.

Second, probability-driven samples are not necessarily what commissions need to gain insight into the perceptions of the most relevant community members relative to commission purposes. For example, a probability-based or "random" sample of some variety will tend to result in a demographic composition that reflects U.S. Census targets for a population. The question for commissions to ask is whether they are interested in knowing about a sample that reflects the general demographics of their entire city (or jurisdiction they serve) or are keener to learn about perceptions relative to specific population subgroups (e.g., Latinos and African Americans, recent immigrants). In many cases, interest will tend toward the specific groups. Note that randomized, representative samples do not often facilitate without spending considerably more money to "oversample" target demographic groups. Again, if commissions are somehow endowed with the money to produce these kind of useful population samples, then they should pursue them. Our assumption, however, is that resource-starved commissions looking to perform useful facilitation-oriented work will often lack these resources.

Third, especially when drilling down for respondents in population subgroups, researchers benefit from a regression to the mean as their sample size increases. This means that the larger a sample is, even if not drawn at random, the more it will take on the characteristics of the population of interest. With smaller, nonprobability samples, the concern is that the derived group of respondents is systematically different from those not included in the sample and that this difference substantially biases the reported survey outcomes. While certainly a concern for commissions to be aware of, an equally valid question is whether there is a realistic basis for the assumption that pockets of targeted subgroups in the sample should be systematically different from those included in the nonprobability sample. For example, in generating the nonprobability sample of African Americans in Cincinnati, we found that reported income, age, sex, and education levels were similar to U.S. Census estimates for African Americans in the area. The question is whether we realistically expect that our nonprobability sample somehow missed a pocket of African Americans in the area whose lived experiences are so distinct from the hundreds of African Americans in the sample that our survey response findings cannot be of use to the commission, community, local elected officials, and so on. Our working assumption is that this is not the case, although every commission should be sure to consider this question of sample difference carefully when interpreting results using nonprobability samples.

Another key point to remember is that, just like with the superordinate/common identity findings reported in the previous chapter, the statistical effects presented are derived from randomly assigned "treatments" in the form of deliberate (i.e., researcher manipulated) question ordering. The point of this randomized ordering is to see if encouraging survey respondents to reflect on particular events or ideas (as contained in the "treatment" survey questions) affects how respondents answer questions that follow the "treatment" in the list of survey questions. The power of inference from this randomized "experimental" design is not derived from a random population sample but instead the integrity of randomly assigning a specific question/treatment and capturing replies from respondents assigned to said treatment. As such, we have confidence in any reported treatment effects in this chapter independent of any faults with sample representativeness of the larger population.

Respondents participated in the survey through an Internet survey link provided between June 2 and September 6, 2017. Residents could also complete the survey at community events where laptops and iPads were provided to facilitate data collection. Since the sample was not drawn at random, we created statistical weights based on 2016 U.S. Census characteristics for Hamilton County (where Cincinnati is located) and applied these weights to the descriptive response percentages and statistical analyses featured below. Weights were created using an iterative raking process that accounted for differences between the U.S. Census information and survey respondent characteristics along age and gender characteristics for African Americans and non–African Americans. In other words, the weighting made the sample correspond to 2016 U.S. Census characteristics on age and gender for both African American and non–African American respondents in Hamilton County. This weighting technique is another way to derive confidence that nonprobability samples can be effectively used to draw conclusions about the larger population.

Our analysis focuses on five questions we asked the survey respondents, each of which taps an underlying concern of the city's Collaborative Agreement and should be a focus of future CHRC facilitation efforts: (1) respondent's trust in the CPD; (2) respondent's trust in the court system; (3) respondent's perception of the CPD as a legitimate authority; (4) respondent's trust in the the CCA; and (5) respondent's perception of whether community–police relations in Cincinnati have improved since the Collaborative Agreement. All survey participants were randomly assigned into two groups with just one of the groups receiving the following questions as the "treatment" BEFORE we asked the questions regarding the five identified city concerns:

(1) Have you ever been treated unfairly or personally experienced discrimination in Cincinnati because of your race, ethnicity, gender, sexuality, being an immigrant, religious heritage, or having an accent?

No (1)

Yes (2)

(2) If yes, in your opinion were you treated unfairly in Cincinnati because of your

> Racial background or ethnicity (1)
> Skin color (2)
> Gender, gender identity, sexuality (3)
> Immigration status (4)
> Religion (5)
> Accent, regardless of whether or not you have an accent (6)
> Other (7)
> I replied "no" to previous question (8)

(3) In the most typical incident you experienced in Cincinnati, what was the race or ethnicity of the person treating you unfairly?

> Black or African American (1)
> Asian (2)
> White (Non-Hispanic) (3)
> Hispanic or Latino/a (4)
> Other (please specify) (5) _____

The point of this very basic effort to prime respondents' thoughts about discrimination was to determine if those with personal discriminatory experiences on their minds when answering survey questions about the CPD, CCA, and so on, have systematically different answers than those not encouraged to think about personal discrimination when responding.

Note that we are not particularly interested in what respondents indicate in response to the discrimination questions used in the treatment battery. Given the nature of survey response bias to questions asking personal information of a sensitive nature, their answers could be subject to a variety of drawbacks related to social desirability and underreporting. More importantly, the point of the experiment is to gauge effects from asking the discrimination questions in the first place—regardless of how one answers. This assumes that the cognitive effect of asking the questions will maintain no matter what someone elects to provide as a direct response.

Concerning what the commission—indeed, also the CCA and CPD—can glean from this exercise, it is useful to know whether basic impressions of key city institutions are subject to more negative evaluations when a resident has thoughts of discriminatory events in her or his mind (from

the act of asking about discrimination). At the least, if this kind of negative relationship exists between the discrimination treatment questions
and outcome measures, it suggests that the CHRC and others should take
into account the ongoing impact of one's past discrimination experiences
in working through public reaction to police and city government as part
of future facilitations. On some level, this may seem like an obvious statement, but given that elected officials want to declare the problems
"solved" as a result of specific policy reforms (e.g., the Collaborative Agreement), it also would indicate that city officials and staff need to be
reminded of the lingering effects associated with discrimination's impact
on how people—especially racial and ethnic minorities—perceive and
engage with local government.

To test for any systematic effects from the discrimination question battery on respondent answers to our five outcome questions, we follow the
same format of reporting results as we did in chapter 5. We first begin by
assessing any statistically significant mean differences in response between
the "treated" group (those receiving the discrimination questions at the
beginning of the survey) and the "control" group (those receiving the discrimination questions near the end of the survey). Among the African
American respondents, 236 of the 470 were randomly assigned to receive
the personal discrimination questions at the start of their survey, while
234 African American respondents answered the discrimination questions near the end of their survey—and after the five outcome questions
of interest in our analysis. In terms of the non–African American
respondents, 305 of the 608 were randomly assigned to the treatment
group, and 303 were in the control group. Table A.6a in the appendix
includes demographic information about the Cincinnati area sample,
which includes a large oversample of African Americans compared to
their percentage in Hamilton County, Ohio.

HOW DOES THINKING ABOUT DISCRIMINATION
INFLUENCE PERCEPTIONS?

Figures 6.1–6.5 show the response percentages for each of the outcome
variables. The first question asks respondents to "please rate how much

you personally trust the Cincinnati Police Department." The respondents could select their level of trust from scaled answers that ranged from 1 ("not at all") to 4 ("a lot"). We used Tukey's Honest Significant Difference (HSD) critical values, which are similar to t-test scores, to determine whether the mean differences between the treated and control groups are larger than we would expect to see by chance among both the African American and non–African American groups. In this case, the control group's mean trust level on the 1–4 scale is 2.51, while the treatment group's mean is 2.19, a difference that is statistically significant at $p < .01$ and suggests that the personal reflection of discriminatory events in one's past has a strong downward or negative effect on African American's sense of trust in the CPD. By contrast in the non–African American respondent group, the mean of the control group is 3.20, which is lower than the treatment mean of 3.32. Although these means are not statistically different (because the difference in size between them is not large enough to exceed the Tukey HSD critical value), it is interesting that non–African Americans asked the discrimination questions at the beginning of their survey trend toward greater trust in CPD compared to those not primed with these questions.

In a second question, respondents were asked, "Please rate how much you personally trust the municipal courts." The provided answers were the same 1–4 response scale as the "trust CPD" measure (1 = "not at all" to 4 = "a lot"), and here we see a similar effect pattern. The mean trust level among African American control respondents is 2.16, while it is only 1.83 among African American treatment respondents. This difference in means is also statistically significant at $p < .01$. The effect pattern is just the opposite among non–African Americans, with those in the control group having a mean trust score of 2.86, in contrast to 3.01 for the discrimination treatment group (a difference significant at $p < .01$). This, again, is striking evidence that when non–African Americans in the Cincinnati area are encouraged to think about personal experiences with discrimination, they actually exhibit statistically higher trust levels in public institutions than their African American counterparts.

Next is the question about respondent views of CPD's legitimacy. This survey question included a 5-point Likert scale ranging from 1 ("strongly

TABLE 6.1 Mean Differences in Cincinnati-Area Resident Perceptions of Local Institutions

	TRUST CINCINNATI POLICE		TRUST COURTS		CPD IS LEGITIMATE	
	AFRICAN AMERICANS ($n = 470$)	NON-AFRICAN AMERICANS ($n = 608$)	AFRICAN AMERICANS	NON-AFRICAN AMERICANS	AFRICAN AMERICANS	NON-AFRICAN AMERICANS
PERCEIVED DISCRIMINATION TREATMENT	2.18*	3.32	1.83*	3.01*	3.11*	4.25*
CONTROL	2.51	3.20	2.16	2.86	3.45	4.01

	TRUST CCA		RELATIONS IMPROVED SINCE COLLABORATIVE AGREEMENT	
	AFRICAN AMERICANS	NON-AFRICAN AMERICANS	AFRICAN AMERICANS	NON-AFRICAN AMERICANS
PERCEIVED DISCRIMINATION TREATMENT	2.67*	3.26	2.90*	3.70
CONTROL	3.00	3.13	3.29	3.63

* = $p < .01$ for Tukey HSD pairwise comparisons between perceived discrimination treatment and control group.

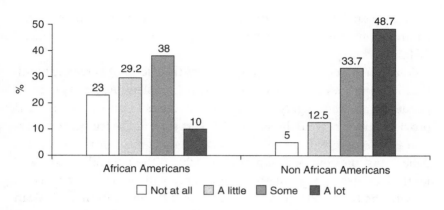

FIGURE 6.1

Trust in Cincinnati Police (CPD); African American, $n = 470$, Non-African American, $n = 608$

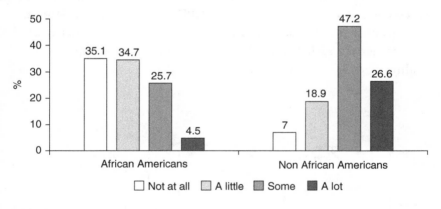

FIGURE 6.2

Trust in Courts; African American, $n = 470$, Non-African American, $n = 608$

disagree") to 5 ("strongly agree") and read: "Overall, the CPD officers in my community are legitimate authorities and people should obey the decisions they make." The control group of African American respondents shows a mean level of agreement with this statement of 3.45, which contrasts with the treatment group's mean of 3.11. As with the previous two outcome items, this mean difference is statistically significant $p < .01$.

Non–African Americans in the sample have the opposite view—with the control group mean of 4.02 significantly lower than the treatment mean of 4.25 (*p* < .01).

The fourth question asked respondents their level of agreement with the following question: "I trust the Citizens Complaint Authority to independently and thoroughly investigate complaints against the CPD." The provided answers were the same 1–5 Likert scale as the legitimacy question (1 = "strongly disagree" to 5 = "strongly agree"). Among African Americans, the control group mean is 3.00 on the 1–5 scale versus 2.67 for the treatment group, a statistically significant difference at *p* < .01. Here, as with the trust CPD question, the mean differences for non–African American respondents are not statistically significant, but the treatment mean of 3.26 is larger than the control of 3.14, suggesting that non–African Americans tend to see local government offices as more trustworthy when they think about personal experience with discrimination. Since the CCA was set up to oversee complaints about CPD conduct, it is interesting and perhaps noteworthy that non–African Americans show greater trust in both rather than what would be the more conventional expectation of finding increased trust in CCA versus the CPD.

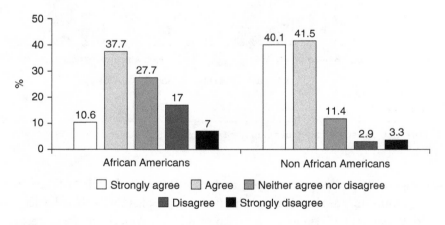

FIGURE 6.3

CPD Is Legitimate Authority; African American, *n* = 470, Non-African American, *n* = 608

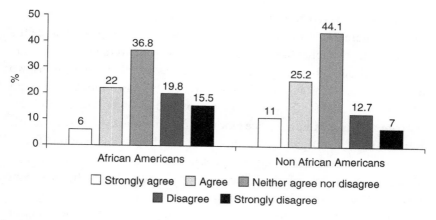

FIGURE 6.4

Trust in Citizens Complaint Authority (CCA); African American, *n* = 470, Non-African American, *n* = 608

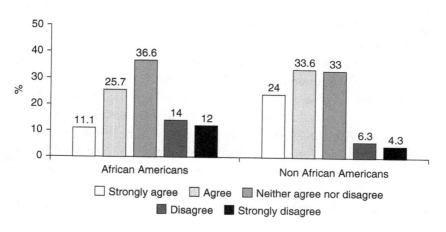

FIGURE 6.5

Community-CPD Relations Improved; African American, *n* = 470, Non-African American, *n* = 608

Finally, we asked respondents their level of agreement with the following statement: "Community/CPD relations have improved since the adoption of the Collaborative Agreement." The answers to this question were scaled using the 1–5 agreement measure as found in the previous two outcomes. The African American control group has a mean agreement of 3.29 versus 2.90 for the treatment group. And, as with the previous four outcomes, this mean difference among African Americans is statistically significant at $p < .01$. The difference in means between the non–African American control and treatment groups is not statistically significant, although, as was the case with the previous four questions, the treatment mean of 3.70 is larger than the control mean of 3.64.

Overall, these mean differences are striking in that they show a clear pattern of opposing perspectives between African Americans and non–African Americans living in Cincinnati area. Of course, one could rightly note that the mean differences between the treatment and control groups for both African Americans and non–African Americans are well within a point of each other on each of the five perception questions—lending credence to the idea that, while differences exist between residents on issues related to the Collaborative Agreement, these differences are not as stark as they could be.

Following the approach we took in the previous chapter's analysis, we also analyzed respondent answers using statistical models that include demographic controls for respondent's gender, age, income, and education level. For ease of interpretation, the 1–4 and 1–5 scaled answers were each collapsed into 0–1 variables, where 0 equals "none to low trust/agreement" and 1 equals "medium to high trust/agreement." The models were run using binary logistic regression with reported predicted probabilities of how likely respondents are to report medium to high trust or agreement, holding all other variables at their means. These full statistical models are reported in table A.7 in the appendix.

Not too surprisingly, there is consistency with the effect pattern seen in the difference of means tests, with African American respondents statistically less likely to have positive responses across the five perception questions if they were assigned to the personal discrimination treatment group. For their part, and again somewhat in line with what we saw in the difference of means section, the non–African American respondents in the discrimination treatment group show a statistically positive response across most of the most questions.

Regarding trust in the CPD, African American respondents in the discrimination treatment group are 18 percent less likely to say they trust the CPD, while non–African Americans in the treatment group are 6 percent more likely to say they have trust in the police. In terms of statistically significant controls, income and age are predictors of police trust, with African Americans reporting higher incomes 16 percent more likely to say they trust CPD, and older non–African Americans are 41 percent more likely to say the same. There is a similar effect pattern for the trust in courts measure, as African Americans in the discrimination question treatment group are 15 percent less likely to express trust in the courts, and non–African Americans receiving the treatment are 8 percent more likely to indicate trust. Meanwhile, older non–African Americans have a 42 percent increase in probability of trust in the courts, and those with higher incomes have a 36 percent increase in indicating trust.

The perception of CPD as a legitimate authority to be obeyed follows this same line of treatment effects, with the African Americans in the treatment group 14 percent less likely to say they perceive CPD as a legitimate authority and non–African Americans 5 percent more likely to do so. The demographic control variables are also significant in this model, with African American women 13 percent less likely to view CPD as legitimate, older African Americans 16 percent more likely to do so, and those with higher incomes 28 percent more likely to perceive CPD as a legitimate. Respondent trust in the CCA follows the same pattern, with African American respondents in the treatment group being 10 percent less likely to say they trust the CCA and non–African Americans receiving the treatment questions being 10 percent more likely to express trust (see table A.8 in the appendix). Yet older African Americans are 22 percent more likely to express trust, while older non–African Americans are only 20 percent more likely to do the same.

Finally, and as it concerns perceptions of improved community–police relations since the Collaborative Agreement in 2002, African Americans in the treatment group primed to think of personal discrimination are, again, statistically less likely to offer a positive response, at 12 percent less likely to agree that relations are better. Interestingly, there is no statistical difference for the treated group of non–African Americans on this question. However, in terms of controls, older respondents in both racial groups are more likely to agree that community–police relations have improved, with African Americans 21 percent more likely and non–African Americans 38 percent more likely to say so. African Americans with higher income are 21 percent more likely and non–African Americans with higher education levels are 29 percent more likely to also see community–police relations as on the upswing since the Collaborative Agreement.

For the CHRC, the ramifications of these survey findings are clear. After almost two decades since the Collaborative Agreement was put into effect, African Americans in the Cincinnati area still respond much differently than non–African Americans to questions of trust in public institutions and the status of community–police relations when they are exposed to a simple survey-embedded priming exercise inquiring about personal experiences with discrimination. The consistent effect of the discrimination questions suggests that African Americans continue to have a different set of lived experiences with police and local government than non–African Americans.

This is not to take anything away from the tangible progress made by public institutions, including the CPD, as a result of the Collaborative Agreement. But if Cincinnati's African Americans are systematic in having a more negative evaluation of community–police relations, there is a clear opening for CHRC to use these data-driven insights to craft programming and intervention efforts around this perception-based difference. Indeed, from a facilitation standpoint, there is hardly a worthier topic for attention by commission staff than probing deeper into the foundational issues that motivate this distrust. Although the experiment leveraged personal experiences with discrimination as a cognitive framework for respondents to use when answering questions about the CPD and related items, we should not take from these results that personal discrimination is alone in motivating these responses. But figuring out how perceived discrimination ties into experiences with actual police encounters, navigating the justice system, and related outcomes requires the kind of in-depth discussion "give and take" that good human relations facilitation provides.

LOS ANGELES: REACHING OUT IN FAITH

As discussed in prior chapters, the issues facing the LAHRC's facilitation work center on identity issues. In the last chapter, we explored how racial and ethnic groups in Los Angeles respond to encouragement to think of themselves as city residents. Now we take up consideration of a different issue: resident trust of different local religious groups. The concern is one that LAHRC has pioneered among commissions nationally, owing both to its strong emphasis on facilitation and the sheer degree of religious diversity in greater Los Angeles. For several years, the LAHRC had a staffer charged with overseeing facilitation efforts in support of the region's religious minorities. The LAHRC has also partnered extensively with the local organization New Ground, which seeks to foster constructive interfaith dialogue focused on Jewish–Muslim relations. Overall, then, the LAHRC is a prime example of a commission that has broadened its facilitation work in areas beyond racial and ethnic relations. We quote here from a report this staffer filed about the commission's efforts on this front.

> Following the 9/11 attacks, the City HRC took immediate steps to address fears of public backlash targeting Arabs, Muslims, and Sikhs. . . . The City HRC fostered personal relationships with leaders in these groups. It also sponsored public forums to elevate understanding of these communities within the general public. . . . The rhetorical framing of "with us or against us" . . . made minority integration in "American" society . . . an imminent expectation for large swaths of the general public. . . . It was evidence that any meaningful and appropriate engagement required partnership formation across government, faith communities, academic institutions, and community-based advocacy groups. . . . In a March 2010 report, the President's Advisory Council on Faith-Based and Neighborhood Partnerships made several recommendations outlining engagement methods, including direct and ongoing communications between the White House and Muslim American and open round tables throughout the country. . . . The City HRC worked with local advocacy groups and members of city council to pass a December 2010 resolution reaffirming religious freedoms and specifically naming the Muslim community in

Los Angeles. Additionally, the HRC hosted an Inter-faith Iftar at City Hall that included different denominations and groups.

. . . The need to create and encourage templates to cultivate healthy inter-group relations is a necessity for the well-being of the city and its people. . . . Though government cannot mandate group integration on a psychological level, the policies that city governments implement can benefit from systematically-derived insight into human and group behavioral motives. . . . The intent . . . is to identify and test hypotheses related to inter- and intra-group trust, motives for engagement in social, religious, and political spheres, acceptance of pluralism and related concepts . . . while not losing the important, group specific aspects of culture and religion that helps to make Los Angeles so vibrantly diverse.[13]

As with the larger community–police issues surrounding the Collaborative Agreement in Cincinnati, the LAHRC's work on religious pluralism initiatives can be approached from various starting points. One way would be to examine how members of religious minorities in greater Los Angeles—including the area's Muslim population—perceives their treatment. Another approach would be to look at what a probability sample of the general public in the region thinks about religious minorities. But in considering the cost involved to a commission in fielding either of those types of studies, it is quickly apparent that both would present challenges for cash-strapped HRCs.

However, a third option leverages HRC contact with minority communities using a nonprobability sampling approach similar to the Cincinnati example in the prior section of this chapter. Going into communities where the commission already has a reputation for facilitation and engagement and soliciting responses to a survey-embedded experiment among those residents not only provides access to data on citizen perceptions but it incorporates a minority-on-minority viewpoint built into the research design. The benefits of using a minority-only group of respondents include an added level of insight useful to a commission like Los Angeles's since the vast majority of HRC facilitation involves members of different minority groups.

Fortunately, an opportunity presented itself for just such a minority group-based data-collection approach. In the spring of 2015, working in tandem with students in statistical research methods classes at California State University, Dominguez Hills, the commission was able to field an online survey experiment using the same basic nonprobability sampling approach as found in the Cincinnati Collaborative Agreement study. Given the Dominguez Hills students' socioeconomic backgrounds and areas of residence, respondents were recruited from the students' social and family networks to participate in a questions-as-treatment survey experiment.

At time the survey was conducted 93 percent of the survey sample of adults resided in South Los Angeles (including the Watts and Compton neighborhoods, where race-related unrest and lingering economic concerns have occupied HRC attention since the commission's inception). Even more useful from a minority-based perspective on religious pluralism is that all of the respondents in this sample identified as either African American or Latino. Moreover, 90 percent of the 758 respondents who completed the survey identified at least nominally as a Christian (including Roman Catholic). This enables us to focus on insights about religious pluralism derived from the survey experiment on the sample's Christian identifiers—all of whom are also African American or Latina/o.

Since the LAHRC is a facilitation-oriented commission, the mechanism tested in the survey experiment should be something that the commission might reference or otherwise use in its community meetings with various groups. One focus for scholars of religious identity has been the impact of different views of lived faith, such as having exclusive or inclusive boundaries, on how people view those outside their faith groups.[14] Paul Djupe and Brian Calfano explain the distinction between the two boundary types:

> Regarding religious exclusivity, Appleby (2003) suggests, "Enclave builders portray their religion's truths, 'rights,' and responsibilities as inherently superior to those of their rivals . . . The strength of a religious community's claim to the loyalty of its adherents rests on the community's ability to present itself as the exclusive bearer of specific moral and/or material benefits." . . . In contrast, religious values relating to inclusion seek openness and communion with others, including and especially those who are not already part of the particular community.[15]

The LAHRC does not concern itself with what people believe as adherents to particular faiths, but it is interested in how different perspectives on religion might impact how local residents perceive others in those faith groups. It might be that, as with their encouragement of a superordinate "Angeleno" identity in promoting political commonality across racial and ethnic groups, the commission could employ similar rhetorical strategies in its facilitation effort to encourage respect for religious pluralism. With this insight in mind, this second Los Angeles–area study used a survey-embedded experiment to test whether a similar type of cognitive suggestion—but this time focusing on religious inclusivity or exclusivity—affects how Christians view those of other faiths.

RELIGIOUS VALUES AND TRUST FOR OTHER RELIGIOUS GROUPS

We follow Djupe and Calfano's religious values survey experiment as our guide for this study.[16] Djupe and Calfano randomly assigned their survey respondents into three groups. The first treatment group read exclusive religious values statements at the beginning of their survey. The second treatment group read inclusive religious value statements at the beginning of their survey. The third group, more commonly described as the control group, were provided with no religious value statements at the beginning of their survey. We followed this same protocol in our survey-embedded experiment.

First, we used a screening question to limit our sample of respondents. Only those stating at the very start of the survey that they have a Christian identity were included in the survey-embedded experiment. Then those Christian respondents were randomly assigned into one of three groups: the exclusive values treatment group (230 respondents), the inclusive values treatment group (225 respondents), or the control group receiving no values statements (227 respondents). The value statements read by the exclusive values treatment group were

> In trying to be a good Christian, it is important to shop as much as possible at stores owned by other Christians.

> In trying to be a good Christian, it is important to keep company with other Christians.

The value statements read by the inclusive values treatment group were

> In trying to be a good Christian, it is important to "love the stranger as yourself."
> In trying to be a good Christian, it is important to invite others to church, even if the church begins to change as a result.

The control group read no value statements before answering the remaining survey questions.

As with the Cincinnati study described earlier in the chapter, the random assignment was accomplished via the Internet survey software program used to collect the survey responses. And, as with the Cincinnati study, survey respondents were solicited through direct recruitment using survey links embedded in email and at public events advertising the survey link. Just like with the perceived discrimination statements in Cincinnati, we are not directly interested in what people said about their level of agreement with the assigned value statements. Instead, the act of reading and thinking about the content in the value statement was intended to shape respondent thinking as they answer a series of follow-on questions about religious groups.

While there are various outcomes of interest related to religious pluralism, Valerie Martinez-Ebers and colleagues show that trust is a key component for improving intergroup relations in urban areas.[17] With this in mind, we focused on expressed levels of trust the Christian respondents have for Muslims, Jews, and atheists. We also included expressed trust levels for other Christians and a nonreligious identity group, LGBT community members, as a way to make points of comparison influence from the religious values statements. The respondent's trust level was measured for each of the five groups as a 1–7 Likert-scaled answer to the following question: "Generally speaking, would you say that the groups in the table below can be trusted, or that you can't be too careful in dealing with them (where 1 means you 'can't be too careful,' and 7 means that the 'group can be trusted')?" Again, the five groups in the referenced table were Muslims, Jews, Atheists, Christians, and LGBT community members.

Table A.6b in the appendix includes sample demographic information, including comparison to U.S. Census targets for Compton, California, which we designate and the population center for the survey respondents. Figures 6.6–6.10 show the response distributions on the individual group trust items, while table 6.2 shows the comparison of mean answers between the exclusive treatment group, the inclusive treatment group, and the control group. Using the Tukey HSD critical value to determine statistically significant mean differences between the three randomly assigned groups, we see that, in terms of the respondents indicating a trust in Muslims, those first encountering the inclusive religious value statements have a mean trust score of 4.60 (on the 1–5 scale), versus 4.16 for the exclusive values treatment group and 4.02 for the control. All three means are statistically different from each other at $p < .01$ and are a strong initial indication that the inclusive value language boosts perceived trust among this minority respondent pool (which is entirely Latino and African

TABLE 6.2 Comparison of Means on Political Commonality with Other Groups, According to Treatments (1–4 Scale)

	INCLUSIVE (n = 230)	EXCLUSIVE (n = 225)	CONTROL (n = 227)
TRUST MUSLIMS	4.60*	4.16	4.02
TRUST JEWS	4.99**	4.78	4.64
TRUST CHRISTIANS	4.71	4.84	4.76
TRUST ATHEISTS	4.25***	3.74	4.11
TRUST LGBT PEOPLE	4.39*	3.81	4.04

Note: * = p <.01 for Tukey HSD pairwise comparisons between the inclusive treatment cue and the other two randomly assigned groups, including the control.
** = p <.01 for Tukey HSD pairwise comparisons between the inclusive treatment cue and control group only.
*** = p<.01 for Tukey HSD pairwise comparisons between the inclusive treatment cue and exclusive treatment cue group only.

American). The mean trust level toward Jew also increases when respondents are exposed to the inclusive language value: 4.99 for that treatment group, 4.78 for the exclusive treatment group, and 4.64 for the control. All three groups show rather high trust levels, which is why the only statistically significant difference is between the inclusive value treatment group and the control group at $p < .01$ (the exclusive treatment group mean is too close in size to the inclusive mean for there to be significant difference between the two).

We included Christians as one of the groups in the trust question primarily as a way to gauge respondent assessment of members of their own faith. Not surprisingly, we found a closer cluster of mean trust scores across the three randomized survey groups. The inclusive treatment mean is 4.71, the exclusive is 4.84, and the control is 4.76. Due to the closeness in size, none of the means is significantly different from each other.

This is not the case in terms of how respondents evaluate their trust levels for those who claim no religion: atheists. Here there is significant mean difference between the inclusive (4.25) and exclusive (3.74) value statements, with the control being 4.11 ($p < .01$). This is the strongest evidence yet that the cognitive considerations encouraged by the two sets of statements contributes to different levels of trust in outgroup members, with the inclusive value treatment having the kind of effect that the

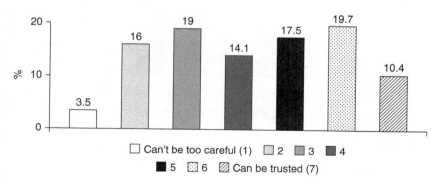

FIGURE 6.6

Trust Muslims; $n = 682$

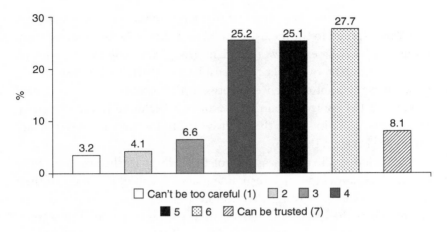

FIGURE 6.7

Trust Jews; $n = 682$

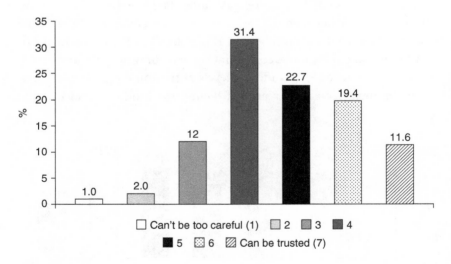

FIGURE 6.8

Trust Christians; $n = 682$

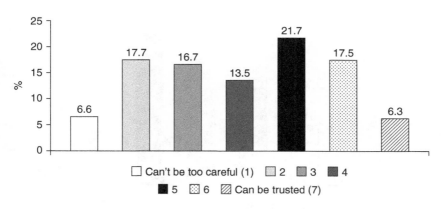

FIGURE 6.9

Trust Atheists; $n = 682$

LAHRC likely wants in terms of moving disparate groups to an increased sense of common ground.

Finally, we included a non-religiously related group as a way to assess how these statements impact trust, specifically toward LGBT persons. In keeping with the pattern found across the prior four outcomes, the inclusive value statement has the highest mean trust score (4.39) compared to the exclusive treatment (3.81), and the control (4.04), and the difference between all three groups is significant at $p < .01$. This particular finding should be encouraging for the LAHRC's facilitation and mediation efforts because it suggests that encouraging people to think about faith in more inclusive terms could increase trust between groups of all kinds, not simply those engaged in interreligious dialogue.

Moving to statistical models, which are fully reported in table A.9 of the appendix, we include additional variables that could influence respondent's trust in the five groups of interest. Specifically, we assess respondent trust controlling for respondents' view of the Bible; identification as a "born again" Christian; the number of friends or coworkers the respondents have who are of a different or no religious identity, sex, age, income level; and whether the respondents are African American (the appendix contains tables with these statistical models and additional information about the covariates). As with the prior results in this and the previous

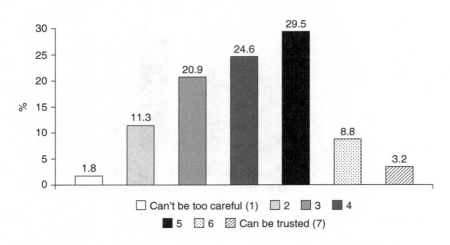

FIGURE 6.10

Trust LGBT people; $n = 682$

chapter, we employ the same logistic regression analysis based on a res-
caling the 1–5 Likert response to a 0/1 outcome, with reported changes in
probability, holding all other variables at their means. We ran a separate
model for each of the five groups of interest.

We find that randomized exposure to the inclusive value treatment in
the Muslim model increases respondent perception of trust in Muslims
by 15 percent, an effect that runs counter to covariate influence from
respondent sex, age, and being African American. Specifically, female
respondents have an 8 percent lower probability of perceiving Muslims
as trustworthy, and older respondents are 26 percent less likely to do the
same. Meanwhile, African American respondents are 13 percent less likely
to perceive Muslims as trustworthy. The inclusive value treatment effect
is virtually the same for respondents' expressed trust in Jews, with those
exposed to the inclusive statements 14 percent more likely to perceive Jews
as trustworthy (no other variables are statistically significant in the model).

Given that this group of respondents identifies as Christian, it is not
surprising that neither of the assigned value treatments have statistical
effects on perceived trust in the Christian model, but believing that the
Bible is the word of God does impact trust. Those who have higher levels

of agreement with the notion that the Bible is God's word are 14 percent more likely to perceive Christians as trustworthy. Interestingly, there is no inclusive values effect for perceiving atheists as trustworthy. Instead, it is the exclusive value treatment that does the work in the Atheist model, with those randomly exposed to exclusive statements at the beginning of their survey 9 percent less likely to perceive atheists as trustworthy (no covariates are significant in that model). A similar effect pattern is found for the LGBT model, with those assigned the exclusive treatment 12 percent less likely to view LGBT persons as trustworthy, while respondents who believe the Bible as God's word are 19 percent less likely to do the same.

As with the political commonality experiment in chapter 5, there is evidence that LAHRC personnel can use inclusive messaging in their facilitation work to impact how people think about other religious groups. This shift in thinking is an important building block to improved intergroup relations, even though changes in thinking may be short-lived or may not actually dictate behavior, at least in all cases. Still, if the LAHRC's focus is on facilitation primarily through dialogue, then the verbal markers commission staff lay down during facilitation activities are important, and there is now data-driven evidence to suggest that key racial and ethnic constituencies in LAHRC's mission can be moved to increased perceptions of trust of other religious groups. What the commission does about trust in Atheists and LGBT residents will likely require a separate remedy.

FORT WORTH AND PITTSBURGH: EXPANDING FROM ENFORCEMENT

The third portion of our chapter concerns the effect of survey-embedded treatments on reports of housing complaints, which are the domain of code enforcement (i.e., commissions like at Pittsburgh and Fort Worth). As discussed in chapter 4, much of the work in investigating complaints of housing discrimination and other landlord issues is the outcome of a series of investigative procedures that these HUD empowered commissions engage in, including conducting interviews with the relevant parties, gathering information, and preparing investigative reports. A similar set of procedures exist for Fort Worth's FEPA enforcement function. Although these enforcement-empowered commissions have more reliable funding available to them for their work, even these commissions face resource challenges in areas that do not directly relate to an expansion into the intergroup facilitation-oriented work discussed by staffers in chapter 4.

Instead, there are pressures on enforcement HRCs that come from beyond local political officials making commissioner appointments of those whose ideological views do not align with commission goals. In the FWHRC's case, it is the Texas legislature that presents a challenge. The executive summary of the commission's 2017 report shows that both local and state elected officials may have substantial impacts on future commission work.

> The biggest legal concern for the FWHRC are the repeated attempts by the Texas State Legislature to limit local municipalities from enforcing expanded anti-discrimination laws. The State's attempt to promote "religious freedom" laws at the expense of anti-discrimination laws is concerning. This concern also impacts the FWHRC's momentum to move forward with needed edits to the city's Human Relations Ordinance. Currently, there is outdated language and language that needs clarification. The FWHRC is concerned that opening the ordinance to revisions may result in certain special interest groups attempting to remove protections for sexual orientation, transgender, gender identity, and gender expression from the ordinance. Additionally the state's passage of SB4 [requiring local law enforcement to engage in federal immigration enforcement activities], and the city council's vote not to join the other large cities in Texas in their lawsuit against SB4, is very disconcerting to the FWHRC. The FWHRC firmly believes that SB4 disproportionately impacts Latino/Hispanic residents for increased scrutiny because of the color of their skin, their accents, and/or their national origin.

In terms of some of the "nuts and bolts" of the code enforcement we have alluded to throughout this book, both the Fort Worth and Pittsburgh commissions track the frequency with which they engage in handing certain kinds of cases, and recently released records by both the FWHRC and Pittsburgh commission provide context on just how much said enforcement the commissions engage in annually. The FWHRC processed 198 fair housing complaints in 2017, 97 percent of which involved "discriminatory terms" in the rental or sale or property. One case even involved an outright refusal by an owner to sell a property based on the prospective buyer's race. By contrast, the Pittsburgh commission had 19 complaints files in 2017. The coding Pittsburgh uses to document the nature of a complaint differs from Fort Worth, as all 19 Pittsburgh cases involved one or more discriminatory terms: 11 were based on disability, 4 on race, 3 on retaliation, 3 on familial status, 2 on color, and 1 for each of the following: sexual orientation, sex, place of birth, national origin, and religion.

FWHRC processed 125 FEPA cases in 2017, with 59 percent dealing with discharge-related issues, 27 percent with general discipline, and 10 percent involving sexual harassment. Investigations of either fair housing or employment complaints are divided into administrative closure, no reasonable cause, or reasonable cause determinations. In the case the commission's investigation establishes that a reasonable cause exists, remedies include the conciliation agreements covered in chapter 4, a fine or monetary settlement, or both. Commissioners work to resolve both the housing and employment disputes within a three- to six-month period.

But, as referenced in the FWHRC's report, the commission has more to worry about in terms of protecting residents than how landlords and employers behave: changes in state and federal policies—driven by political agendas—make for a changing enforcement landscape. Concerns are similar among the Pittsburgh Commission on Human Relations (CHR), although the Pennsylvania General Assembly has not taken up the kind of immigration enforcement legislation seen in Texas and has been more content to allow the City of Pittsburgh, which was in receivership for several years due to financial difficulties, more leeway in charting its own policy course through home rule. As the CHR chair recently stated in a recent report to the city,

> These days, it seems like civil rights are being eroded on the national level: travel bands, rescinded protections for transgender people,

suspension of data collection on the gender wage gap. This is not an exhaustive list. In the City of Pittsburgh, however, we can insulate ourselves from these national trends. Our City Code defines more protected classes than federal law, and we can add protected classes and protections as we see fit and necessary through City Council. We can enforce our anti-discrimination and equal-protection laws through the CHR without relying on federal or state agencies.[18]

The last sentence is telling given that HUD pays the commission for its code enforcement work. But if HUD decided to curtail its funding for this purpose, the commission has support from the Pittsburgh City Council to fund the type of code enforcement that protects housing access. However, council funding is a political decision by local elected officials that can be overturned rather quickly, and the council has not been as interested in increasing the CHR's funding for initiatives beyond code enforcement. And even with its success as a HUD enforcement agency, we saw in our chapter 4 interviews that Pittsburgh commission staffers desire to expand the CHR's mandate into facilitation work. This desire is seen in a later section of the commission report. "The commission is tasked with not only investigating claims of discriminatory treatment and enforcing equal protection laws, but also holding public hearings, investigating problems of prejudice, intolerance bigotry, and discrimination, instituting and conducting educational or other programs to promote equal rights and opportunities, recommending legislation to promote equal rights and opportunities, and more."

The "more" in this case, including the general shift to a facilitation-based commission, requires resources that the CHR does not have yet. In garnering a more resourced and wider commission mandate, the CHR, like its three counterparts in this book, needs data-driven understanding of where some of its nascent facilitation-based efforts might complement its existing code enforcement programs. So, like the Cincinnati and Los Angeles examples above, we next turn attention to insights from another community survey featuring a survey-embedded experiment and a sample of city residents.

In 2017 the Pittsburgh commission initiated the same kind of non-probability survey of residents (featuring an embedded questions-as-treatment experiment), as featured in the Cincinnati and Los Angeles examples referenced earlier in the chapter. In Pittsburgh's case, however, interest focused on a diverse set of outcomes ranging from both what the commission already handles in terms of housing complaints as well as city residents' perceptions of discrimination by city workers and an overall assessment of race relations in the city. Of the surveys described in this book, the Pittsburgh version represents perhaps the best example of a commission using data collection to both assess the work it performs under its current mandate and resource structure.

The results reported from the Pittsburgh survey experiment are based on answers from 1,789 total respondents, all of whom were city residents. We helped facilitate the Pittsburgh study, primarily in the development of the survey questionnaire. The commission was persuaded by our argument that encouraging reflection on personal experiences with racial discrimination might impact survey responses along an array of outcomes. Commission interest was to see whether and how the perceived discrimination impacts responses to housing-related survey questions (which were not part of the Cincinnati study given the nature of that commission's mandate). As with the Cincinnati study, Pittsburgh's survey respondents were randomly assigned to two groups: 900 respondents in the treatment group answered the discrimination questions toward the beginning of the survey, while 899 respondents in the control group answered the discrimination questions at the end. Unlike the Cincinnati and Los Angeles surveys, however, we were not responsible for administering the survey. Pittsburgh's commission contracted with the Internet survey firm Qualtrics Panels to field the study. Table A.6c in the appendix contains demographic information for the Pittsburgh sample and compares it to U.S. Census targets for Allegheny County, Pennsylvania.

Regarding housing issues, the Pittsburgh commission chose to include a long series of items that residents might complain about in terms of landlord treatment. The commission already sees itself as having a good handle on the reporting of HUD-related code violations, so it wanted to use survey space to ask residents about their interactions with landlords more generally as a way to gauge community satisfaction. In terms of experiences with landlords, respondents were asked:

If you rent, during the last year have you had a difficult time getting your landlord to repair/replace:

TABLE 6.3

	YES	NO	N/A
Air conditioner/heater			
Broken/frozen pipes			
Damaged/broken doors and/or screens			
Damaged/broken windows and/or screens			
Damaged/broken/missing sidewalks, entry ways			
Damaged/old carpet			
Leaky faucet			
Lighting			
Locks			
Refrigerator			
Roof leaks			
Stove			
Toilet			
Water heater			
Washer/dryer			

Since only 30 percent of the survey identified as renters, we limited our first outcome analysis to these 524 respondents. We examined which renters were having the most problems using a count estimator model (i.e., negative binomial regression). Table A.10 of the appendix contains the full statistical model results for these Pittsburgh data.

For a variety of reasons (e.g., findings in the housing literature and the demographics of renters versus nonrenters[19]), we suspect that those who were primed to remember their personal discrimination experiences would be more likely to report property owner problems. This is exactly what we find. Those assigned to the perceived discrimination treatment questions report, on average, 1.72 more items that they had a hard time getting their landlord to fix versus control group respondents. Even controlling for the respondent's race/ethnicity (i.e., African American or Latino), sex, income level, and age, the treatment effect is still essentially the same—1.60 more items—and remains statistically significant. Meanwhile, African American respondents reported .81 more item problems and Latino respondents 1.34 more item problems than white respondents. Interestingly, the landlord realities are different for women respondents, as they report .74 fewer cases of landlord difficulty than men, while older respondents report 1.60 fewer incidents than younger renters.

While we should be cautious in interpreting these results for how they relate to commission work, it is intriguing that reflection on personal discrimination affects the number of repair issues that respondents identify as problems with their landlords. Landlord repairs are not a topic directly related to discrimination, at least in an overt sense, but repairs clearly relate to housing issues and the quality of one's housing experience. As such, the finding suggests that the commission might incorporate opportunities for residents to think about and express perceived discrimination during facilitation meetings or as part of a revised complaint procedure process along a variety of topics, as the treatment effect found here suggests that repair problems with landlords are underreported. Given this, it might be that other problems are also underreported.

The CHR is also interested in knowing the types of discrimination that respondents encounter at work. This moves into FEPA territory, even though the Pittsburgh commission presently does not have responsibility to address these types of complaints directly. Respondents were asked:

In the past year, did YOU experience a difference in treatment at work (from coworkers, supervisors/managers, company owners, etc.) because of:

TABLE 6.4

	NO	YES
Age (over 40)		
Skin color		
Ethnicity		

(*continued*)

	NO	YES
Gender		
Gender expression		
Gender identity		
Mental disability		
National origin or your birthplace		
Physical disability/handicap		
Race		
Religion or religious preferences		
Sexual orientation		
The way you were dressed		
Use of a language other than English		

To systematically evaluate those who experiencing discrimination at work, we used the same count-based outcome approach as we did for the property owner problem, but this time all survey respondents were included in the analysis. We find that those exposed to the perceived discrimination questions at the beginning of the survey report, on average, said they experienced .57 more types of discrimination at work than the control group of respondents (and the effect is statistically significant at $p < .01$). Adding the demographic control variables lowers the treatment effect to .45 more types of discrimination, but with the same level of significance. The only demographic characteristic that was significant in the count model was age, with older respondents reporting they encountered 1.69 fewer types of discrimination than younger respondents did.

A similar question—using the same fourteen discrimination types—was asked of respondents regarding problems encountered with services offered by the City of Pittsburgh. Here, similar to the findings in previous questions, those exposed to the personal discrimination treatment reported .31 more types of discrimination experiences in dealing with the city, which increased to .33 when demographic controls are included in the model. Interestingly, none of the demographic characteristics of the respondents was statistically significant.

The Pittsburgh results, like the Cincinnati and Los Angeles examples before them, paint a mixed picture for commissions. Part of this is due to the reality that no research design or data-collection method is pristine enough to provide quick and consistent answers to questions of what commissions need to do to maintain their current level of effective mandate implementation and expand their reach into those human relations topics of relative need in their jurisdictions. Still, with the degree to which HRCs are resource poor (HUD and FEPA funding notwithstanding), the general insight that these small and inexpensive research designs provide are invaluable in giving commissions some sense of a road map for future initiatives, whether in terms of facilitation and advisory functions, approaching external funders and potential community partners for resources, or both.

7

IMAGINING HUMAN RELATIONS
FOR THE FUTURE

We began this book asking three guiding questions to help structure our examination of HRCs. First, how do commissions react
to and manage their ever-expanding mission? Second, what are
the structural opportunities and challenges facing HRCs? Third, and
finally, what constitute the most promising, evidence-based strategies for
assisting HRCs and similar organizations in improving intergroup relations and limiting discrimination?

The historical overviews of both race relations and the development of
commissions in our early chapters set the stage for describing the critical
need for permanent commissions empowered to take on the responsibility of working to improve intergroup relations and limit discrimination
within the communities they serve. Tracing the process of simply getting
local and state governments to see value in commission work shows that
the nature of human relations work requires two key ingredients: patience
and commitment. This is seen especially in the management of expanding commission missions—our first question.

Note that we do not use the term "mandate" in this question, as a commission's mission is likely seen as something broader and less determined
by the specifics imposed by local statutes and budgets. If the mission
of all commissions centers on improving intergroup relations, albeit
through different means, then given the state of society and the intergroup
tensions therein, the mission is clearly expanding. With the ongoing tensions between police and communities of color, the aggressive campaign
by federal agents to deport undocumented immigrants, and the continued epidemics of housing and food insecurity for many in impoverished

areas of America's cities, the HRC mandate shows no signs of shrinking, at least from a topical standpoint. But, critically, also expanding are the daily, work-related demands on HRC staffers and commissioners. Not only is the "make do with less" status quo entrenched in these human relations offices (often imposed by budgetary decisions from above) but so is the expectation among community groups airing their frustrations that commissions are there to function as a sounding board for the hashing and rehashing of grievances (i.e., embodied by the "regulars" who often appear at commission hearings and events).

HRC commissioners and staffers work hard to perform almost impossible tasks when it comes to making progress in improving the state of intergroup relations and reducing discrimination. In various cases, the commissions have reason to celebrate successes, ranging from breakthroughs between groups at odds with each other, to resolutions between landlords and tenants, to policy changes in how police engage with communities of color. But sometimes the tasks before commissions can seem insurmountable, and this perception takes a toll. Our interviews from personnel across commissions show dedicated professionals working to come to grips with the cycle of elation and disappointment inherent in attempting to move members of society toward productive ways of coexisting. The mental and emotional strain of the work that staff perform is a reminder that human relations takes a toll on those trying to improve conditions on the ground for marginalized and displaced groups (and, by extension, entire communities). By and large, then, HRC commissioners and staffers manage their mission, but we did not find evidence that they feel confident that their efforts are stemming macro-level tides. In some ways, of course, this is to be expected given the subject areas commissions deal with, but it is perhaps human nature to want to feel like one's efforts are "making a difference." Commission efforts likely are doing so, even if individual staffers and commissioners do not always perceive it.

Another aspect of human nature as it pertains to human relations work, or any bureaucratically entrenched function for that matter, is the reality of executing work duties against the backdrop of statutory limitations and available resources. Here the topic of commission "mandates" dovetails well with what we discovered in relation to our second question about opportunities and challenges. We explored mandates in chapter 4 as a way to delineate structural differences between commissions according to functions that are primarily quasi-judicial, facilitation-based, or advisory. Using our four case study commissions, we found some degree of overlap between the three types in that almost all commissions fulfill the advisory role. But the difference between the quasi-judicial and facilitation types is where the structural nature of challenges outside of dealing with their broader mission seem to manifest.

Yet, as we repeatedly found, movement toward enlarging commission mandates, or even doubling down on efforts covered by existing commission statues, requires access to resources that are not exactly in long supply. Indeed, to the extent that elected officials seem more inclined to enhance budgets for police—even shifting commission resources away in the process—there can be no illusion that the work HRCs perform is valued enough to justify increased resource expenditures from municipal budgets. Meanwhile, commissions in the mold of Los Angeles and Cincinnati are likely not to come into opportunities to function as HUD or FEPA enforcers (as their counterparts in Fort Worth and Pittsburgh do).

And as we completed this book, we learned that the City of Los Angeles elected not to empower the LAHRC with enforcement capacity but instead set up an entirely new body to perform those tasks: the Civil and Human Rights Commission. This new commission will not replace the LAHRC's work as an intergroup facilitator body, which is good news given the importance of this type of emphasis. However, the creation of a separate government structure to handle antidiscrimination investigation and enforcement functions, while perhaps warranted in some ways, leads invariably to questions about bureaucratic turf tensions, competition for city resources, and public confusion over which body should be involved in dealing with specific issues that arise in communities (e.g., the commission names are so similar that it is hard to see how the missions are not confused even by attentive residents). These potential drawbacks aside, to the extent that the LAHRC is substantially geared toward facilitation work, it might be that adding enforcement work to the LAHRC's existing portfolio would have not positioned the commission for success in this new role. Indeed, in some cases, bringing in a new entity with new personnel to do a different type of job may make for more effective implementation for both the existing and new bodies. As such, the Los Angeles approach may be something worth considering in the reverse for cities like Fort Worth and Pittsburgh, where newer bodies could take on an intergroup facilitator role with the existing commissions continuing their antidiscrimination enforcement agenda.

Whatever the future holds for the breadth of mission of HRCs in these and other municipalities, however, all will still face challenges with resource access. So what can commissions do with the resources in hand to increase their cache? Based on our findings across chapters, we make the following recommendations:

- Be knowledgeable and always mindful of the history of discrimination and conflict that constituents have experienced. This recommendation may seem obvious for HRC staff, but appointed commissioners may not be as educated or aware. When commission representatives have and apply this knowledge, their interactions with constituents as well as elected officials are likely to be more successful. Constituents will feel respected, and officials are more likely to respect the HRC messenger.

- Test and implement different collective identity messaging with constituents, remembering to be sensitive and respectful of their subgroup identities, including residency. This strategy should increase perceptions of commonality among residents, especially those in diverse communities.

- Look for ways that resident perceptions of discrimination may impact how they view various items related to commission work, both core and periphery. One of the strengths of those data collected by the Pittsburgh commission as covered in chapter 6 is the ability to link personal feelings of discrimination to systematic responses about landlord complaints. In this example, discrimination as a general, individual level perception might be considered a bit tangential for the Pittsburgh commission's HUD-based focus, but our data analysis shows that cognitively highlighting discrimination as a topic for residents may lead them to reveal concerns about a variety of issues more central to a commission's work. The Pittsburgh case is but one example, and each commission should pursue its own study of linkages as opportunities allow.

In line with these recommendations, the future of these commissions seems based on how effectively and creatively they can leverage resource partnerships with outside entities to expand their work scope, if not their official mandates. To be sure, it is more likely that the quasi-judicial commissions will find ways to expand into intergroup relations work than facilitation commissions taking on quasi-judicial functions. We do not have a quick or easy remedy for how facilitation HRCs might become more like their code enforcer cousins, absent a political patron who finds such mandate realignment desirable. However, we do offer two suggestions about how all commissions, especially the facilitator bodies, might best position their efforts to be ready to fulfill their potentials. In doing so, an increase in a commission's perceived competence and usefulness to its political masters and constituent communities might lead to other opportunities within local government structures. Although these improvements might never result in wholesale commission transformations (e.g., from a facilitator to a quasi-judicial role), they stand to expand a commission's profile nonetheless.

IT'S ALL ACADEMIC

Perhaps the resource with the greatest leveraging potential by commissions is the establishment of partnerships with academics and academic institutions. Although some academics and institutions will want payment for their work in relation to commission missions, commissions should not be shy about exploring alternatives to taking on additional financial obligations—particularly where budgets are too tight to allow the addition of full-time staffers. Instead of money for services, HRCs might think creatively about offering opportunities for faculty and students to work with commissions in fulfilling duties related to enforcement, facilitation, and advisement. Some tasks will require confidentiality in terms of complaints and conciliation agreements related to HUD and FEPA processes, but much of the other work that commissions perform will not be under the same kind of restrictions.

Arguably, the best example of how a commission–academic partnership might play out is in the collection, analysis, and dissemination of data related to one or more community-oriented challenges germane to commission work. The three data-based assessments discussed in chapter 6 are examples of studies that can easily be carried out by academics and the findings disseminated to commissions and interested constituencies. In each of those cases, academic researchers lent their expertise for no monetary compensation (and instead counted the experience as community or university service or research), while commissions assisted with the provision of resources to generate respondent samples for data collection. The relative drawbacks of a nonprobability sample and the advantages of a randomly assigned treatment were covered in the last chapter. We do not recite those items here except to say that the insights generated from the Los Angeles, Cincinnati, and Pittsburgh studies have proven useful to each commission or their community partners, and they were performed at minimum cost. And the three studies really only scratched the surface in terms of issues of interest to commissions—meaning that replications and extensions of the three designs (and the intergroup identity design in chapter 5, for that matter) are ready-made starting points for how commissions of all kinds across the United States might engage with academic institutions to advance commission missions.

The enticement for academics and their institutions—if not money, or at least not much of it—would be access to the inner workings of a government body. Here, what commissions lack in terms of available monetary resources they should be prepared to provide in terms of material that academics can use as both teachers and researchers. Although urban politics, urban affairs, public administration, and public policy (to name a few of the fields that intersect with HRC work) are not necessarily the core interests of even a majority of academics in political science, public administration, and sociology departments, it is likely that at least one faculty member in one of these fields and departments has a broad interest in the kind of intergroup and antidiscrimination work that commissions engage in. The trick will be for commissions and academics to make the connection, make it mutually beneficial, and, if possible, find a way to secure funds for a commission–academic collaboration. Although the logistics of networking can be hard enough, given the challenges with personalities and work schedules, figuring out funding (and coming to peace with the notion that, for academics, this work will not be like a lucrative consulting side gig) may be the bigger obstacle.

Of course, one potential funding source is a government agency. Our Los Angeles study with the LAHRC featured in chapter 5 was wholly funded by the National Science Foundation in 2015. But that approach to generating support should be considered the exception, given the small number of studies funded in this way. Much more likely is that academics and commissions can find educational buy-in in the form of monetary or in-kind support from institutions if there is a curricular purpose to the collaboration. While universities are not necessarily the cash cows that some assume, their core mission is delivering an educational experience for students. However, the external pressures on universities to come up with courses and training experiences that mirror "real world" situations means that greater educational resources—especially internal institutional grants—are available to help faculty retool their teaching and courses.

We suggest that academics can leverage the resources available for curricular innovation to pursue collaborations with HRC in their institution's proximity by adding any one of the following course-related activities. The first, and most obvious, is an internship option for individual students. Although internships for academic credit are often administered at the departmental or college levels, interested faculty can serve as advisors (formally or informally) for interested students. With the growing popularity of service-learning programs across universities (which tend to function as a cross between a co-op and traditional internship), faculty might also see if adding these type of learning components to their courses might make sense for their students and wider curriculum. Faculty might also consider modifying the "study away" model used by universities to focus student time on an intense weeks-long project over a summer or intersemester period.

Then there is the more traditional option of embedding an active learning experience within an existing course in political science, public administration, public policy, or related field. The setup in this case would entail faculty devising a project that students could work on in real time during a semester, ideally by putting into practice core areas of course material. Here is where the data-driven examples of the previous two chapters may best come into play, with students in research methods classes working on developing research designs to capture and analyze data on an array of commission-related concerns, including intergroup relations, code enforcement strategies, and even public knowledge and perception of HRCs. Of course, an equally enlightening opportunity for faculty, students, and commissions would be to engage in qualitatively oriented research that complements survey and related research designs (and might generate thickly descriptive data in the process). If possible, faculty could dovetail course projects with existing commission programs aimed at generating community understanding of group relations and discrimination. For its part, the LAHRC has partnered extensively with local universities in having students work as language interpreters, interview transcribers, and data analysts on different community-oriented projects of interest. The benefit to students was access to a hands-on learning project that provides skills and experience for future job searches while providing the commission with invaluable information as it conducts its facilitation function.

Just as impactful would be a collaboration between faculty, students, and commissions in the quasi-judicial work carried out by commissions like the Pittsburgh and Fort Worth examples. In these instances, students in local government and management courses could learn about the policies and procedures that guide enforcement of code for HUD and FEPA. As stated, efforts will be needed to maintain confidentiality for the parties involved, but the students would gain invaluable insight into the implementation of federal policies through local bureaucratic implementation. Students might also undertake research projects aimed at evaluating any differences between how local commission members and staffers interpret portions of the code being enforced, perhaps as a way to assess Meier and O'Toole's findings on value-driven bureaucratic action at the local level.[1] And, as seen in the previous chapters, political control, while Meier and O'Toole have argued is something from which local bureaucrats have a degree of latitude in avoiding, is a reality that all commissions must contend with as they directly exercise their current mandates, expand their responsibilities and powers, or enlarge their pool of resources.

Faculty can position student learning opportunities by situating the discussion of commissions in the wider bureaucratic and jurisdiction framework we used in prior chapters, but students may also use the opportunity to think and engage commissions creatively. Specifically, students might be encouraged through course assignments to propose ways that academic and commission collaborations can be institutionalized to provide more regular collaborations. To that end, students might also look for private organizational partnerships that can serve as the third leg of a stool supporting commission work. Students—with faculty supervision—can establish contact networks across area nonprofits with missions and constituencies similar to commissions' scope of work. What is more, students and faculty can serve as expert witnesses and similar types of community voices before city councils in advocating for expanded commission resources and jurisdiction. To be sure, many commissions have likely already sought to use public–private partnerships to advance specific initiatives and commission reach on key issues and among core constituency groups. The difference with our recommendation, however, is that assistance to a commission's mission becomes a regular part of the academy's commitment to these government bodies by incorporating collaboration and service into college courses.

GROW WITHIN AND WITHOUT

For HRCs to thrive, becoming enmeshed with higher education or expanding on existing public–private partnerships is only part of the answer. Commissions must think about the best ways to bring about greater resource support and mandate expansion. And, realistically, the best way to realize these goals is for commissions to become better advocates not simply for the needy in their communities but also for their collective work in the area of human relations and human rights. Commissioners and commission staffers will need to do more to sell elected officials and the public on the importance of their work—they must be advocates not just for the society they serve but for the profession they are in.

There is already a national organizational infrastructure in place to promote HRCs and their work: The Washington, D.C.–based International Association of Official Human Rights Agencies (IAOHRA) is an umbrella organization devoted to the promotion of "equality and diversity through public policy and legislation."[2] Like the California-specific California

Association of Human Relations Organizations (CAHRO), the IAOHRA provides resources to member commissions on areas ranging from intergroup conflict to mediation to team building and community organizing. Both the IAOHRA and CAHRO run member meetings that allow for human relations professionals to obtain in-person instruction on best practices and to share experiences related to work in the field.

The IAOHRA also sees the development of its reach as a professional organization as paramount to promoting commission work, including support for commissions facing political challenges to the scope and method of mission implementation. This is in addition to goals related to the development of the IAOHRA as an organization with a growing member list and donor base. Although one might suggest that the IAOHRA should choose one of these goals as a first priority, we recommend moving ahead with both an IAOHRA expansion and a broader campaign to educate the public and politicians about HRCs because commission work, as we discovered in chapter 4, is not linear in terms of progress. Instead, progress feeds on simultaneously occurring events that require commissions to work on multiple issues and fronts at once. And there is also a "chicken and egg" component at work: expanding IAOHRA membership and reach may (or may not) precede successful advocacy on behalf of commissions.

The concern about growing the IAOHRA's organizational presence is not misplaced. As of 2018 the IAOHRA's active membership consisted of 66 commissions out of the more than 150 known to exist at the state and local government levels around the country (see commission list in the appendix). Not even the four case studies examined in this book are all represented, with the Pittsburgh commission lacking an active membership. It might be that the commissions without the IAOHRA's membership have good reasons for not having a formal organizational tie, and perceived problems of the IAOHRA's ability to effectively represent commission interests may be part of that decision. In four interviews with commission staff at each of our commission case study cites, none offered what might be considered an enthusiastic endorsement of IAOHRA's work. This is seemed partly due to lack of awareness on the part of our interviewees as to what the organization does to impact the daily work of commissions (and perhaps because it is a state-level organization, the LAHRC, reports a stronger, more regular working relationship with the

CAHRO). It is not hard to understand this reaction to the IAOHRA, given that the organization's location is Washington, D.C., but it is also the case that neither the local commissions nor state associations have the same potential to represent commissions interests at the national level. This is why we recommend both an expansion of the IAOHRA's organizational strength as it relates to commission membership and a simultaneous expansion of the IAOHRA's national profile and ties to local commissions as a way to bolster commission work in the field.

Part of the path forward in these respects might require solving a collective-action problem related to having commissions in stronger political positions and with greater relative resources encourage collaboration and other forms of interaction with other HRCs. Likely candidates for this type of coordinator role are the state-wide commissions that, at least in name, have responsibility to ensure positive intergroup relations across a much larger area than city or county commissions. Of course, it might also be that commissions in large urban areas can also (or instead) serve in this coordinating capacity to bring smaller HRCs into the fold of state-based coalitions similar to the CAHRO. Just which existing commissions take up this coordinating mantle will depend on specifics related to an HRC's capacity to undertake this kind of extra institutional goal. If there is any conclusion to draw from the insights offered in the preceding chapters, it is that there is no likely relationship between the type of commission (i.e., quasi-judicial, facilitator, advisory) and service as a hub of commission efforts regionally. This is because even those well-endowed commissions using federal dollars for code enforcement face stark resource restrictions in operating outside of established policy lanes.

So perhaps the spark for specific commissions to take up the role of coordinating action on behalf of their fellow bodies will come from this and other scholarly examinations of HRCs. Such work helps showcase the worth of commissions to the business of government in ensuring social justice and a host of other important outcomes. The good news is really the same as the bad news on this front: there is no precedent or roadmap to follow, which means whatever new action is undertaken may set benchmarks for commission coordination. And such coordination at the state level should occur with an eye not only toward deepening ties with other commissions in the same state or region but also toward fortifying the membership and overall activities the IAOHRA undertakes.

We view an expanded and strengthened IAOHRA as essential because, whatever elements of federalism remain critical to our system of government, there is no denying that the federal government has the monetary resources to spend on initiatives it determines are worthwhile. At this point, the vast bulk of the regularly appropriated resources are tied up in support HUD enforcement, with certain, one-time funds available through grants offered by the Department of Justice and Department of Homeland Security. The goal for an invigorated IAOHRA should be to compel Congress to appropriate new budget lines for enhanced commission responsibilities in the facilitation and advisory roles. We suspect that by dangling the monetary carrot of federal dollars, municipalities will be more willing to enlarge commission mandates and perhaps even match federal dollars with local general fund revenue.

It is more than likely that this idea has already occurred to the capable folks at the IAOHRA, but the relatively short commission membership list is a key impediment to the organization's lobby clout. This is why the localized networking of commissions at the state and regional levels and the subsequent joining of IAOHRA are critical. Even though improved membership and organizational health does not guarantee success, the chances for government support in expanded commission mandates and resources should, invariably, increase the stronger IAOHRA becomes.

A FINAL IDEA TO THINK ABOUT

And here is where academic and private organizational collaborations with commissions may come full circle in helping HRCs improve their profiles. By assisting with reports and other data-related products regarding outcomes critical to commission activities, academic and private organizational partnerships can provide HRCs with a wide supply of material to push on commission websites and social media platforms and to directly distribute to elected officials and their staff. These external partners may also function as a "brain trust" of sorts to help tackle community problems that are both directly and tangentially related to a commission's mandate. In the process, commissions should seek to position themselves as key advisory bodies for as many government departments

and offices as possible, working to make the commission a hub of expertise and deliberation on behalf of the various intersecting issues under the
"human relations" banner.

As the case studies in Los Angeles and Cincinnati suggest, the greatest
challenge in this regard might be the broad mandates and resources
directed at municipal police forces. It is unrealistic to expect commissions
to have the same level of investment as police departments. Still, the trend
to source mediation, intergroup relations, and discrimination issues to
police agencies in cities where HRCs lack the quasi-judicial function can
only be slowed or reversed by commissions and their external allies making a strong and consistent case for HRCs to take their rightful place as
the bodies responsible for working on these issues. Indeed, the Los Angeles example of setting up a separate body is one way to address this
(although it remains to be seen if the new Civil and Human Rights Commission runs into similar resource competition issues with other city
departments, especially the LAPD).

But external partners alone cannot bolster commissions. In order for
these efforts to be successful, commission staff and the appointed commissioners themselves will need to step up their efforts to promote, defend,
and work to expand commission footprints in local government (and in
state and national associations, for that matter). A major theme throughout this book is that commissions of all types are hemmed in and feel the
strain of too few resources and variable levels of political support for their
work. We also show that commissioners and commission staff can often
feel overburdened with the nature of their work, leading to feelings of job
dissatisfaction and burnout. Asking these dedicated volunteers and professionals to give more of themselves may seem like asking too much.
Unfortunately, just as there seem to be a select few who are aware that
issues of human relations are critical for local governments to address, this
same select few will have to be part of the solution to bring the importance of HRC work to a wider array of constituencies. On the positive side,
with the continued efforts of those accustomed to working creatively for
solutions that are nonlinear and open-ended in nature, expansion of commission purviews and success may be in closer reach than we think.

APPENDIX

LIST OF HUMAN RELATIONS COMMISSIONS AND HUMAN RIGHTS COMMISSIONS IN THE UNITED STATES

1. Abington Township (PA) Human Relations Commission
2. Alaska Commission for Human Rights
3. Albany (OR) Human Relations Commission
4. Alexandria (VA) Human Rights Office
5. Ames (IO) Human Relations Commission
6. Anchorage (AK) Equal Rights Commission
7. Annapolis (MD) Human Relations Commission
8. Arizona Civil Rights Division
9. Atlanta (GA) Human Relations Commission
10. Aurora (IN) Human Relations Commission
11. Austin (TX) Human Relations Commission
12. Austin (TX) Human Rights Commission
13. Baltimore (MD) Community Relations Commission
14. Billings (MT) Human Rights Commission
15. Boston (MA) Human Rights Commission
16. Boulder (CO) Human Relations Commission
17. Brookings (SD) Human Rights Commission
18. Broward County (FL) Human Relations Commission
19. Buffalo Citizens Commission on Human Rights
20. California Department of Fair Employment and Housing
21. Clearwater (FL) Office of Community Relations
22. Carbondale (IL) Human Relations Commission

23. Cincinnati (OH) Human Relations Commission
24. Chandler (AR) Human Relations Commission
25. Chaska (MN) Human Rights Commission
26. Chula Vista Human Relations Commission
27. Clarksville (TN) Human Relations Commission
28. Colorado Civil Rights Division
29. Colorado Spring Human Relations Commission
30. Connecticut Commission on Human Rights and Opportunity
31. Corpus Christi Human Relations Commission
32. Dade County (FL) Fair Housing and Employment Commission
33. DeKalb (IL) Human Relations Commission
34. District of Columbia Office of Human Rights
35. East Chicago (IN) Human Rights Commission
36. East Lansing (MI) Human Relations Commission
37. El Cerrito (CA) Human Relations Commission
38. Elkhart (IN) Human Relations Commission
39. Erie County (PA) Human Relations Commission
40. Fairfax County (VA) Human Rights Commission
41. Fargo (ND) Human Relations Commission
42. Fayetteville-Cumberland Human Relations Commission
43. Ferguson (MO) Human Rights Commission
44. Florida Commission on Human Rights
45. Fort Collins (CO) Human Relations Commission
46. Fort Wayne (IN) Metropolitan Human Relations Commission
47. Fort Worth (TX) Human Relations Commission
48. Gary (IN) Human Relations Commission
49. Greenville (SC) Human Relations Commission
50. Haddonfield (NJ) Human Relations Commission
51. Haverford Township Human Relations Commission
52. Hawaii Department of Labor and Industrial Relations
53. Humboldt County (CA) Human Rights Commission
54. Hutchinson (KS) Human Relations Commission
55. Idaho Human Rights Commission
56. Illinois Department of Human Rights
57. Indiana Civil Rights Commission
58. Iowa City Human Rights Commission

59. Iowa Civil Rights Commission
60. Jacksonville (FL) Equal Employment Opportunity Commission
61. Kansas Commission on Civil Rights
62. Kirkwood (MO) Human Rights Commission
63. Lafayette (CO) Human Rights Commission
64. Lancaster (PA) Human Relations Commission
65. Lawrence (KS) Human Relations Commission
66. Long Beach (CA) Human Relations Commission
67. Los Angeles Citizens Commission on Human Rights
68. Lower Merion Township (PA) Human Relations Commission
69. Lexington–Fayette (KY) Urban County Human Rights Commission
70. Louisville and Jefferson County (KY) Human Relations Commission
71. Maine Human Rights Commission
72. Maryland Commission on Human Relations
73. Massachusetts Commission Against Discrimination
74. Melrose (MA) Human Rights Commission
75. Michigan Department of Civil Rights
76. Minneapolis Commission on Civil Rights
77. Minneapolis Department of Civil Rights
78. Minnesota Department of Human Rights
79. Missouri Commission on Civil Rights
80. Monmouth County Human Relations Commission
81. Montana Human Rights Division
82. Moorhead Human Rights Commission
83. Mountainview (CA) Human Relations Commission
84. Nashville (TN) Citizens Commission on Human Rights
85. Nebraska Equal Opportunity Commission
86. Nevada Commission on Equal Rights of Citizens
87. Newburgh (NY) Human Rights Commission
88. Newburyport (MA) Human Rights Commission
89. Newton (MA) Human Rights Commission
90. New Hampshire Commission for Human Rights
91. New Hanover County (NC) Human Relations Commission
92. New Jersey Division on Civil Rights
93. New Mexico Department of Work Force Solutions
94. New Mexico Human Rights Commission

95. New York City Commission on Human Rights
96. New York State Division on Human Rights
97. Norwalk (CT) Human Relations Commission
98. Ohio Civil Rights Commission
99. Oklahoma Human Rights Commission
100. Omaha (NE) Human Relations Department
101. Orange County (NC) Human Relations Commission
102. Oregon Bureau of Labor
103. Oregon Citizens Commission on Human Rights
104. Orlando (FL) Human Relations Department
105. Pasadena Human Relations Commission
106. Peekskill (NY) Human Relations Commission
107. Pennsylvania Human Relations Commission
108. Philadelphia Commission on Human Relations
109. Pittsburgh Commission on Human Relations
110. Portland (OR) Human Rights Commission
111. Pueblo (CO) Human Relations Commission
112. Puerto Rico Department of Labor and Human Resources
113. Redlands Human Relations Commission
114. Raleigh (NC) Human Relations Commission
115. Reading (PA) Human Relations Commission
116. Rhode Island Commission for Human Rights
117. Rocky Mount (NC) Human Relations Commission
118. Sacramento Citizens Commission on Human Rights
119. San Diego Human Relations Commission
120. San Francisco (CA) Human Rights Commission
121. San Luis Obispo (CA) Human Relations Commission
122. Scottsdale (AZ) Human Relations Commission
123. Seattle (OR) Citizens Commission on Human Rights
124. Shorewood (WI) Human Relations Commission
125. Sioux City (IO) Human Rights Commission
126. South Florida Citizens Commission on Human Rights
127. St. Louis Civil Rights Enforcement Agency
128. St. Petersburg (FL) Human Relations Department
129. Seattle Human Rights Commission
130. Skokie (IL) Human Relations Commission

131. Sommerville (MA) Human Rights Commission
132. South Bend (IN) Human Rights Commission
133. South Carolina Human Affairs Commission
134. South Dakota Division of Human Rights
135. Suffolk County (NY) Human Rights Commission
136. Sullivan County (NY) Human Rights Commission
137. Tacoma (WA) Human Relations Division
138. Tennessee Human Rights Commission
139. Texas Commission on Human Rights
140. Texas Health and Human Services Commission Civil Rights Office
141. Toledo (OH) Human Relations Commission
142. Topeka (KS) Human Relations Commission
143. University City (MO) Human Relations Commission
144. Utah Industrial Commission, Anti-Discrimination Division
145. Vermillion (SD) Human Relations Commission
146. Vermont Attorney General's Office, Civil Rights Division
147. Virgin Islands Department of Labor
148. Virginia Division of Human Rights Office of the Attorney General
149. Virginia Beach Human Rights Commission
150. Wakefield (MA) Human Rights Commission
151. Washington Human Rights Commission
152. West Orange (NJ) Human Relations Commission
153. West Virginia Human Rights Commission
154. Wilmington / New Hanover County (NC) Community Relations Advisory Committee
155. Winston-Salem Human Relations Commission
156. Wisconsin Equal Rights Division, Department of Industry, Labor and Human Relations
157. Wyoming Fair Employment Practices Commission

TABLES PERTAINING TO CHAPTER 5

TABLE A.1 Sample Demographics

	SAMPLE	U.S. CENSUS, LOS ANGELES COUNTY
FEMALE (%)	63	51
LATINO (%)	43	48
AFRICAN AMERICAN (%)	13	9
ASIAN (%)	11	15
ANGLO (%)	32	26
MEDIAN AGE	43	37
BACHELOR DEGREE OR HIGHER	35	32

TABLE A.2 Comparison of Means on Political Commonality with Other Groups, According to Treatments (1–4 Scale)

SUBJECTS' TREATMENT CUES	PERCEIVED COMMONALITY WITH		
ANGLOS (N=419)	**AFRICAN AMERICANS**	**ASIANS**	**LATINOS**
COLLECTIVE IDENTITY	3.39*	3.30*	2.97ф
SUBGROUP DISTINCTIVE	2.50	2.75	2.69
COMBINED IDENTITY	2.41	2.70	2.63
CONTROL	2.36	2.59	2.49
LATINOS (N=533)	**AFRICAN AMERICANS**	**ASIANS**	**ANGLOS**
COLLECTIVE IDENTITY	3.10*	3.05*	3.23*
SUBGROUP DISTINCTIVE	2.75	2.37	2.45
COMBINED IDENTITY	2.65	2.33	2.31
CONTROL	2.67	2.33	2.49
AFRICAN AMERICANS (N=155)	**ASIANS**	**LATINOS**	**ANGLOS**
COLLECTIVE IDENTITY	3.21*	3.06	3.41*
SUBGROUP DISTINCTIVE	2.06	2.94	2.22
COMBINED IDENTITY	2.29	3.07	2.26
CONTROL	2.39	3.11	2.40

Note: * = $p < .01$ for Tukey HSD pairwise comparisons between the Collective Identity treatment cue and the other three randomly assigned groups, including the control. ф = $p < .01$ for Tukey HSD pairwise comparisons between the Collective Identity treatment cue and Combined Identity treatment cue and control groups only.

TABLE A.3 Anglo Subjects' Perceived Commonality with African Americans, Asians, and Latinos

	AFRICAN AMERICANS		ASIANS		LATINOS	
	COEFF. (ROBUST SE)	MIN → MAX PROBABILITY	COEFF. (ROBUST SE)	MIN → MAX PROBABILITY	COEFF. (ROBUST SE)	MIN → MAX PROBABILITY
COLLECTIVE IDENTITY CUE	2.23*** (0.36)	.41	1.43*** (0.35)	.24	.612** (0.29)	.13
SUBGROUP IDENTITY CUE	.079 (0.29)	.02	.144 (0.32)	.03	.013 (0.31)	.003
COMBINED CUE	-.127 (0.28)	-.03	.134 (0.30)	.03	.100 (0.29)	.03
INTERGROUP CONTACT	.172 (0.13)	.16	.178 (0.13)	.14	.093 (0.13)	.08
KNOWLEDGE OF WATTS	.057 (0.11)	.05	.163 (0.11)	.12	.180* (.103)	.16
AGE	-.003 (0.01)	-.03	.003 (0.01)	.04	-.007 (0.01)	-.09
FEMALE	-.300 (0.23)	-.05	-.673** (0.30)	-.13	-.528** (0.22)	-.12

DEMOCRAT	.340 (0.26)	.08	-.300 (0.28)	-.06	.154 (0.25)	.04
REPUBLICAN	-.269 (0.29)	-.06	-.663** (0.30)	-.14	-.224 (0.28)	-.05
COLLEGE GRADUATE	-.012 (0.24)	.00	.102 (0.25)	.02	.157 (0.23)	.04
INCOME < 50K	-.304 (0.25)	-.07	-.794*** (0.27)	.02	.134 (0.25)	.03
CONSTANT	-.416 (0.75)		.257 (0.78)		.168 (0.72)	
BASELINE	.64		.73		.65	
LOG-LIKELIHOOD	-243.5		-226.1		-259.2	
WALD CHI²	60.6		45.9		17.5	
PROB > F	.000		.000		.100	
PSEUDO R²	.13		.10		.03	
N	418		411		410	

* = $p < .10$, ** = $p < .05$, *** = $p < .01$ in two-tailed tests. Unstandardized logistic regression coefficients.

TABLE A.4 Latino Subjects' Perceived Commonality with African Americans, Asians, and Anglos

	AFRICAN AMERICANS		ASIANS		ANGLOS	
	COEFF. (ROBUST SE)	MIN → MAX PROBABILITY	COEFF. (ROBUST SE)	MIN → MAX PROBABILITY	COEFF. (ROBUST SE)	MIN → MAX PROBABILITY
COLLECTIVE IDENTITY	.970*** (0.28)	.19	1.15*** (0.26)	.27	1.19*** (0.28)	.28
SUBGROUP IDENTITY	.055 (0.26)	.01	.077 (0.26)	.02	-.153 (0.26)	-.04
COMBINED	-.021 (0.25)	-.01	.197 (0.25)	.05	-.128 (0.26)	-.03
INTERGROUP CONTACT	.045 (0.10)	.04	.090 (0.10)	.09	.069 (0.11)	.07
KNOWLEDGE OF WATTS	.319 (0.25)	.07	.207 (0.24)	.05	.296 (0.24)	.07
AGE	-.010 (0.01)	-.08	-.010 (0.01)	-.09	.010 (0.01)	.06
FEMALE	-.076 (0.21)	-.02	-.622** (0.20)	-.15	-.506** (0.21)	-.12

DEMOCRAT	−.110 (0.21)	−02	.063 (0.20)	.02	.168 (0.21)	.04
REPUBLICAN	−.088 (0.31)	−.02	.545 (0.30)	.13	.833** (0.34)	.20
COLLEGE GRADUATE	.184 (0.20)	.04	.115 (0.19)	.03	.090 (0.20)	.02
INCOME <50K	−.140 (0.20)	−.04	−.138 (0.19)	−.03	−.526** (0.20)	−.13
CONSTANT	.706 (.596)		−.042 (0.58)		−.244 (0.60)	
BASELINE	.67		.49		.54	
LOG-LIKELIHOOD	−329.8		−347.0		−319.3	
WALD CHI²	19.7		41.6		52.7	
PROB > F	.050		.000		.000	
PSEUDO R²	.03		.06		.09	
N	533		534		508	

* = $p < .10$, ** = $p < .05$, *** = $p < .01$ in two-tailed tests. Unstandardized logistic regression coefficients.

TABLE A.5 African American Subjects' Perceived Commonality with Latinos, Asians, and Anglos

	LATINOS		ASIANS		ANGLOS	
	COEFF. (ROBUST SE)	MIN → MAX PROBABILITY	COEFF. (ROBUST SE)	MIN → MAX PROBABILITY	COEFF. (ROBUST SE)	MIN → MAX PROBABILITY
COLLECTIVE IDENTITY	-1.00 (0.67)	-.15	1.49** (0.53)	.35	1.91** (0.59)	.41
SUBGROUP IDENTITY	-.732 (0.65)	-.10	-.472 (0.50)	-.12	-.449 (0.49)	-.11
COMBINED	-1.16 (0.63)	-.17	-.210 (0.49)	-.05	-.335 (0.47)	-.08
INTERGROUP CONTACT	.520** (0.26)	.29	.148 (0.17)	.15	-.071 (0.18)	.07
KNOWLEDGE OF WATTS	.549** (.23)	.30	-.128 (.145)	-.13	.144 (.144)	.14
AGE	-.014 (0.02)	-.09	.019 (0.19)	.24	-.012 (0.02)	-.16
FEMALE	-.519 (0.50)	-.06	.883** (0.44)	.21	.094 (0.41)	.02

220

	.455 (0.56)	.06	.528 (0.43)	.13	.402 (0.45)	.10
DEMOCRAT	.455 (0.56)	.06	.528 (0.43)	.13	.402 (0.45)	.10
REPUBLICAN	−.030 (1.07)	−.01	1.51 (1.03)	.33	2.17* (1.22)	.39
COLLEGE GRADUATE	−1.22** (0.53)	−.18	.520 (0.39)	.13	−.218 (0.41)	−.05
INCOME<50K	−.663* (0.50)	−.09	−.186 (0.38)	−.05	−.169 (0.38)	−.05
CONSTANT	.227 (1.52)		−2.29** (1.17)		−.123 (1.17)	
BASELINE		.84		.47		.53
LOG-LIKELIHOOD	−63.3		−93.6		−92.3	
WALD CHI²	19.5		23.2		20.5	
PROB > F	.15		.020		.040	
PSEUDO R²	.05		.13		.13	
N	154		155		154	

* = $p < .10$, ** = $p < .05$, *** = $p < .01$ in two-tailed tests. Unstandardized logistic regression coefficients.

TABLES PERTAINING TO CHAPTER 6

TABLE A.6A

2018 U.S. CENSUS ESTIMATES: HAMILTON COUNTY, OHIO			HAMILTON COUNTY, OHIO ($N = 1078$)		
AFRICAN AMERICAN	ANGLO	FEMALE	AFRICAN AMERICAN	ANGLO	FEMALE
27%	68%	52%	44%	56%	58%

TABLE A.6B

2018 U.S. CENSUS ESTIMATES: COMPTON, CALIFORNIA			COMPTON, CALIFORNIA ($N = 682$)		
AFRICAN AMERICAN	LATINO	FEMALE	AFRICAN AMERICAN	LATINO	FEMALE
31%	67%	51%	17%	83%	56%

TABLE A.6C

2018 U.S. CENSUS ESTIMATES: PITTSBURGH, PENNSYLVANIA			PITTSBURGH, PENNSYLVANIA ($N = 1754$)		
AFRICAN AMERICAN	ANGLO	FEMALE	AFRICAN AMERICAN	ANGLO	FEMALE
24%	67%	51%	16%	76%	53%

TABLE A.7 Cincinnati Resident Perceptions of CPD and Local Courts

	TRUST CINCINNATI POLICE COEFF. (ROBUST SE) MIN → MAX		TRUST COURTS COEFF. (ROBUST SE) MIN → MAX		CPD IS LEGITIMATE COEFF. (ROBUST SE) MIN → MAX	
	AFRICAN AMERICANS	NON-AFRICAN AMERICANS	AFRICAN AMERICANS	NON-AFRICAN AMERICANS	AFRICAN AMERICANS	NON-AFRICAN AMERICANS
PERCEIVED DISCRIMINATION TREATMENT	-.735** (0.19)	.434* (.23)	-.742*** (0.21)	.450** (.20)	-.548*** (0.19)	.373* (.22)
	.18	.06	.15	.08	.14	.05
FEMALE	.077 (0.20)	-.037 (.23)	.020 (0.22)	-.021 (.20)	-.518*** (0.20)	-.176 (.222)
	.02	-.01	.003	.004	.13	-.02
AGE	.069 (0.05)	.396** (.08)	-.100 (0.30)	.336*** (.07)	.105* (0.56)	.191** (.082)
	.10	.41	.11	.42	.16	.18
INCOME	.100** (0.05)	.222 (.05)	.062 (0.05)	.254*** (.05)	.165*** (0.48)	.139*** (.05)
	.16	.25	.09	.36	.28	.15
EDUCATION	-.001 (.07)	-.153 (.09)	-.100 (.079)	-.003 (.08)	-.024 (.072)	.023 (.09)
	.002	-.10	.11	.003		.02
CONSTANT	-.478 (0.38)	-1.03 (.55)	.044 (0.39)	-2.28 (.52)	-.551 (0.38)	-.402 (.57)

(continued)

223

TABLE A.7 Cincinnati Resident Perceptions of CPD and Local Courts (Continued)

	TRUST CINCINNATI POLICE COEFF. (ROBUST SE) MIN → MAX		TRUST COURTS COEFF. (ROBUST SE) MIN → MAX		CPD IS LEGITIMATE COEFF. (ROBUST SE) MIN → MAX	
	AFRICAN AMERICANS	NON-AFRICAN AMERICANS	AFRICAN AMERICANS	NON-AFRICAN AMERICANS	AFRICAN AMERICANS	NON-AFRICAN AMERICANS
BASELINE	.48	.85	.29	.76	.48	.83
LOG-LIKELIHOOD	−314.1	−256.4		−314.4		
WALD CHI²	22.1	46.0	17.6	58.8	34.8	20.1
PROB > F	.000	.000	.004	.000	.000	.001
PSEUDO R²	.03	.09	.03	.10	.06	.04
N	470	608	470	608	470	608

* = $p < .10$, ** = $p < .05$, *** = $p < .01$ in two-tailed tests. Unstandardized negative binomial regression coefficients.

TABLE A.8 Cincinnati Resident Perceptions of CCA

	TRUST COMPLAINT AUTHORITY COEFF. (ROBUST SE) MIN → MAX		RELATIONS IMPROVED SINCE COLLABORATIVE AGREEMENT COEFF. (ROBUST SE) MIN → MAX	
PERCEIVED DISCRIMINATION TREATMENT	−.520*** (0.21) −.10	.452*** (.17) .10	−.511*** (0.20) −.12	−.094 (.17) .03
FEMALE	.026 (0.22) .01	−.211 (.175) −.05	.040 (0.21) .01	−.066 (.18) −.02
AGE	.197*** (0.10) .22	.153** (.07) .20	.154** (0.06) .21	.270*** (.07) .38
INCOME	.050 (0.05) .07	.028 (.04) .04	.128*** (0.05) .21	.054 (.04) .09
EDUCATION	−.181** (.08) .23	.073 (.07) .10	−.021 (.07) −.03	.201*** (.07) .29
CONSTANT	−.946 (0.44)	−2.07 (.50)	−1.47 (0.43)	−2.43 (.49)
BASELINE	.27	.36	.36	.58
LOG-LIKELIHOOD	−268.7	−387.8	−297.1	−393.9
WALD CHI²	17.0	18.7	20.5	36.1
PROB > F	.010	.002	.000	.000
PSEUDO R²	.03	.02	.04	.05
N	470	608	470	608

* = $p < .10$, ** = $p < .05$, *** = $p < .01$ in two-tailed tests. Unstandardized negative binomial regression coefficients.

TABLE A.9 Angeleno Respondent Trust in Group

	COEFF. (ROBUST SE) MIN → MAX				
	TRUST MUSLIMS	TRUST JEWS	TRUST CHRISTIANS	TRUST ATHEISTS	TRUST LGBT
INCLUSIVE TREATMENT	.615*** (0.19) .15	.603*** (0.20) .14	−.183 (0.19) −.05	.068 (0.19) .02	.278 (0.19) .07
EXCLUSIVE TREATMENT	.061 (0.19) .02	.094 (0.19) .02	.073 (0.19) .02	−.364* (0.19) −.09	−.499*** (0.20) .12
BIBLE IS GOD'S WORD	.030 (0.07) .03	.033 (0.07) .03	.146** (0.07) .14	−.037 (0.07) −.04	−.200*** (0.07) .19
BORN AGAIN	−.1330 (0.09) .13	−.144 (0.09) .14	−.092 (0.10) −.09	.049 (0.09) .05	.116 (0.09) .11
FRIENDS/ COWORKERS DIFFERENT	−.236 (0.11) .17	−.092 (0.11) −.07	−.134 (0.11) −.10	.155 (0.11) .12	.143 (0.11) .10
SEX	−.338** (0.17) −.08	.102 (0.17) .02	.079 (0.16) .02	−.387 (0.16) .10	−.082 (0.17) −.02
AGE	−.286*** (0.11) .26	−.111 (0.11) −.11	−.004 (0.11) −.004	−.048 (0.11) −.05	−.018 (0.11) −.02
INCOME	−.141 (0.09) .17	.125 (0.09) .15	−.144 (0.09) .18	−.004 (0.01) −.01	.001 (.09) .001
AFRICAN AMERICAN	−.523** (0.22) −.13	.059 (0.23) .01	−.015 (0.22) −.004	−.029 (0.22) −.01	−.183 (0.23) −.04
CONSTANT	1.48*** (0.43)	.367 (0.43)	.558 (0.42)	−.170 (0.41)	−.262 (0.42)
BASELINE	.47	.61	.54	.45	.14
LOG-LIKELIHOOD	−453.44	−448.2	−464.9	−462.4.4	−449.9
WALD CHI²	36.9	15.5	11.3	14.5	24.5
PROB > F	.000	.08	.25	.11	.004
PSEUDO R²	.03	.02	.01	.02	.03
N	682	682	682	682	682

$* = p < .10$, $** = p < .05$, $*** = p < .01$ in two-tailed tests. Unstandardized negative binomial regression coefficients.

TABLE A.10 Pittsburgh Resident Reports of Discrimination and Landlord Problems

	TOTAL LANDLORD REPAIR PROBLEMS	TOTAL WORKER DISCRIMINATION	TOTAL CITY DISCRIMINATION
	COEFF. (ROBUST SE) MIN → MAX		
PERCEIVED DISCRIMINATION TREATMENT	.464*** (0.08) 1.60	.453*** (0.10) .45	.309* (0.17) .33
AFRICAN AMERICAN	.198*** (0.07) .81	.567 (0.14) .69	−.042 (0.25) −.04
LATINO	.301** (0.15) 1.34	.082 (0.31) .08	−.360 (0.53) −.33
SEX	−.190*** (0.06) −.74	−.044 (0.10) .04	−.092 (0.10) −.09
INCOME	−.024 (0.02) −.63	−.00001 (0.03) −.0004	−.057 (0.04) −.42
AGE	−.087*** (0.03) −1.60	−.286*** (0.04) −1.69	.024 (0.06) .19
CONSTANT	1.37*** (0.13)	.668*** (0.18)	.227 (0.32)
TREATMENT EFFECT W/O CONTROLS	.493*** (0.08) 1.72	.514*** (0.10) .57	.291* (.172) .31
ALPHA	.247*** (0.03)	3.58 (0.22)	10.2 (0.74)
PROB > = CHIBAR²	.000	.000	.000
BASELINE	3.88	.99	1.08
LOG-LIKELIHOOD	−1206.7	−2304.5	−1592.2
WALD CHI²	70.3	100.3	7.01
PROB > CHI²	.000	.000	.320
PSEUDO R	.03	.02	.002
N	524	1771	1,509

* = $p < .10$, ** = $p < .05$, *** = $p < .01$ in two-tailed tests. Unstandardized negative binomial regression coefficients.

NOTES

INTRODUCTION

The events related in this chapter are from the authors' firsthand accounts as they attended Watts Gang Task Force meetings with LAHRC and LAPD personnel from 2013 to 2015.

1. HUMAN RELATIONS COMMISSIONS

1. Kenneth L. Saunders and Hyo Eun (April) Bang, "A Historical Perspective on U.S. Human Rights Commissions," in *Executive Session Papers: Human Rights Commissions and Criminal Justice*, no. 3, ed. by Marea L. Beeman (Cambridge, Mass.: Kennedy School of Government, Harvard University, 2007).
2. U.S. Department of Justice, "Guidelines for Effective Human Relations Commissions," rev. September 1998, updated March 2003, https://www.justice.gov/archive/crs/pubs/gehrc.htm#2.
3. Paul M. Ong, Andre Comandon, Alycia Cheng, and Sylvia González, *South Los Angeles Since the Sixties: Half a Century of Progress?* (Los Angeles: Center for Neighborhood Knowledge, UCLA Luskin School of Public Affairs, n.d.), 4. http://www.aasc.ucla.edu/news/SLA_Since_The_60s_FullRpt.pdf.
4. Governor's Commission on the Los Angeles Riots, "Violence in the City—An End or A Beginning: A Report" (Sacramento: State of California, 1965), 38.
5. See Ong et al., "South Los Angeles Since the Sixties."
6. Ong et al., "South Los Angeles Since the Sixties."
7. Ong et al., "South Los Angeles Since the Sixties."
8. See Judith Taylor, "The Emotional Contradictions of Identity Politics: A Case Study of a Failed Human Relations Commission," *Sociological Perspectives* 49, no. 2 (2006): 217–37, https://doi.org/10.1525%2Fsop.2006.49.2.217.

9. Philip J. Ethington and Christopher D. West, *The Challenge of Intergroup Relations in Los Angeles: An Historical and Comparative Evaluation of the Los Angeles City Human Relations Commission, 1966–1998*, Department of History and The Southern California Studies Center of the University of Southern California, Los Angeles City Human Relations Commission, 1998.

10. On trust in institutions, see Angus Campbell, Philip E. Converse, and Willard L. Rodgers, *The Quality of American Life: Perceptions, Evaluations, and Satisfactions* (New York: Russell Sage Foundation, 1976); and Karen S. Cook, Russell Hardin, and Margaret Levi, *Cooperation Without Trust?* (New York: Russell Sage Foundation, 2005). On connectedness between residents, see Mark Baldassare, *The Growth Dilemma: Residents' Views and Local Population Change in the United States* (Berkeley: University of California Press, 1981).

11. Laurence J. O'Toole Jr. and Robert S. Montjoy, "Interorganizational Policy Implementation: A Theoretical Perspective," *Public Administration Review* 44, no. 6 (November–December 1984): 491–503.

12. Terry Nichols Clark and Lorna Crowley Ferguson, *City Money: Political Processes, Fiscal Strain, and Retrenchment* (New York: Columbia University Press, 1983); and Jack Citrin, "Comment: The Public Relevance of Trust in Government," *American Political Science Review* 68, no. 3 (September 1974): 973–88, https://doi.org/10.2307/1959141.

13. Louis Wirth, "Urbanism as a Way of Life," *American Journal of Sociology* 44, no. 1 (July 1938): 1–24. http://www.jstor.org/stable/2768119.

14. Janet L. Abu-Lughod, *Race, Space, and Riots in Chicago, New York, and Los Angeles* (New York: Oxford, 2007), 270–71.

15. See Robert B. Denhardt and Janet Vinzant Denhardt, "The New Public Service: Serving Rather Than Steering," *Public Administration Review* 60, no. 6 (November–December 2000): 549–59. https://doi.org/10.1111/0033-3352.00117.

16. Renée A. Irvin and John Stansbury, "Citizen Participation in Decision Making: Is It Worth the Effort?" *Public Administration Review* 64, no. 1 (February 2007): 55–65. https://doi.org/10.1111/j.1540-6210.2004.00346.x.

17. Abu-Lughod, *Race, Space, and Riots*, 270–71.

18. See Kenneth Meier and Laurence J. O'Toole, "Political Control Versus Bureaucratic Values: Reframing the Debate," *Public Administration Review* 66, no. 2 (2006): 177–92, https://doi.org/10.1111/j.1540-6210.2006.00571.x.

19. On "creativity" as market-driven, economically focused developments in urban planning, see Mark Pennington, *Planning and the Political Market: Public Choice and the Politics of Failure* (New Brunswick, N.J.: Athlone Press, 2000). On Healy's use of "creativity" in urban governance as a process with spiritual or cultural dimensions, see Patsy Healey, "Creativity and Urban Governance," Policy Studies 25, no. 2 (June 2004): 87–102. https://dx.doi.org/10.1080/0144287042000262189.

20. Meier and O'Toole, "Political Control versus Bureaucratic Values."

21. See Ray H. MacNair, Russell Caldwell, and Leonard Pollane, "Citizen Participants in Public Bureaucracies: Foul-Weather Friends," *Administration & Society* 14, no. 4 (1983):

507–24. https://dx.doi.org/10.1177%2F009539978301400405. See also Ronald K. Mitchell, Bradley R. Agle, and Donna J. Wood, "Toward a Theory of Stakeholder Identification and Salience: Defining the Principle of Who and What Really Counts," *Academy of Management Review* 22, no. 4 (October 1997): 853–886. https://dx.doi.org/10.2307/259247.

22. Gary J. Miller, "The Political Evolution of Principal-Agent Models," *Annual Review of Political Science* 8 (2005): 203–225, https://doi.org/10.1146/annurev.polisci.8.082103.104840.

23. Meier and O'Toole, "Political Control versus Bureaucratic Values," 180.

24. James Q. Wilson, *What Government Agencies Do and Why They Do It* (New York: Basic Books, 1989).

25. Ethington and West, "The Challenge of Intergroup Relations in Los Angeles."

26. Saunders and Bang, "A Historical Perspective on U.S. Human Rights Commissions."

27. Ed Cairns, Jared Kenworthy, Andrea Campbell, and Miles Hewstone, "The Role of in-Group Identification, Religious Group Membership and Intergroup Conflict in Moderating In-Group and Out-Group Affect," *British Journal of Social Psychology* 45, no. 4 (2006): 701–16, https://doi.org/10.1348/014466605X69850.

28. Abu-Lughod, *Race, Space, and Riots*, 270–71.

29. We use black and African American interchangeably. When we use Anglo, we specifically refer to people who are non-Latino or non-Hispanic whites.

2. THE HISTORY OF INTERGROUP RELATIONS IN AMERICA

1. Michael Omi and Howard Winant. *Racial formation in the United States* (New York: Routledge, 2014).

2. See, e.g., Barbara Fields, "Ideology and Race in American History," in *Region, Race, and Reconstruction: Essays in Honor of C. Vann Woodward*, ed. by J. Morgan Kousser and James M. McPherson, 143–77. (New York: Oxford University Press, 1982). See also Rodney Hero, *Latinos and the U.S. Political System* (Philadelphia: Temple University Press, 1992).

3. John E. Bodnar, *Immigration and Industrialization: Ethnicity in an American Mill Town, 1870–1940* (Pittsburgh: University of Pittsburgh Press, 1977); and Joan Wallach Scott, *Gender and the Politics of History*, rev. ed. (New York: Columbia University Press, 1999).

4. Ronald H. Bayor, "Historical Encounters: Intergroup Relations in a 'Nation of Nations.'" *Annals of the American Academy of Political and Social Science* 530, no. 1 (1993): 15, https://doi.org/10.1177%2F0002716293530001002.

5. See Gary R. Mormino and George E. Pozzetta, *The Immigrant World of Ybor City: Italians and Their Latin Neighbors in Tampa, 1885–1985* (Champaign: University of Illinois Press, 1987); and Aidan McGarry and James M. Jasper, eds., *The Identity Dilemma: Social Movements and Collective Identity* (Philadelphia: Temple University Press, 2015).

6. Thomas J. Archdeacon, *New York City, 1664–1710: Conquest and Change* (Ithaca, N.Y.: Cornell University Press, 1976).

7. Michael J. Feldberg, *The Philadelphia Riots of 1844: A Study of Ethnic Conflict* (Westport, Conn.: Greenwood, 1975).

8. Bayor, "Historical Encounters."

9. Paul A. Gilje, *The Road to Mobocracy: Popular Disorder in New York City, 1763–1834.* (Chapel Hill: University of North Carolina Press, 2014), 137.

10. Nikki Marie Taylor, *Frontiers of Freedom: Cincinnati's Black Community, 1802–1866* (Columbus: Ohio University Press, 2005).

11. Bayor, "Historical Encounters."

12. We use the term "American Indians" or just "Indians" rather than "Native Americans" to separate this group from the anti-immigrant term used by the nativist elements described previously, including the political party known as the Native American Party.

13. Joanne Nagel, *American Indian Ethnic Renewal: Red Power and the Resurgence of Identity and Culture* (New York: Oxford University Press, 1997).

14. U.S. Department of Interior, Indian Affairs. "FAQs: Why Tribes Exist Today in the United States," n.d., https://www.bia.gov/FAQs/.

15. David Wilkins, *American Indian Politics and the American Political System* (Lanham, Md.: Rowman & Littlefield, 2007).

16. Nagel, *American Indian Ethnic Renewal.*

17. A federally recognized tribe is an American Indian or Alaska Native tribal entity that is recognized as having a government-to-government relationship with the United States, with the responsibilities, powers, limitations, and obligations attached to that designation, and is eligible for funding and services from the Bureau of Indian Affairs.

18. Kenneth R. Philp, *Termination Revisited: American Indians on the Trail to Self-Determination, 1933–1953* (Lincoln: University of Nebraska Press, 2002), 21–33.

19. Kenneth R. Philp, "Stride toward Freedom: The Relocation of Indians to Cities, 1952–1960," *Western Historical Quarterly* 16, no. 2 (April 1985): 175–90.

20. Dennis Banks, *Ojibwa Warrior: Dennis Banks and the Rise of the American Indian Movement* (Norman: University of Oklahoma Press, 2005).

21. National Congress of American Indians (NCAI) and the U.S. Department of Interior, Office of Indian Energy and Economic Development, "Native American Economic Policy Report: Developing Tribal Economies to Create Healthy, Sustainable and Culturally Vibrant Communities," 2007, http://www.ncai.org/resources/ncai-publications/native-american-economic-policy-report.pdf.

22. Henry Louis Gates Jr., "Slavery by the Numbers," *The Root*, February 10, 2014, https://www.theroot.com/slavery-by-the-numbers-1790874492.

23. James M. McPherson, *Battle Cry of Freedom: The Civil War Era* (Cambridge: Oxford University Press, 1988).

24. McPherson, *Battle Cry of Freedom.*

25. James Marten, "Slavery and Causes of the American Civil War." *Encyclopedia Britannica Blog,* April 11, 2011, http://blogs.britannica.com/2011/04/slavery-american-civil-war/.

26. Christopher A. Bracey, "Civil Rights Act of 1866," n.d., http://www.encyclopedia.com/social-sciences-and-law/law/law/civil-rights-act-1866.

27. Lynching Statistics by Year, http://law2.umkc.edu/faculty/projects/ftrials/shipp/lynchingyear.html.

28. Isabel Wilkerson, *The Warmth of Other Suns: The Epic Story of America's Great Migration* (New York: Random House, 2010).

29. Stewart E. Tolnay, "Jim Crow's Legacy: The Lasting Impact of Segregation," *Contemporary Sociology: A Journal of Reviews* 4, no. 1 (2017): 114.

30. Robert VanGiezen and Albert E. Schwenk, "Compensation from Before World War I Through the Great Depression," U.S. Bureau of Labor Statistics, January 30, 2003, https://www.bls.gov/opub/mlr/cwc/compensation-from-before-world-war-i-through-the-great-depression.pdf.

31. Gail Lumet Buckley, *American Patriots: The Story of Blacks in the Military from the Revolution to Desert Storm* (New York: Random House, 2002).

32. Wilkerson, *The Warmth of Other Suns.*

33. Cameron McWhirter, *Red Summer: The Summer of 1919 and the Awakening of Black America* (New York: Henry Holt, 2011).

34. Sheila Fitzpatrick, *The Russian Revolution* (New York: Oxford University Press, 2008).

35. William M. Tuttle, *Race Riot: Chicago in the Red Summer of 1919* (University of Illinois Press, 1996); and Janet L. Abu-Lughod, *Race, Space, and Riots in Chicago, New York, and Los Angeles* (New York: Oxford, 2007).

36. Chicago Commission on Race Relations (CCRR), *The Negro in Chicago: A Study of Race Relations and a Race Riot* (Chicago: University of Chicago, 1922).

37. CCRR, *The Negro in Chicago*; Tuttle, *Race Riot*; and Abu-Lughod, *Race, Space, and Riots.*

38. Annette McDermott, "Did World War II Launch the Civil Rights Movement?" History Channel, October 19, 2018, https://www.history.com/news/did-world-war-ii-launch-the-civil-rights-movement.

39. Beth Bailey and David Farber, "The "Double-V" Campaign in World War II Hawaii: African Americans, Racial Ideology, and Federal Power," *Journal of Social History* 26, no. 4 (1993): 817–43.

40. Roger Daniels, *Prisoners Without Trial: Japanese Americans in World War II* (New York: Hill and Wang, 2004).

41. Luis R. Fraga, John J. Garcia, Rodney Hero, Michael Jones-Correa, Valerie Martinez-Ebers, and Gary Segura, *Latino Lives in America: Making It Home* (Philadelphia: Temple University Press, 2010).

42. A very small number of wealthy residents in New Mexico were allowed to stay and retain their Mexican citizenship.

43. Renata Keller, *Mexico's Cold War: Cuba, the United States, and the Legacy of the Mexican Revolution* (Cambridge: Cambridge University Press, 2015).

44. Jason Steinhauer, "The History of Mexican Immigration to the U.S. in the Early 20th Century," *Insights: Scholarly Work at the John W. Klug Center* (blog), March 11, 2015, https://blogs.loc.gov/kluge/2015/03/the-history-of-mexican-immigration-to-the -u-s-in-the-early-20th-century/.

45. Susan Currell and Christina Cogdell, *Popular Eugenics: National Efficiency and American Mass Culture in the 1930s* (Athens: Ohio University Press, 2006).

46. Quoted in Steinhauer, "The History of Mexican Immigration to the U.S."

47. Steinhauer, "The History of Mexican Immigration to the U.S."

48. Maurico Mazón, *The Zoot-Suit Riots: The Psychology of Symbolic Annihilation* (Austin: University of Texas Press, 2010).

49. With the exception of the 65th Infantry Regiment from Puerto Rico.

50. Richard Steele, "The Federal Government Discovers Mexican Americans," in *World War II and Mexican American Civil Rights*, ed. by Richard Griswold del Castillo, 19–33 (Austin: University of Texas Press, 2008).

51. Kelly Lytle Hernández, "The Crimes and Consequences of Illegal Immigration: A Cross-Border Examination of Operation Wetback, 1943 to 1954," *Western Historical Quarterly*, 37, no. 4 (2006): 421–44, https://doi.org/10.2307/25443415.

52. Greta Weber, "Cuba's 'Peter Pans' Remember Childhood Exodus," *National Geographic*, August 14, 2015, https://news.nationalgeographic.com/2015/08/150814-cuba -operation-peter-pan-embassy-reopening-Castro/.

53. Robert L. Bach, "The Cuban Exodus: Political and Economic Motivations." In *The Caribbean Exodus*, ed. Barbara B. Levine, 106–30 (New York: Praeger, 1987).

54. Jorge Duany, "Cuban Migration: A Postrevolution Exodus Ebbs and Flows," *Migration Information Resource*, July 6, 2017, https://www.migrationpolicy.org/article/cuban -migration-postrevolution-exodus-ebbs-and-flows.

55. Duany, "Cuban Migration."

56. Duany, "Cuban Migration."

57. Bach, "The Cuban Exodus."

58. Duany, "Cuban Migration."

59. Darrel Wanzer-Serano, *The New York Young Lords and the Struggle for Liberation* (Philadelphia: Temple University Press, 2015).

60. Lisa García Bedolla, *Latino Politics* (Hoboken NJ: Wiley, 2015).

61. Abu-Lughod, *Race, Space, and Riots*.

62. Gary Orfield, *Must We Bus? Segregated Schools and National Policy* (Washington, D.C.: Brookings Institution Press, 1978).

63. See Gunner Myrdal, *An American Dilemma: The Negro Problem and Modern Democracy*, 2 vols. (New York: Harper, 1944).

64. Herbert Roof Northup, Richard L. Rowan, Darold T. Barnum, and John C. Howard, *Negro Employment in Southern Industry* (Philadelphia: University of Pennsylvania, 1970); William Cohen, "Negro Involuntary Servitude in the South." *Journal of Southern*

History 42, no. 1 (February 1976): 31–60; and Gavin Wright, *Old South, New South: Revolutions in the Southern Economy Since the Civil War* (New York: Basic Books, 1986).

65. David R. James, "The Transformation of the Southern Racial State: Class and Race Determinants of Local-State Structures," *American Sociological Review* 53, no. 2 (April 1988): 191–208.

66. Pamela Irving Jackson and Leo Carroll, "Race and the War on Crime: The Sociopolitical Determinants of Municipal Police Expenditures in 90 non-Southern U.S. Cities," *American Sociological Review* 46, no. 3 (June 1981): 290–305. https://www.jstor.org/stable/2095061.

67. Richard Quinney and John Wildeman, *The Problem of Crime: A Critical Introduction to Criminology* (New York: HarperCollins, 1977).

68. Peter B. Kraska, "Militarization and Policing—Its Relevance to 21st Century Police," *Policing* 1, no. 4 (2007): 501–13. https://doi.org/10.1093/police/pam065.

69. William H. Frey and Reynolds Farley, "Latino, Asian, and Black Segregation in U.S. Metropolitan Areas: Are Multiethnic Metros Different?" *Demography* 33, no. 1 (1996): 35–50.

70. See Joe William Trotter, *The Great Migration in Historical Perspective: New Dimensions of Race, Class, and Gender* (Bloomington: University of Indiana Press, 1991); Mark Ellis and Richard Wright "Assimilation and Differences Between the Settlement Patterns of Individual Immigrants and Immigrant Households," *Proceedings of the National Academy of Sciences* 102 (October 2005): 15325–30; and Dennis R. Judd and Dick W. Simpson, eds., *The City, Revisited: Urban Theory from Chicago, Los Angeles, and New York* (Minneapolis: University of Minnesota Press, 2011).

71. Paula McClain, "Coalition and Competition: Patterns of Black-Latino Relations in Urban Politics," in *The Politics of Minority Coalitions: Race, Ethnicity, and Shared Uncertainties*, ed. by Wilbur Rich (New York: Praeger, 1996).

72. John H. Mollenkopf and Manuel Castells, eds., *Dual City: Restructuring New York* (New York: Russell Sage Foundation, 1991); and Raphael Sonenshein, *Politics in Black and White: Race and Power in Los Angeles* (Princeton, N.J.: Princeton University Press, 1993).

73. Anna Brown, "Key Takeaways on U.S. Immigration: Past, Present and Future" (Washington, D.C.: Pew Research Center, 2015), http://pewrsr.ch/1P15CEb.

74. George C. Galster, "Black Suburbanization: Has It Changed the Relative Location of Races?" *Urban Affairs Reviews* 26, no. 4 (1991): 621–28. https://doi.org/10.1177%2F004208169102600410.

75. Kenneth J. Meier and Joseph Stewart Jr., "Cooperation and Conflict in Multiracial School Districts," *Journal of Politics* 53, no. 4 (199): 1123–33, https://dx.doi.org/10.2307/2131870; and Paula D. McClain and Steven C. Tauber, "Black and Latino Socioeconomic and Political Competition: Has a Decade Made a Difference?" *American Politics Research* 26, no. 2 (1998): 237–52. https://dx.doi.org/10.1177/1532673X9802600206.

76. C. Henry and Carlos Munoz Jr., "Ideological and Interest Linkages in California Rainbow Politics." In *Racial and Ethnic Politics in California*, ed. by Bryan O. Jackson and Michael B. Preston. Berkeley, Calif.: IGS Press, 1991); and Paula D. McClain, "The Changing Dynamics of Urban Politics: Black and Hispanic Municipal Employment—Is There Competition?" *Journal of Politics* 55, no. 2 (1993): 399–414, https://doi.org/10.2307/2132272.

77. Douglas S. Massey and Nancy A. Denton, *American Apartheid: Segregation and the Making of the Underclass* (Cambridge, Mass.: Harvard University Press, 1993).

78. Jolene Kirschenman and Kathryn M. Neckerman, "'We'd Love to Hire Them, But . . .': The Meaning of Race for Employers." In *The Urban Underclass*, ed. by Christopher Jencks and Paul E. Peterson (Washington, D.C.: Brookings Institution Press, 1991).

79. Michael Jones-Correa, ed., *Governing American Cities: Inter-Ethnic Coalitions, Competition, and Conflict* (New York: Russell Sage Foundation, 2001).

80. Bernard H. Ross and Myron A. Levine, *Urban Politics: Power in Metropolitan America* (Itasca, Ill.: F.E. Peacock, 1996).

81. Sonenshein, *Politics in Black and White*.

82. Jones-Correa, *Governing American Cities*.

83. Jones-Correa, *Governing American Cities*; and Sonenshein, *Politics in Black and White*.

3. ORIGINS AND DEVELOPMENT OF ORGANIZED HUMAN RELATIONS EFFORTS

1. Philip Ethington and Christopher West, "The Challenge of Intergroup Relations in Los Angeles: An Historical and Comparative Evaluation of the Los Angeles City Human Relations Commission, 1966–1998," Department of History and The Southern California Studies Center of the University of Southern California, Los Angeles City Human Relations Commission, 1998.

2. Ethington and West, "The Challenge of Intergroup Relations," 11.

3. Chicago Commission on Race Relations (CCRR), *The Negro in Chicago: A Study of Race Relations and a Race Riot* (Chicago: University of Chicago Press, 1922).

4. CCRR, *The Negro in Chicago*, 645.

5. Robert E. Park, *Race and Culture* (Glencoe, Ill.: Free Press, 1950).

6. St. Claire Drake and Horace R. Cayton, *Black Metropolis: A Study of Negro Life in a Northern City* (Chicago: University of Chicago, 1945).

7. Ethington and West, "The Challenge of Intergroup Relations."

8. State of Maryland, Commission on Civil Rights, "About MCCR," n.d., https://mccr.maryland.gov/Pages/About-MCCR.aspx.

9. State of Maryland, Commission on Civil Rights, "About MCCR."

10. Kenneth R. Janken, "The Civil Rights Movement: 1919–1960s," TeacherServe, National Humanities Center, n.d., accessed July 2, 2019, http://nationalhumanitiescenter.org/tserve/freedom/1917beyond/essays/crm.htm.

11. Phillip J. Obermiller and Thomas Wagner, *The Cincinnati Human Relations Commission: A History, 1943–2013* (Columbus: Ohio University Press, 2014), 3.

12. Obermiller and Wagner, *The Cincinnati Human Relations Commission*, 5.

13. New York City Human Rights Commission, "Commission's History," n.d., accessed April 9, 2019, https://www1.nyc.gov/site/cchr/about/commissions-history.page.

14. Dan W. Dodson, "The Mayor's Committee on Unity of New York City," *Journal of Educational Sociology* 19, no. 5 (1946): 289, https://doi.org/10.2307/2263229.

15. Ethington and West, "The Challenge of Intergroup Relations," 18.

16. Ralph Bunche, the first African American to receive a Ph.D. in political science, was Myrdal's lead research assistant in the study's first year, when research questions and design were developed. Bunche's influence is reflected in the attention paid to the exclusion of African Americans from political deliberations.

17. Kenneth L. Saunders and Hyo Eun (April) Bang, "A Historical Perspective on U.S. Human Rights Commissions," in *Executive Session Papers: Human Rights Commissions and Criminal Justice*, no. 3, ed. by Marea L. Beeman (Cambridge, MA: Kennedy School of Government, Harvard University, 2007).

18. The ACRR was underwritten by the Julius Rosenwald's Foundation, the same benefactor who provided the bulk of funding for the comprehensive study of the 1919 Chicago riot.

19. "For Policemen: Plan Course in Race Relations" *Pittsburgh Courier*, March 30, 1946. https://www.newspapers.com/clip/1707726/american_council_on_race_relations/.

20. Edwin R. Embree, "The American Council on Race Relations," *Journal of Negro Education* 13, no. 4 (1944): 562–64. www.jstor.org/stable/2292514.

21. Quoted in Ethington and West, "The Challenge of Intergroup Relations," 15.

22. Saunders and Bang, "A Historical Perspective on U.S. Human Rights Commissions."

23. José Angel Gutiérrez, *The Making of a Chicano Militant: Lessons from Cristal* (Madison: University of Wisconsin Press, 1998); and Stokely Carmichael, Charles V. Hamilton, and Kwame Ture, *Black Power: The Politics of Liberation in America* (New York: Vintage, 1992).

24. Ronald Takaki, *Iron Cages: Race and Culture in Nineteenth-Century America* (New York: Knopf, 1979).

4. THE HUMANS WHO MUST RELATE

1. Robert S. Montjoy and Laurence J. O'Toole, "Toward a Theory of Policy Implementation: An Organizational Perspective." *Public Administration Review* 39, no. 5 (1979): 465–476.

2. City of Fort Worth, "Human Relations Commission," n.d., accessed January 18, 2020, http://fortworthtexas.gov/boards/human-relations/.

3. City of Fort Worth, Texas, Code of Ordinances, ch. 17, § 17-49(a), Investigation of Alleged Violations; Filing Complaint, http://library.amlegal.com/nxt/gateway.dll

/Texas/ftworth_tx/cityoffortworthtexascodeofordinances/partiicitycode /chapter17humanrelations?f=templates$fn=default.htm$3.0$vid=amlegal:fort worth_tx$anc=JD_Ch.17Art.IIIDiv.2.

4. The City of Pittsburgh, "Chapter 653: Human Relations Commission," n.d., accessed December 6, 2019, https://library.municode.com/pa/pittsburgh/codes/code_of_ordinances?nodeId=COOR_TITSIXCO_ARTVDI_CH653HURECO.

5. City of Los Angeles, Office of the City Clerk, *General Information on City Commissions*. Last revised October 2016, https://clerk.lacity.org/sites/g/files/wph606/f/City%20 Commissions%20General%20Information.pdf.

6. Montjoy and O'Toole, "Toward a Theory of Policy Implementation."

7. Montjoy and O'Toole, "Toward a Theory of Policy Implementation."

8. Patsy Healey, "Creativity and Urban Governance," *Policy Studies* 25, no. 2 (June 2004): 87–102.

9. Healey, "Creativity and Urban Governance," 97.

10. Healey, "Creativity and Urban Governance."

11. Torill Strand, "Metaphors of Creativity and Workplace Learning," *Scandinavian Journal of Educational Research* 55, no. 4 (2011): 346.

12. Strand, "Metaphors of Creativity and Workplace Learning," 346.

13. See Geoff Mulgan, "The Process of Social Innovation," *Innovations* (MIT Press), Spring 2006: 145–62.

14. Mark Matthews, Chris Lewis, and Grahame Cook. 2009. "Public Sector Innovation: A Review of the Literature." In *Innovation in the Public Sector: Enabling Better Performance, Driving New Directions: Better Practice Guide* (Canberra, Australia: ANAO, 2009), 60–62.

15. Fiona Patterson, Máire Kerrin, and Geraldine Gatto-Roissard, "Characteristics and Behaviours of Innovative People in Organisations: Literature Review," paper prepared for NESTA Policy and Research Unit, London, December 9, 2009. https://media.nesta .org.uk/documents/characteristics_behaviours_of_innovative_people.pdf.

16. Charles Landry, *The Creative City: A Toolkit for Urban Innovators* (New York: Routledge, 2008). See also John Howard, *Innovation, Ingenuity, and Initiative: The Adoption and Application of New Ideas in Australian Local Government* (Canberra: ANSZOG Institute for Governance; and Sydney: Australian Centre of Excellence for Local Government, September 12, 2012), http://hdl.handle.net/10453/42114; and Mark Evans, Chris Aulich, Anne Howard, Megan Peterson, and Richard Reid, *Innovation in Local Government: Defining the Challenge, Making the Change* (Sydney: ACLEG, University of Technology Sydney; and Canberra: ANZSOG Institute for Governance, 2012).

17. Montjoy and O'Toole, "Toward a Theory of Policy Implementation."

18. Robert Alan Dahl, *A Preface to Democratic Theory*, 2nd. ed. (Chicago: University of Chicago Press, 1970).

19. Kenneth Meier and Laurence J. O'Toole, "Political Control Versus Bureaucratic Values: Reframing the Debate" *Public Administration Review* 66, no. 2 (2006): 178, https:// doi.org/10.1111/j.1540-6210.2006.00571.x. See also John Brehm and Scott Gates, *Working,*

Shirking, and Sabotage: Bureaucratic Response to a Democratic Public (Ann Arbor: University of Michigan Press, 1997).

20. Lorraine Bradley, interviewed by Brian Calfano and Valerie Martinez-Ebers, May 15, 2016, Los Angeles, Calif.

21. Christopher Connelly, "Fort Worth Is the Largest City in Texas Not Opposing SB4," *KERA National Public Radio*, August 2, 2017, https://www.kut.org/post/fort-worth-largest-city-texas-not-opposing-sb4.

22. Luke Ranker, "Fort Worth Anti-Discrimination Official Accused of Posting Racist Content on Facebook." *Fort Worth Star Telegram*, July 2, 2019, https://www.star-telegram.com/news/local/fort-worth/article232189932.html.

23. Luke Ranker, "For Years Fort Worth Officials Knew of Anti-Racism Commissioner's Offensive Posts," *Fort Worth Star Telegram*, July 3, 2019, https://www.star-telegram.com/news/local/fort-worth/article232253907.html.

24. Ranker, "For Years Fort Worth Officials Knew."

25. Ranker, "For Years Fort Worth Officials Knew."

26. Ranker, "Fort Worth Anti-Discrimination Official."

5. EXPERIMENTING WITH THE DYNAMICS OF INTERGROUP IDENTITY

1. Gordon W. Allport, *The Nature of Prejudice* (Reading, Mass.: Addison Wesley, 1954); Patricia Villasenor, director, Los Angeles Human Relations Commission, interview, April 29, 2015, Los Angeles, Calif.

2. Interview with Patricia Villasenor, director, Los Angeles Human Relations Commission on April 29, 2015, Los Angeles, CA.

3. Samuel L. Gaertner, J. A. Mann, A. Murrell, and John F. Dovidio, "Reducing Intergroup Bias: The Benefits of Re-categorization," *Journal of Personality and Social Psychology* 57, no. 2 (1989): 239–49, https://psycnet.apa.org/doi/10.1037/0022-3514.57.2.239; John E. Transue, "Identity Salience, Identity Acceptance, and Racial Policy Attitudes: American National Identity as a Uniting Force," *American Journal of Political Science* 51, no. 1 (2007): 78–91, https://doi.org/10.1111/j.1540-5907.2007.00238.x; and Thomas F. Pettigrew, Linda R. Tropp, Ulrich Wagner, and Oliver Christ, "Recent Advances in Intergroup Contact Theory," *International Journal of Intercultural Relations* 35, no. 3 (2011): 271–80, https://doi.org/10.1016/j.ijintrel.2011.03.001.

4. Manuela Barreto and Naomi Ellemers, "The Impact of Respect Versus Neglect of Self-Identities on Identification and Group Loyalty," *Personality and Social Psychology Bulletin* 28, no. 5 (2002): 629–39, https://doi.org/10.1177%2F0146167202288007; Roberto González and Rupert Brown, "Dual Identities in Intergroup Contact: Group Status and Size Moderate the Generalization of Positive Attitude Change," *Journal of Experimental Social Psychology* 42, no. 6 (2006): 753–67, https://doi.org/10.1016/j.jesp.2005.11.008; and Jack Citrin and David O. Sears, *American Identity and the Politics of Multiculturalism* (New York: Cambridge University Press, 2014).

5. Jeffrey C. Dixon and Michael S. Rosenbaum, "Nice to Know You? Testing Contact, Cultural, and Group Threat Theories of Anti-Black and Anti-Hispanic Stereotypes," *Social Science Quarterly* 85, no. 2 (June 2004): 257–80, https://doi.org/10.1111/j.0038 -4941.2004.08502003.x; and Jeffrey C. Dixon, "The Ties That Bind and Those That Don't: Toward Reconciling Group Threat and Contact Theories of Prejudice," *Social Forces* 84, no. 4 (June 2006): 2179–204, https://doi.org/10.1353/sof.2006.0085.

6. Henri Tajfel, *Human Groups and Social Categories: Studies in Social Psychology* (Cambridge: Cambridge University Press, 1981).

7. Sonia Roccas and Marilynn B. Brewer, "Social Identity Complexity," *Personality and Social Psychology Review* 6, no. 2 (2002): 88–106, https://doi.org/10.1207%2FS153 27957PSPR0602_01.

8. Henri Tajfel and John L. M. Dawson, *Disappointed Guests: Essays by African, Asian, and West Indian Students* (London: Oxford University Press, 1965); and Donald R. Kinder and David O. Sears, "Prejudice and Politics: Symbolic Racism versus Racial Threats to the Good Life, *Journal of Personality and Social Psychology* 40, no. 3: 414–31, https://psycnet.apa.org/doi/10.1037/0022-3514.40.3.414.

9. For theories from social psychology, see Matthew J. Hornsey and Michael A. Hogg, "Subgroup Relations: A Comparison of Mutual Intergroup Differentiation and Common Ingroup Identity Models of Prejudice Reduction," *Personality and Social Psychology Bulletin* 26, no. 2 (2000): 242–25, https://doi.org/10.1177%2F0146167200264010; and González and Brown, "Dual Identities in Intergroup Contact." On identity as a variable construct, see John F. Dovidio, Samuel L. Gaertner, and Tamar Saguy, "Commonality and the Complexity of 'We': Social Attitudes and Social Change," *Personality and Social Psychology Review* 13, no. 1 (2009): 3–20, https://doi.org/10.1177%2F1088868 308326751.

10. Henri Tajfel, "Cognitive Aspects of Prejudice," *Journal of Social Issues* 25, no. 4 (1969): 79–97, https://doi.org/10.1111/j.1540-4560.1969.tb00620.x; and Michael A. Hogg and John C. Turner, "Interpersonal Attraction, Social Identification and Psychological Group Formation," *European Journal of Social Psychology* 15, no. 1 (1985): 51–66.

11. David A. Wilder, "Perceiving Persons as a Group: Categorization and Intergroup Relations," in *Cognitive Processes in Stereotyping and Intergroup Behavior*, ed. by David L. Hamilton, 213–58 (Hillsdale, N.J.: Erlbaum, 1981).

12. John F. Dovidio, Samuel L. Gaertner, Ana Validzic, Kimberly Matoka, Brenda Johnson, and Stacy Frazier, "Extending the Benefits of Recategorization: Evaluations, Self-Disclosure, and Helping," *Journal of Experimental Social Psychology* 33, no. 4 (1997): 401–40.

13. Dovidio, Gaertner, and Saguy, "Commonality and the Complexity of 'We,'" 5.

14. Samuel L. Gaertner and John F. Dovidio, *Reducing Intergroup Bias: The Common Ingroup Identity Model* (Philadelphia: Psychology Press, 2000).

15. Gaertner and Dovidio, *Reducing Intergroup Bias*; and Dovidio, Gaertner, and Saguy, "Commonality and the Complexity of 'We.'"

16. Hornsey and Hogg, "Subgroup Relations."

17. González and Brown, "Dual Identities in Intergroup Contact"; Hornsey and Hogg, "Subgroup Relations"; and Citrin and Sears, *American Identity and the Politics of Multiculturalism*.

18. Transue, "Identity Salience, Identity Acceptance, and Racial Policy Attitudes."

19. Luigi Castelli, Luciano Arcuri, and Luciana Carraro, "Projection Processes in the Perception of Political Leaders," *Basic and Applied Social Psychology* 31, no. 3 (2009): 189–96, https://doi.org/10.1080/01973530903058151.

20. Barreto and Ellemers, "The Impact of Respect Versus Neglect of Self-Identities."

21. Allport, *The Nature of Prejudice*; Miles Hewstone and Rupert Brown, "Contact Is Not Enough: An Intergroup Perspective on the 'Contact hypothesis,'" in *Contact and Conflict in Intergroup Encounters*, ed. by M. Hewstone and R. Brown (Oxford: Blackwell, 1986); and Pettigrew et al., "Recent Advances in Intergroup Contact Theory."

22. Allport, *The Nature of Prejudice*.

23. Everett, Jim A. C., "Intergroup Contact Theory: Past, Present, and Future," *Inquisitive Mind* 17, no. 2 (2013).

24. Hewstone and Brown, "Contact Is Not Enough"; and W. Scott Ford, "Favorable Intergroup Contact May Not Reduce Prejudice: Inconclusive Journal Evidence, 1960–1984," *Sociology and Social Research* 70 (1986): 256–58.

25. Pettigrew et al., "Recent Advances in Intergroup Contact Theory," 271.

26. Allport, *The Nature of Prejudice*.

27. Sandra Jovchelovitch, "Trust and Social Representations: Understanding the Relations Between Self and Other in the Brazilian Public Sphere," in *Trust and Distrust: Sociocultural Perspectives*, ed. by Ivana Marková and Alex Gillispie, 105–20 (Charlotte, N.C.: Information Age Publishing, 2008); Pierre Nora, "Between Memory and History: Les lieux de mémoire," *Representations*, no. 26 (Spring 1989): 7–24; James H Liu and Denis J. Hilton, "How the Past Weighs on the Present: Social Representations of History and Their Role in Identity Politics," *British Journal of Social Psychology* 44, no. 4 (2005): 537–56; Leonie Huddy, "From Social to Political Identity: A Critical Examination of Social Identity Theory," *Political Psychology* 22, no. 1 (2001): 127–56; and Peter J. Verovšek, "Collective Memory, Politics, and the Influence of the Past: The Politics of Memory as a Research Paradigm," *Politics, Groups, and Identities* 4, no. 3 (2016): 529–53.

28. Jovchelovitch, "Trust and Social Representations," 115.

29. Liu and Hilton, "How the Past Weighs on the Present," 537.

30. On international or subnational conflict, see Verovšek, "Collective Memory, Politics, and the Influence of the Past." On the relationship of historical events with individuals' policy preferences, see Michael Dawson, *Behind the Mule: Race and Class in African American Politics* (Princeton, N.J.: Princeton University Press, 1994); and Leonie Huddy and Stanley Feldman, "Americans Respond Politically to 9/11: Understanding the Impact of the Terrorist Attacks and Their Aftermath," *American Psychologist* 66 (2011): 455–67.

31. Dawson, *Behind the Mule*.

32. Gabriel R. Sanchez and Eduardo Vargas, "Taking a Closer Look at Group Identity: The Link Between Theory and Measurement of Group Consciousness and Linked Fate," *Political Research Quarterly* 69 (2016): 160–74.

33. See Philip J. Ethington, William H. Frey, and Dowell Myers, "The Racial Resegregation of Los Angeles County, 1940–2000," Race Contours 2000 Study, Public Research Report No. 2001-04 (University of Southern California and University of Michigan, 2001).

34. Gerald Horne, *Fire this Time: The Watts Uprising and the 1960s* (Charlottesville: University of Virginia Press, 1995).

35. Livia Gershon, "Did The 1965 Watts Riots Change Anything?" *JSTOR Daily*, July 13, 2016, https://daily.jstor.org/did-the-1965-watts-riots-change-anything/.

36. Vincent Jeffries, Ralph H. Turner, and Richard T. Morris, "The Public Perception of the Watts Riot as Social Protest," *American Sociological Review* 36, no. 3 (June 1971): 443–51, https://dx.doi.org/10.2307/2093084.

37. Brian J. Gaines, James H. Kuklinski, and Paul J. Quirk, "The Logic of the Survey Experiment Revisited." *Political Analysis* 15, no. 1 (2007): 1–20. https://doi.org/10.1093/pan/mpl008.

38. U.S. Census Bureau, American Community Survey 1-Year Estimates, Los Angeles County Estimates for Age, Sex, Education, Income and Homeownership, generated by Valerie Martinez-Ebers on June 1, 2018 using American FactFinder, https://factfinder.census.gov/faces/nav/jsf/pages/community_facts.xhtml.

39. But see Kevin Wallsten and Tatishe M. Nteta, "Race, Partisanship, and Perceptions of Inter-minority Commonality," *Politics, Groups, and Identities* 4, no. 2 (2017): 298–320.

40. Following standard protocols for "opt-in" panels, our sample is composed of people who previously agreed to participate in online surveys for compensation. The compensation for survey participation is negotiated and paid by Qualtrics. We paid Qualtrics a set price per completed survey.

41. Kevin J. Mullinix, Thomas J. Leeper, James N. Druckman, and Jeremy Freese, "The Generalizability of Survey Experiments," *Journal of Experimental Political Science* 2, no. 2 (2015): 109, https://doi.org/10.1017/XPS.2015.19.

42. Miliaikeala Heen, Joel Lieberman, and Terance Miethe, "A Comparison of Different Online Sampling Approaches for Generating National Samples," *Center for Crime and Justice Policy*, September 2014, 1–8; and Taylor C. Boas, Dino P. Christenson, and David M. Glick, "Recruiting Large Online Samples in the United States and India: Facebook, Mechanical Turk and Qualtrics," *Political Science Research and Methods*, August 8, 2018, https://doi.org/10.1017/psrm.2018.28.

43. U.S. Census Bureau, American Community Survey 1-Year Estimates.

44. Transue, "Identity Salience, Identity Acceptance, and Racial Policy Attitudes."

45. Allport, *The Nature of Prejudice*.

46. The open-ended question read: "How comfortable were you in in answering the question [treatment cue assigned to the subject]?"

47. Responses: 1= "Nothing," "2" = "Little," "3" = "Some," and 4 = "A lot."
48. Elze G. Ufkes, Sabine Otten, Karen I. Van Der Zee, Ellen Giebels, and John F. Dovidio, "Urban District Identity as a Common Ingroup Identity: The Different Role of Ingroup Prototypicality for Minority and Majority Groups," *European Journal of Social Psychology* 42, no. 6 (October 2012): 706–16, https://doi.org/10.1002/ejsp.1888.
49. Ufkes et al., "Urban District Identity as a Common Ingroup Identity."
50. Luis Ricardo Fraga, John A. Garcia, Rodney E. Hero, Michael Jones-Correa, Valerie Martinez-Ebers, and Gary M. Segura, *Latino Lives in America: Making It Home* (Philadelphia: Temple University Press, 2010); Sanchez and Vargas, "Taking a Closer Look at Group Identity"; and Leonie Huddy, "Group Identity and Political Cohesion," in *The Oxford Handbook of Political Psychology*, 2nd ed., ed. by David O Sears, Leonie Huddy, and Robert Jervis, 511–58 (New York: Oxford University Press, 2003).
51. Claudine Gay, Jennifer Hochschild, and Ariel White, "Americans' Belief in Linked Fate: Does the Measure Capture the Concept?" *Journal of Race, Ethnicity, and Politics* 1, no. 1 (March 2016): 117–44, https://dx.doi.org/10.1017/rep.2015.3.
52. Pettigrew et al., "Recent Advances in Intergroup Contact Theory."
53. Betina Cutaia Wilkinson, "Perceptions of Commonality and Latino–Black, Latino–White Relations in a Multiethnic United States," *Political Research Quarterly* 67, no. 4 (2014): 905–16, https://doi.org/10.1177%2F1065912914540217; and Paula McClain and Joseph Stewart Jr., *Why Can't We All Get Along? Racial and Ethnic Minorities in American Politics* (Boulder, Colo.: Westview, 2002).
54. Transue, "Identity Salience, Identity Acceptance, and Racial Policy Attitudes"; and Wallsten and Nteta, "Race, Partisanship, and Perceptions of Inter-Minority Commonality."
55. Huddy, "From Social to Political Identity."

6. REPORTING AND RESPONDING TO COMMUNITY

1. Phillip J. Obermiller and Thomas Wagner, *The Cincinnati Human Relations Commission: A History, 1943–2013* (Columbus: Ohio University Press, 2014), 67.
2. See, e.g., *Protests over Police Violence*, CBS News, last visited October 25, 2018, http://www.cbsnews.com/feature/protests-over-police-violence/; and Ashley Fantz and Steve Visser, "Hundreds Arrested in Protests over Shootings by Police," CNN, August 4, 2016, https://www.cnn.com/2016/07/10/us/black-lives-matter-protests/.
3. Obermiller and Wagner, *The Cincinnati Human Relations Commission*, 65.
4. Thomas, quoted in Obermiller and Wagner, *The Cincinnati Human Relations Commission*, 70–71.
5. Quoted in Obermiller and Wagner, *The Cincinnati Human Relations Commission*, 76.
6. United States District Court, Southern District of Ohio, Western Division, In Re Cincinnati Policing, Case No. C-1-99-317, https://www.cincinnati-oh.gov/police/linkservid/27A205F1-69E9-4446-BC18BD146CB73DF2/showMeta/0/.

7. Saul Green, Joseph E. Brann, Jeffrey A. Fagan, and John E. Eck, "Progress Report: City of Cincinnati Collaborative Agreement Bias-Free Policing and Officer Accountability," September 21, 2017, p. 1–2, accessed at https://www.cincinnati-oh.gov/police/assets /File/Bias-Free%20Policing%20%26%20Officer%20Accountability%20Progress%20 Report%20-%20Saul%20Green%209-21-17.pdf.

8. See, e.g., President's Task Force on 21st Century Policing, Department of Justice, *Final Report of the President's Task Force on 21st Century Policing*, May 2015, https://cops .usdoj.gov/pdf/taskforce/taskforce_finalreport.pdf.

9. C. Thomas and J. Hyman, "Perceptions of Crime, Fear of Victimization, and Public Perceptions of Police Performance," *Journal of Police Science and Administration* 5 (September 1977): 305–17; and Ben Brown and Wm Reed Benedict, "Perceptions of the Police: Past Findings, Methodological Issues, Conceptual Issues and Policy Implications," *Policing: An International Journal of Police Strategies & Management*, 25, no. 3 (2002): 543–80.

10. Liqun Cao, James Frank, and Francis T. Cullen, "Race, Community Context and Confidence in the Police," *American Journal of Police* 15, no. 1 (1996): 3–22, https://doi.org /10.1108/07358549610116536.

11. Elaine B. Sharp and Paul E. Johnson, "Accounting for Variation in Distrust of Local Police," *Justice Quarterly* 26, no. 1 (2009): 157–82, https://doi.org/10.1080/07418820 802290496.

12. Robert J. Sampson and Dawn Jeglum Bartusch, "Legal Cynicism and (Subcultural?) Tolerance of Deviance: The Neighborhood Context of Racial Differences," *Law & Society Review* 32, no. 4 (1988): 777–804

13. Joumana Silyan-Saa, "Government Community Engagement Methods: City of Los Angeles Case Study," *Journal of the Moroccan Interdisciplinary Center for Strategic and International Studies*, 2012.

14. Rodney Stark and Roger Finke, *Acts of Faith: Explaining the Human Side of Religion* (Berkeley: University of California Press, 2000).

15. Paul A. Djupe and Brian Robert Calfano, *God Talk: Experimenting with the Religious Causes of Public Opinion* (Philadelphia: Temple University Press, 2013), 171. See also R. Scott Appleby, "Religions, Human Rights and Social Change," in *The Freedom to Do God's Will: Religious Fundamentalism and Social Change*, ed. by James Busuttil and Gerrie ter Harr (New York: Routledge, 2003), 181–82.

16. Djupe and Calfano, *God Talk*.

17. Valerie Martinez-Ebers, Brian Calfano, and Regina Branton, "Bringing People Together: Improving Intergroup Relations via Group Identity Cues," *Urban Affairs Review*, online first, June 9, 2019, http://dx.doi.org/10.1177/1078087419853390.

18. Megan Stanley and Carlos Torres. "Pittsburgh Commission on Human Relations: Pittsburgh Human Rights Assessment." October 2018. Unpublished Report.

19. Bernie Hogan and Brent Berry, "Racial and Ethnic Biases in Rental Housing: An Audit Study of Online Apartment Listings," *City and Community* 10, no. 4 (2011): 351–72, https://doi.org/10.1111/j.1540-6040.2011.01376.x.

7. IMAGINING HUMAN RELATIONS FOR THE FUTURE

1. Kenneth J. Meier, Laurence J. O'Toole Jr., and Alisa Hicklin, "I've Seen Fire and I've Seen Rain: Public Management and Performance after a Natural Disaster," *Administration & Society* 41, no. 8 (2010): 979–1003.
2. "Promoting Civil and Human Rights Around the World," International Association of Official Human Rights Agencies, accessed November 1, 2019, https://www.iaohra.org/about-us.

BIBLIOGRAPHY

Abu-Lughod, Janet L. *Race, Space, and Riots in Chicago, New York, and Los Angeles.* New York: Oxford, 2007.

Allport, Gordon W. *The Nature of Prejudice.* Reading, Mass.: Addison Wesley, 1954.

Appleby, R. Scott. "Religions, Human Rights and Social Change." In *The Freedom to Do God's Will: Religious Fundamentalism and Social Change*, ed. by James Busuttil and Gerrie ter Harr, 197–229. New York: Routledge, 2003.

Archdeacon, Thomas J. *New York City, 1664–1710: Conquest and Change.* Ithaca, N.Y.: Cornell University Press, 1976.

Bach, Robert L. "The Cuban Exodus: Political and Economic Motivations." In *The Caribbean Exodus*, ed. Barbara B. Levine, 106–30. New York: Praeger, 1987.

Bailey, Beth, and David Farber. "The "Double-V" Campaign in World War II Hawaii: African Americans, Racial Ideology, and Federal Power." *Journal of Social History* 26, no. 4 (1993): 817–43.

Baldassare, Mark. *The Growth Dilemma: Residents' Views and Local Population Change in the United States.* Berkeley: University of California Press, 1981.

Banks, Dennis. *Ojibwa Warrior: Dennis Banks and the Rise of the American Indian Movement.* Norman: University of Oklahoma Press, 2005.

Barreto, Manuela, and Ellemers, Naomi. "The Impact of Respect Versus Neglect of Self-Identities on Identification and Group Loyalty." *Personality and Social Psychology Bulletin* 28, no. 5 (2002): 629–39. https://doi.org/10.1177%2F0146167202288007.

Bayor, Ronald H. "Historical Encounters: Intergroup Relations in a 'Nation of Nations.'" *Annals of the American Academy of Political and Social Science* 530, no. 1 (1993): 14–27. https://doi.org/10.1177%2F0002716293530001002.

Bedolla, Lisa García. *Latino Politics.* Hoboken NJ: Wiley, 2015.

Bernstein, Iver. *The New York City Draft Riots: Their Significance for American Society and Politics in the Age of the Civil War.* New York: Bison, 2010.

Boas, Taylor C., Dino P. Christenson, and David M. Glick. "Recruiting Large Online Samples in the United States and India: Facebook, Mechanical Turk and Qualtrics."

Political Science Research and Methods, August 8, 2018. https://doi.org/10.1017/psrm .2018.28.

Bobo, Lawrence D., Melvin L. Oliver, James H. Johnson Jr., and Abel Valenzuela Jr. "Analyzing Inequality in Los Angeles." In *Prismatic Metropolis: Inequality in Los Angeles*, ed. by Lawrence D. Bobo, Melvin L. Oliver Jr., James H. Johnson, and Abel Valenzuela Jr., 3–50. New York: Russell Sage Foundation, 2000.

Bodnar, John E. *Immigration and Industrialization: Ethnicity in an American Mill Town, 1870–1940*. Pittsburgh: University of Pittsburgh Press, 1977.

Brehm, John, and Scott Gates. *Working, Shirking, and Sabotage: Bureaucratic Response to a Democratic Public*. Ann Arbor: University of Michigan Press, 1997.

Brewer, Marilyn B., and Norman Miller. "Beyond the Contact Hypothesis: Theoretical Perspectives on Desegregation." In *Groups in Contact: The Psychology of Desegregation*, ed. by Norman S. Miller and Marilyn B. Brewer, 281–302. San Diego, CA: Academic Press, 1984.

Brown, Anna. "Key Takeaways on U.S. Immigration: Past, Present and Future." Washington, D.C.: Pew Research Center, 2015. http://pewrsr.ch/1P15CEb.

Brown, Ben, and Benedict, Wm Reed. "Perceptions of the Police: Past Findings, Methodological Issues, Conceptual Issues and Policy Implications." *Policing: An International Journal of Police Strategies & Management* 25, no. 3 (2002): 543–80.

Buckley, Gail Lumet. *American Patriots: The Story of Blacks in the Military from the Revolution to Desert Storm*. New York: Random House, 2002.

Cairns, Ed, Jared Kenworth, Andrea Campbell, and Miles Hewstone. "The Role of Ingroup Identification, Religious Group Membership, and Intergroup Conflict in Moderating In-Group and Out-Group Affect." *British Journal of Social Psychology* 45, no. 4 (2006): 701–16. https://doi.org/10.1348/014466605X69850.

Camarillo, Albert M. "Cities of Color: The New Racial Frontier in California's Minority-Majority Cities." In *The City Reader*, 6th ed., ed by. Richard T. LeGates and Frederic Stout, 139–48. New York: Routledge, 2015.

Campbell, Angus, Philip E. Converse, and Willard L. Rodgers. *The Quality of American Life: Perceptions, Evaluations, and Satisfactions*. New York: Russell Sage Foundation, 1976.

Cao, Liqun, James Frank, and Francis T. Cullen. "Race, Community Context and Confidence in the Police." *American Journal of Police* 15, no. 1 (1996): 3–22. https://doi .org/10.1108/07358549610116536.

Carmichael, Stokely. *Stokely Speaks: From Black Power to Pan-Africanism*. Chicago: Chicago Review Press, 2007.

Carmichael, Stokely, Charles V. Hamilton, and Kwame Ture. *Black Power: The Politics of Liberation in America*. New York: Vintage, 1992.

Carrigan, William D., and Clive Webb. "The Lynching of Persons of Mexican Origin or Descent in the United States, 1848 to 1928." *Journal of Social History* 37, no. 2 (2003): 411–38. https://doi.org/10.1353/jsh.2003.0169.

Castelli, Luigi, Luciano Arcuri, and Luciana Carraro. "Projection Processes in the Perception of Political Leaders." *Basic and Applied Social Psychology* 31, no. 3 (2009): 189–96. https://doi.org/10.1080/01973530903058151.

Chicago Commission on Race Relations (CCRR). *The Negro in Chicago: A Study of Race Relations and a Race Riot.* Chicago: University of Chicago, 1922.

Citrin, Jack. "Comment: The Public Relevance of Trust in Government." *American Political Science Review* 68, no. 3 (September 1974): 973–88. https://doi.org/10.2307/1959141.

Citrin, Jack, and David O. Sears. *American Identity and the Politics of Multiculturalism.* New York: Cambridge University Press, 2014.

Clark, Terry Nichols, and Lorna Crowley Ferguson. *City Money: Political Processes, Fiscal Strain, and Retrenchment.* New York: Columbia University Press, 1983.

Cohen, William. "Negro Involuntary Servitude in the South." *Journal of Southern History* 42, no. 1 (February 1976): 31–60.

Cook, Karen S., Russell Hardin, and Margaret Levi. *Cooperation Without Trust?* New York: Russell Sage Foundation, 2005.

Currell, Susan, and Christina Cogdell. *Popular Eugenics: National Efficiency and American Mass Culture in the 1930s.* Athens: Ohio University Press, 2006.

Dahl, Robert Alan. *A Preface to Democratic Theory.* 2nd. ed. Chicago: University of Chicago Press, 1970.

Daniels, Roger. *Prisoners Without Trial: Japanese Americans in World War II.* New York: Hill and Wang, 2004.

Dawson, Michael. *Behind the Mule: Race and Class in African American Politics.* Princeton, N.J.: Princeton University Press, 1994.

Denhardt, Robert B., and Janet Vinzant Denhardt. "The New Public Service: Serving Rather Than Steering." *Public Administration Review* 60, no. 6 (November–December 2000): 549–59. https://doi.org/10.1111/0033-3352.00117.

Dixon, Jeffrey C. "The Ties That Bind and Those That Don't: Toward Reconciling Group Threat and Contact Theories of Prejudice." *Social Forces* 84, no. 4 (June 2006): 2179–204. https://doi.org/10.1353/sof.2006.0085.

Dixon, Jeffrey C., and Michael S. Rosenbaum. "Nice to Know You? Testing Contact, Cultural, and Group Threat Theories of Anti-Black and Anti-Hispanic Stereotypes." *Social Science Quarterly* 85, no. 2 (June 2004): 257–280. https://doi.org/10.1111/j.0038-4941.2004.08502003.x.

Djupe, Paul A., and Brian Robert Calfano. *God Talk: Experimenting with the Religious Causes of Public Opinion.* Philadelphia: Temple University Press, 2013.

Dodson, Dan W. "The Mayor's Committee on Unity of New York City." *Journal of Educational Sociology* 19, no. 5 (1946): 289–98. https://doi.org/10.2307/2263229.

Dovidio, John F., Samuel L. Gaertner, and Tamar Saguy. "Commonality and the Complexity of 'We': Social Attitudes and Social Change." *Personality and Social Psychology Review* 13, no. 1 (2009): 3–20. https://doi.org/10.1177%2F1088868308326751.

Dovidio, John F., Samuel L. Gaertner, Ana Validzic, Kimberly Matoka, Brenda Johnson, and Stacy Frazier. "Extending the Benefits of Recategorization: Evaluations, Self-Disclosure, and Helping." *Journal of Experimental Social Psychology* 33, no. 4 (1997): 401–40.

Downey, Dennis J. "Organizational Models and Social Movement Transitions: Promoting Civic Unity Through Local Race Relations Committees During World War II." American Sociological Association, Montreal, Quebec, Canada, 2006. http://citation .allacademic.com//meta/p_mla_apa_research_citation/1/0/4/5/9/pages104595 /p104595-1.php.

Drake, St. Claire, and Horace R. Cayton. *Black Metropolis: A Study of Negro Life in a Northern City.* Chicago: University of Chicago, 1945.

Duany, Jorge. "Cuban Migration: A Postrevolution Exodus Ebbs and Flows." *Migration Information Resource.* July 6, 2017. https://www.migrationpolicy.org/article /cuban-migration-postrevolution-exodus-ebbs-and-flows.

Ellis, Mark, and Richard Wright. "Assimilation and Differences Between the Settlement Patterns of Individual Immigrants and Immigrant Households." *Proceedings of the National Academy of Sciences* 102 (October 2005): 15325–30.

Embree, Edwin R. "The American Council on Race Relations." *Journal of Negro Education* 13, no. 4 (1944): 562–64. www.jstor.org/stable/2292514.

Ethington, Philip J., William H. Frey, and Dowell Myers. "The Racial Resegregation of Los Angeles County, 1940–2000." Race Contours 2000 Study, Public Research Report No. 2001-04. University of Southern California and University of Michigan, 2001.

Ethington, Philip J., and Christopher D. West. *The Challenge of Intergroup Relations in Los Angeles: An Historical and Comparative Evaluation of the Los Angeles City Human Relations Commission, 1966–1998.* Department of History and The Southern California Studies Center of the University of Southern California, Los Angeles City Human Relations Commission, 1998.

Evans, Mark, Chris Aulich, Anne Howard, Megan Peterson, and Richard Reid. *Innovation in Local Government: Defining the Challenge, Making the Change.* Sydney: ACLEG, University of Technology Sydney; and Canberra: ANZSOG Institute for Governance, 2012.

Everett, Jim A. C. "Intergroup Contact Theory: Past, Present, and Future." *Inquisitive Mind* 17, no. 2 (2013).

Feldberg, Michael J. *The Philadelphia Riots of 1844: A Study of Ethnic Conflict.* Westport, Conn.: Greenwood, 1975.

Fields, Barbara. "Ideology and Race in American History." In *Region, Race, and Reconstruction: Essays in Honor of C. Vann Woodward,* ed. by J. Morgan Kousser and James M. McPherson, 143–77. New York: Oxford University Press, 1982.

Fitzpatrick, Sheila. *The Russian Revolution.* New York: Oxford University Press, 2008.

Ford, W. Scott. "Favorable Intergroup Contact May Not Reduce Prejudice: Inconclusive Journal Evidence, 1960–1984." *Sociology and Social Research* 70 (1986): 256–58.

Fraga, Luis R., John J. Garcia, Rodney Hero, Michael Jones-Correa, Valerie Martinez-Ebers, and Gary Segura. *Latino Lives in America: Making It Home.* Philadelphia: Temple University Press, 2010.

Frey, William H., and Reynolds Farley. "Latino, Asian, and Black Segregation in U.S. Metropolitan Areas: Are Multiethnic Metros Different?" *Demography* 33, no. 1 (1996): 35–50.

Gaertner, Samuel L., and John F. Dovidio. *Reducing Intergroup Bias: The Common Ingroup Identity Model.* Philadelphia: Psychology Press, 2000.

Gaertner, Samuel L., J. A. Mann, A. Murrell, and John F. Dovidio. "Reducing Intergroup Bias: The Benefits of Re-Categorization." *Journal of Personality and Social Psychology* 57, no. 2 (1989): 239–49. https://psycnet.apa.org/doi/10.1037/0022-3514.57.2 .239.

Gaertner, Samuel L., Mary C. Rust, John F. Dovidio, Betty A. Bachman, and Phyllis A. Anastasio. "The Contact Hypothesis: The Role of Common Ingroup Identity on Reducing Intergroup Bias." *Small Group Research* 25, no. 2 (1994): 267–77. https:// doi.org/10.1177%2F1046496494252005.

Gaines, Brian J., James H. Kuklinski, and Paul J. Quirk. "The Logic of the Survey Experiment Revisited." *Political Analysis* 15, no. 1 (2007): 1–20. https://doi.org/10.1093 /pan/mpl008.

Galster, George C. "Black Suburbanization: Has It Changed the Relative Location of Races?" *Urban Affairs Reviews* 26, no. 4 (1991): 621–28. https://doi.org/10 .1177%2F004208169102600410.

García Bedolla, Lisa. *Latino Politics.* Hoboken, N.J.: Wiley, 2015.

Gay, Claudine, Jennifer Hochschild, and Ariel White. "Americans' Belief in Linked Fate: Does the Measure Capture the Concept?" *Journal of Race, Ethnicity, and Politics* 1, no. 1 (March 2016): 117–44. https://dx.doi.org/10.1017/rep.2015.3.

Gershon, Livia. "Did The 1965 Watts Riots Change Anything?" *JSTOR Daily,* July 13, 2016. https://daily.jstor.org/did-the-1965-watts-riots-change-anything/.

Gilje, Paul A. "The Development of an Irish American Community in New York City Before the Great Migration." In *The New York Irish,* ed. by Ronald H. Bayor and Timothy J. Meagher, 70–86. Baltimore: Johns Hopkins University Press, 1997.

——. *The Road to Mobocracy: Popular Disorder in New York City, 1763–1834.* Chapel Hill: University of North Carolina Press, 2014.

González, Roberto, and Brown, Rupert. "Dual Identities and Intergroup Contact: Group Status and Size Moderate the Generalization of Positive Attitude Change." *Journal of Experimental Social Psychology* 42, no. 6 (2006): 753–67. https://doi.org/10.1016/j .jesp.2005.11.008.

Governor's Commission on the Los Angeles Riots. "Violence in the City—An End or A Beginning: A Report." Sacramento: State of California, 1965.

Gutiérrez, José Angel. *A Gringo Manual on How to Handle Mexicans.* Houston: Arte Publico Press, 2001.

——. *The Making of a Chicano Militant: Lessons from Cristal.* Madison: University of Wisconsin Press, 1998.

Healey, Patsy. "Creativity and Urban Governance." Policy Studies 25, no. 2 (June 2004): 87–102. https://dx.doi.org/10.1080/0144287042000262189.

Heen, Miliaikeala, Joel Lieberman, and Terance Miethe. "A Comparison of Different Online Sampling Approaches for Generating National Samples." *Center for Crime and Justice Policy*, September 2014, 1–8.

Henry, C., and Carlos Munoz Jr. "Ideological and Interest Linkages in California Rainbow Politics." In *Racial and Ethnic Politics in California*, ed. by Bryan O. Jackson and Michael B. Preston. Berkeley, Calif.: IGS Press, 1991.

Hernández, Kelly Lytle. "The Crimes and Consequences of Illegal Immigration: A Cross-Border Examination of Operation Wetback, 1943 to 1954." *Western Historical Quarterly* 37, no. 4 (2006): 421–44. https://doi.org/10.2307/25443415.

Hero, Rodney. *Latinos and the U.S. Political System.* Philadelphia: Temple University Press, 1992.

Hewstone, Miles. "Contact and Categorization: Social Psychological Interventions to Change Intergroup Relations." In *Stereotypes and Stereotyping*, ed. by C. Neil Macrae, Charles Stangor, and Miles Hewstone, 323–368. New York: Guilford, 1996.

Hewstone, Miles, and Rupert Brown. "Contact Is Not Enough: An Intergroup Perspective on the 'Contact Hypothesis.'" In *Contact and Conflict in Intergroup Encounters*, ed. by Miles Hewstone and Rupert Brown. Oxford: Blackwell, 1986.

Hogan, Bernie, and Brent Berry. "Racial and Ethnic Biases in Rental Housing: An Audit Study of Online Apartment Listings." *City and Community* 10, no. 4 (2011): 351–72. https://doi.org/10.1111/j.1540-6040.2011.01376.x.

Hogg, Michael A., and John C. Turner. "Interpersonal Attraction, Social Identification and Psychological Group Formation." *European Journal of Social Psychology* 15, no. 1 (1985): 51–66.

Horne, Gerald. *Fire this Time: The Watts Uprising and the 1960s.* Charlottesville: University of Virginia Press, 1995.

Hornsey, Matthew J., and Michael A. Hogg. "Subgroup Relations: A Comparison of Mutual Intergroup Differentiation and Common Ingroup Identity Models of Prejudice Reduction." *Personality and Social Psychology Bulletin* 26, no. 2 (2000): 242–25. https://doi.org/10.1177%2F0146167200264010.

Howard, John. *Innovation, Ingenuity, and Initiative: The Adoption and Application of New Ideas in Australian Local Government.* Canberra: ANSZOG Institute for Governance; and Sydney: Australian Centre of Excellence for Local Government, September 12, 2012. http://hdl.handle.net/10453/42114.

Huddy, Leonie. "From Social to Political Identity: A Critical Examination of Social Identity Theory." *Political Psychology* 22, no. 1 (2001): 127–56.

——. "Group Identity and Political Cohesion." In *The Oxford Handbook of Political Psychology*, 2nd ed., ed. by David O Sears, Leonie Huddy, and Robert Jervis, 511–58. New York: Oxford University Press, 2003.

Huddy, Leonie, and Stanley Feldman. "Americans Respond Politically to 9/11: Understanding the Impact of the Terrorist Attacks and Their Aftermath." *American Psychologist* 66 (2011): 455–67.

Irvin, Renée A., and John Stansbury. "Citizen Participation in Decision Making: Is It Worth the Effort?" *Public Administration Review* 64, no. 1 (February 2007): 55–65. https://doi.org/10.1111/j.1540-6210.2004.00346.x.

Jackson, Pamela Irving, and Leo Carroll. "Race and the War on Crime: The Sociopolitical Determinants of Municipal Police Expenditures in 90 Non-Southern U.S. Cities." *American Sociological Review* 46, no. 3 (June 1981): 290–305. https://www.jstor.org/stable/2095061.

James, David R. "The Transformation of the Southern Racial State: Class and Race Determinants of Local-State Structures." *American Sociological Review* 53, no. 2 (April 1988): 191–208. https://www.jstor.org/stable/2095687.

Jeffries, Vincent, Ralph H. Turner, and Richard T. Morris. "The Public Perception of the Watts Riot as Social Protest." *American Sociological Review* 36, no. 3 (June 1971): 443–51. https://dx.doi.org/10.2307/2093084.

Jones-Correa, Michael, ed. *Governing American Cities: Inter-Ethnic Coalitions, Competition, and Conflict.* New York: Russell Sage Foundation, 2001.

Jovchelovitch, Sandra. "Trust and Social Representations: Understanding the Relations Between Self and Other in the Brazilian Public Sphere." In *Trust and Distrust: Sociocultural Perspectives*, ed. by Ivana Marková and Alex Gillispie, 105–20. Charlotte, N.C.: Information Age Publishing, 2008.

Judd, Dennis R., and Dick W. Simpson, eds. *The City, Revisited: Urban Theory from Chicago, Los Angeles, and New York.* Minneapolis: University of Minnesota Press, 2011.

Keller, Renata. *Mexico's Cold War: Cuba, the United States, and the Legacy of the Mexican Revolution.* Cambridge: Cambridge University Press, 2015.

——. "U.S.-Mexican Relations from Independence to the Present." *American History,* March 2016. https://dx.doi.org/10.1093/acrefore/9780199329175.013.269.

Kinder, Donald R., and David O. Sears. "Prejudice and Politics: Symbolic Racism versus Racial Threats to the Good Life. *Journal of Personality and Social Psychology* 40, no. 3 (1981): 414–31. https://psycnet.apa.org/doi/10.1037/0022-3514.40.3.414.

Kirschenman, Jolene, and Kathryn M. Neckerman. "'We'd Love to Hire Them, But . . .': The Meaning of Race for Employers." In *The Urban Underclass*, ed. by Christopher Jencks and Paul E. Peterson. Washington, D.C.: Brookings Institution Press, 1991.

Kraska, Peter B. "Militarization and Policing—Its Relevance to 21st Century Police." *Policing* 1, no. 4 (2007): 501–13. https://doi.org/10.1093/police/pam065.

Landry, Charles. *The Creative City: A Toolkit for Urban Innovators.* New York: Routledge, 2008.

Levin, Shana, Stacey Sinclair, Jim Sidanius, J., and Colette Van Laar. "Ethnic and University Identities Across the College Years: A Common In-Group Identity Perspective." *Journal of Social Issues* 65, no. 2 (2009): 287–306. https://doi.org/10.1111/j.1540-4560.2009.01601.x.

Liu, James H., and Denis J. Hilton. "How the Past Weighs on the Present: Social Representations of History and Their Role in Identity Politics." *British Journal of Social Psychology* 44, no. 4 (2005): 537–56.

MacNair, Ray H., Russell Caldwell, and Leonard Pollane. "Citizen Participants in Public Bureaucracies: Foul-Weather Friends." *Administration & Society* 14, no. 4 (1983): 507–24. https://doi.org/10.1177%2F009539978301400405.

Marten, James. "Slavery and Causes of the American Civil War." *Encyclopedia Britannica Blog.* April 11, 2011. http://blogs.britannica.com/2011/04/slavery-american-civil-war/.

Martinez-Ebers, Valerie, Brian Calfano, and Regina Branton. "Bringing People Together: Improving Intergroup Relations via Group Identity Cues." *Urban Affairs Review,* online first, June 9, 2019. http://dx.doi.org/10.1177/1078087419853390.

Massey, Douglas S., and Nancy A. Denton. *American Apartheid: Segregation and the Making of the Underclass.* Cambridge, Mass.: Harvard University Press, 1993.

Matthews, Mark, Chris Lewis, and Grahame Cook. 2009. "Public Sector Innovation: A Review of the Literature." In *Innovation in the Public Sector: Enabling Better Performance, Driving New Directions: Better Practice Guide.* Canberra, Australia: ANAO, 2009.

Mazón, Maurico. *The Zoot-Suit Riots: The Psychology of Symbolic Annihilation.* Austin: University of Texas Press, 2010.

McClain, Paula D. "The Changing Dynamics of Urban Politics: Black and Hispanic Municipal Employment—Is There Competition?" *Journal of Politics* 55, no. 2 (1993): 399–414. https://doi.org/10.2307/2132272.

——. "Coalition and Competition: Patterns of Black-Latino Relations in Urban Politics." In *The Politics of Minority Coalitions: Race, Ethnicity, and Shared Uncertainties,* ed. by Wilbur Rich. New York: Praeger, 1996.

McClain, Paula, and Joseph Stewart Jr. *Why Can't We All Get Along? Racial and Ethnic Minorities in American Politics.* Boulder, Colo.: Westview, 2002.

McClain, Paula D., and Steven C. Tauber. "Black and Latino Socioeconomic and Political Competition: Has a Decade Made a Difference?" *American Politics Research* 26, no. 2 (1998): 237–52. https://dx.doi.org/10.1177/1532673X9802600206.

McDermott, Annette. "Did World War II Launch the Civil Rights Movement?" History Channel, October 19, 2018. https://www.history.com/news/did-world-war-ii -launch-the-civil-rights-movement.

McGarry, Aidan, and James M. Jasper, eds. *The Identity Dilemma: Social Movements and Collective Identity.* Philadelphia: Temple University Press, 2015.

McPherson, James M. *Battle Cry of Freedom: The Civil War Era.* Cambridge: Oxford University Press, 1988.

McWhirter, Cameron. *Red Summer: The Summer of 1919 and the Awakening of Black America.* New York: Henry Holt, 2011.

Meier, Kenneth, and Laurence J. O'Toole. "Political Control Versus Bureaucratic Values: Reframing the Debate." *Public Administration Review* 66, no. 2 (2006): 177–92. https://doi.org/10.1111/j.1540-6210.2006.00571.x.

Meier, Kenneth J., Laurence J. O'Toole Jr., and Alisa Hicklin. "I've Seen Fire and I've Seen Rain: Public Management and Performance after a Natural Disaster." *Administration & Society* 41, no. 8 (2010): 979–1003.

Meier, Kenneth J., and Joseph Stewart Jr. "Cooperation and Conflict in Multiracial School Districts." *Journal of Politics* 53, no. 4 (199): 1123–33. https://dx.doi.org/10.2307/2131870.

Miller, Gary J. "The Political Evolution of Principal-Agent Models." *Annual Review of Political Science* 8 (2005): 203–225. https://doi.org/10.1146/annurev.polisci.8.082103.104840.

Mitchell, Ronald K., Bradley R. Agle, and Donna J. Wood. "Toward a Theory of Stakeholder Identification and Salience: Defining the Principle of Who and What Really Counts." *Academy of Management Review* 22, no. 4 (October 1997): 853–886. https://dx.doi.org/10.2307/259247.

Mollenkopf, John H., and Castells, Manuel, eds. *Dual City: Restructuring New York.* New York: Russell Sage Foundation, 1991.

Montjoy, Robert S. and Laurence J. O'Toole. "Toward a Theory of Policy Implementation: An Organizational Perspective." *Public Administration Review* 39, no. 5 (1979): 465–76.

Mormino, Gary R., and George E. Pozzetta. *The Immigrant World of Ybor City: Italians and Their Latin Neighbors in Tampa, 1885–1985.* Champaign: University of Illinois Press, 1987.

Mulgan, Geoff. "The Process of Social Innovation." *Innovations* (MIT Press), Spring 2006: 145–62.

Mullinix, Kevin J., Thomas J. Leeper, James N. Druckman, and Jeremy Freese. "The Generalizability of Survey Experiments." *Journal of Experimental Political Science* 2, no. 2 (2015): 109–38. https://doi.org/10.1017/XPS.2015.19.

Myrdal, Gunner. *An American Dilemma: The Negro Problem and Modern Democracy,* 2 vols. New York City: Harper, 1944.

Nagel, Joanne. *American Indian Ethnic Renewal: Red Power and the Resurgence of Identity and Culture.* New York: Oxford University Press, 1997.

National Congress of American Indians (NCAI) and the U.S. Department of Interior, Office of Indian Energy and Economic Development. "Native American Economic Policy Report: Developing Tribal Economies to Create Healthy, Sustainable and Culturally Vibrant Communities." 2007. http://www.ncai.org/resources/ncai-publications/native-american-economic-policy-report.pdf.

Nora, Pierre. "Between Memory and History: Les lieux de mémoire." *Representations,* no. 26 (Spring 1989): 7–24.

Northup, Herbert Roof, Richard L. Rowan, Darold T. Barnum, and John C. Howard. *Negro Employment in Southern Industry.* Philadelphia: University of Pennsylvania, 1970.

Obermiller, Phillip J., and Thomas Wagner. *The Cincinnati Human Relations Commission: A History, 1943–2013.* Columbus: Ohio University Press, 2014.

Omi, Michael, and Howard Winant. *Racial formation in the United States.* New York: Routledge, 2014.

Ong, Paul M., Andre Comandon, Alycia Cheng, and Sylvia González. *South Los Angeles Since the Sixties: Half a Century of Progress?* Los Angeles: Center for Neighborhood Knowledge, UCLA Luskin School of Public Affairs, n.d. http://www.aasc.ucla.edu/news/SLA_Since_The_60s_FullRpt.pdf.

Orfield, Gary. *Must We Bus? Segregated Schools and National Policy.* Washington, D.C.: Brookings Institution Press, 1978.

O'Toole, Laurence J., Jr., and Robert S. Montjoy. "Interorganizational Policy Implementation: A Theoretical Perspective." *Public Administration Review* 44, no. 6 (November–December 1984): 491–503.

Park, Robert E. *Race and Culture.* Glencoe, Ill.: Free Press, 1950.

Patterson, Fiona, Maire Kerrin and Geraldine Gatto-Roissard. "Characteristics and Behaviours of Innovative People in Organizations: Literature Review." Paper prepared for NESTA Policy and Research Unit, London, December 9, 2009. https://media.nesta.org.uk/documents/characteristics_behaviours_of_innovative_people.pdf.

Pennington, Mark. *Planning and the Political Market: Public Choice and the Politics of Failure.* New Brunswick, N.J.: Athlone Press, 2000.

Pettigrew, Thomas F., and Linda R. Tropp. "How Does Intergroup Contact Reduce Prejudice? Meta-Analytic Tests of Three Mediators." *European Journal of Social Psychology* 38, no. 6 (2008): 922–34. https://doi.org/10.1002/ejsp.504.

Pettigrew, Thomas F., Linda R. Tropp, Ulrich Wagner, and Oliver Christ. "Recent Advances in Intergroup Contact Theory." *International Journal of Intercultural Relations* 35, no. 3 (2011): 271–80. https://doi.org/10.1016/j.ijintrel.2011.03.001.

Philp, Kenneth R. "Stride toward Freedom: The Relocation of Indians to Cities, 1952–1960." *Western Historical Quarterly* 16, no. 2 (April 1985): 175–90.

——. *Termination Revisited: American Indians on the Trail to Self-Determination, 1933–1953.* Lincoln: University of Nebraska Press, 1999.

Quinney, Richard. *The Social Reality of Crime.* Boston: Little, Brown, 1970.

Quinney, Richard, and John Wildeman. *The Problem of Crime: A Critical Introduction to Criminology.* New York: HarperCollins, 1977.

Roccas, Sonia, and Marilynn B. Brewer. "Social Identity Complexity." *Personality and Social Psychology Review* 6, no. 2 (2002): 88–106. https://doi.org/10.1207%2FS15327957PSPR0602_01.

Rodriguez, Nestor. "U.S. Immigration and Intergroup Relations in the Late 20th Century: African Americans and Latinos." *Social Justice* 23, no. 3 (1996): 111–25.

Ross, Bernard H., and Myron A. Levine. *Urban Politics: Power in Metropolitan America.* Itasca, Ill: F. E. Peacock, 1996.

Sampson, Robert J., and Dawn Jeglum Bartusch. "Legal Cynicism and (Subcultural?) Tolerance of Deviance: The Neighborhood Context of Racial Differences." *Law & Society Review* 32, no. 4 (1998): 777–804.

Sanchez, Gabriel R., and Eduardo Vargas. "Taking a Closer Look at Group Identity: The Link Between Theory and Measurement of Group Consciousness and Linked Fate." *Political Research Quarterly* 69 (2016): 160–74.

Saunders, Kenneth L. and Hyo Eun (April) Bang. "A Historical Perspective on U.S. Human Rights Commissions." In *Executive Session Papers: Human Rights Commissions and Criminal Justice*, no. 3, ed. by Marea L. Beeman. Cambridge, Mass.: Kennedy School of Government, Harvard University, 2007.

Scott, Joan Wallach. *Gender and the Politics of History*, rev. ed. New York: Columbia University Press, 1999.

Sharp, Elaine B., and Paul E. Johnson. 2009. "Accounting for Variation in Distrust of Local Police." *Justice Quarterly* 26, no. 1 (2009): 157–82. https://doi.org/10.1080/07418820802290496.

Silyan-Saa, Joumana. "Government Community Engagement Methods: City of Los Angeles Case Study." *Journal of the Moroccan Interdisciplinary Center for Strategic and International Studies*, 2012.

Sonenshein, Raphael J. *Politics in Black and White: Race and Power in Los Angeles.* Princeton, N.J.: Princeton University Press, 1993.

Stark, Rodney, and Roger Finke. *Acts of Faith: Explaining the Human Side of Religion.* Berkeley: University of California Press, 2000.

Steele, Richard. "The Federal Government Discovers Mexican Americans." In *World War II and Mexican American Civil Rights*, ed. by Richard Griswold del Castillo, 19–33. Austin: University of Texas Press, 2008.

Steinhauer, Jason. "The History of Mexican Immigration to the U.S. in the Early 20th Century." *Insights: Scholarly Work at the John W. Klug Center* (blog), March 11, 2015. https://blogs.loc.gov/kluge/2015/03/the-history-of-mexican-immigration-to-the-u-s-in-the-early-20th-century/.

Strand, Torill. "Metaphors of Creativity and Workplace Learning." *Scandinavian Journal of Educational Research* 55, no. 4 (2011): 341–55.

Tajfel, Henri. "Cognitive Aspects of Prejudice." *Journal of Social Issues* 25, no. 4 (1969): 79–97. https://doi.org/10.1111/j.1540-4560.1969.tb00620.x.

——. *Human Groups and Social Categories: Studies in Social Psychology.* Cambridge: Cambridge University Press, 1981.

Tajfel, Henri, and John L. M. Dawson. *Disappointed Guests: Essays by African, Asian, and West Indian Students.* London: Oxford University Press, 1965.

Takaki, Ronald. *Iron Cages: Race and Culture in Nineteenth-Century America.* New York: Knopf, 1979.

Taylor, Donald M., and Fathali M. Moghaddam. *Theories of Intergroup Relations: International Social Psychological Perspectives.* 2nd ed. Westport, Conn.: Praeger, 1994.

Taylor, Judith. "The Emotional Contradictions of Identity Politics: A Case Study of a Failed Human Relations Commission." *Sociological Perspectives* 49, no. 2 (2006): 217–37. https://doi.org/10.1525%2Fsop.2006.49.2.217.

Taylor, Nikki Marie. *Frontiers of Freedom: Cincinnati's Black Community, 1802–1866.* Columbus: Ohio University Press, 2005.

Thomas, C., and Hyman, J. "Perceptions of Crime, Fear of Victimization, and Public Perceptions of Police Performance." *Journal of Police Science and Administration* 5 (September 1977): 305–17.

Tolnay, Stewart E. "Jim Crow's Legacy: The Lasting Impact of Segregation." *Contemporary Sociology: A Journal of Reviews* 4, no. 1 (2017): 114–66.

Transue, John E. "Identity Salience, Identity Acceptance, and Racial Policy Attitudes: American National Identity as a Uniting Force." *American Journal of Political Science* 51, no. 1 (2007): 78–91. https://doi.org/10.1111/j.1540-5907.2007.00238.x.

Trotter, Joe William, ed. *The Great Migration in Historical Perspective: New Dimensions of Race, Class, and Gender.* Bloomington: University of Indiana Press, 1991.

Tuttle, William M. *Race Riot: Chicago in the Red Summer of 1919.* Champaign: University of Illinois Press, 1996.

Ufkes, Elze G., Sabine Otten, Karen I. Van Der Zee, Ellen Giebels, and John F. Dovidio. "Urban District Identity as a Common Ingroup Identity: The Different Role of Ingroup Prototypicality for Minority and Majority Groups." *European Journal of Social Psychology* 42, no. 6 (October 2012): 706–16. https://doi.org/10.1002/ejsp.1888.

VanGiezen, Robert, and Albert E. Schwenk. "Compensation from Before World War I Through the Great Depression." U.S. Bureau of Labor Statistics, January 30, 2003. https://www.bls.gov/opub/mlr/cwc/compensation-from-before-world-war-i -through-the-great-depression.pdf.

Verovšek, Peter J. "Collective Memory, Politics, and the Influence of the Past: The Politics of Memory as a Research Paradigm." *Politics, Groups, and Identities* 4, no. 3 (2016): 529–53.

Wallsten, Kevin, and Tatishe M. Nteta. "Race, Partisanship, and Perceptions of Interminority Commonality." *Politics, Groups, and Identities* 4, no. 2 (2017): 298–320.

Wanzer-Serano, Darrel. *The New York Young Lords and the Struggle for Liberation.* Philadelphia: Temple University Press, 2015.

Weber, Greta. "Cuba's 'Peter Pans' Remember Childhood Exodus." *National Geographic.* August 14, 2015, https://news.nationalgeographic.com/2015/08/150814 -cuba-operation-peter-pan-embassy-reopening-Castro/.

Wilder, David A. "Perceiving Persons as a Group: Categorization and Intergroup Relations." In *Cognitive Processes in Stereotyping and Intergroup Behavior,* ed. by David L. Hamilton, 213–58. Hillsdale, N.J.: Erlbaum, 1981.

Wilkinson, Betina Cutaia. "Perceptions of Commonality and Latino–Black, Latino–White Relations in a Multiethnic United States." *Political Research Quarterly* 67, no. 4 (2014): 905–16. https://doi.org/10.1177%2F1065912914540217.

Wilkerson, Isabel. *The Warmth of Other Suns: The Epic Story of America's Great Migration.* New York: Random House, 2010.

Wilkins, David. *American Indian Politics and the American Political System.* Lanham, Md.: Rowman & Littlefield, 2007.

Wilson, James Q. *What Government Agencies Do and Why They Do It*. New York: Basic Books, 1989.

Wirth, Louis. "Urbanism as a Way of Life." *American Journal of Sociology* 44, no. 1 (July 1938): 1–24. http://www.jstor.org/stable/2768119.

Wright, Gavin. *Old South, New South: Revolutions in the Southern Economy Since the Civil War*. New York: Basic Books, 1986.

INDEX

Note: Page numbers with an *f* indicate figures; those with a *t* indicate tables.